Non-Wage Benefits

Michael Cunningham

Non-Wage Benefits

'Fringe Benefits':
What they are and
how to win them

Pluto  Press

First published 1981 by Pluto Press Limited,
Unit 10 Spencer Court, 7 Chalcot Road, London NW1 8LH

Copyright © Michael Cunningham 1981

ISBN 0 86104 334 0

Cover designed by Colin Bailey

Photoset and printed in Great Britain by
Photobooks (Bristol) Limited, 28 Midland Road,
St Philips, Bristol

Contents

Acknowledgements

In writing this book, I have had enormous help from a large number of sources. My main thanks are due to Sue Ward, without whose encouragement and expert assistance the book would not have been finished in time. Also I must thank Mark Panto who provided me with many useful and penetrative suggestions in the later stages of writing. I have also received valuable advice on legal matters from Barbara Roche and the North Lewisham Law Centre and on income tax matters from Alfie Garfield.

For much of the information appearing in the various chapters, I am indebted to the Labour Research Department (which gives guidance to trade union negotiators on *all* terms and conditions of employment), Incomes Data Services, the *Industrial Relations Review and Report* and to surveys produced by the GMWU and the NUJ.

Finally, I am also grateful to Peter Ayrton, Andrew Bovey, Mike Kidron, Linda Milbourne, Jerry Tilston and Amanda Woolley, to the NUPE Research Department and to many NUPE colleagues and shop stewards – all of whom have been kind enough to give me assistance and ideas whenever I asked.

Michael Cunningham
April 1981

Introduction

This book is all about benefits provided by the employer that are *not* wages/salary (or bonus, commission or allowances for such things as shift, overtime etc). These benefits come in different forms:

- *cash* (e.g. subsistence allowances, mileage allowances);
- *loans* (e.g. personal loans, mortgages, relocation expenses);
- *in kind* (e.g. holidays, sick leave, study leave, workplace nurseries – or a car).

This book will concentrate on non-wage benefits for manual workers and for those white-collar workers who are *not* executives.

This introduction is divided into the following sections:

- What are non-wage benefits?
- 'Total remuneration';
- Why have non-wage benefits become so popular?
- The spread of non-wage benefits;
- The value of non-wage benefits to employees;
- Drawbacks of non-wage benefits for employees;
- Cost of non-wage benefits to the employer;
- Income tax on non-wage benefits;
- How to use this book.

What are non-wage benefits?

Non-wage benefits are all the items dealt with in this book – from holidays to canteens, sick leave to sports clubs and company discounts to company cars. There are also many other non-wage benefits not dealt with here, like clothing, tool allowances and free telephones – these are not dealt with in this book for reasons of space.

They are already becoming very important in negotiations with employers for two reasons:

■ most of them involve a low unit cost (i.e. the amount of money that the employer spends on each employee – on average – is very low);

■ as employers are becoming more and more difficult to budge on wages, trade unionists are looking to these areas in an attempt to improve their terms and conditions of employment.

Non-wage benefits have been described by the British Institute of Management as:

■ 'Items over and above basic remuneration which increase the well-being or wealth of employees at some cost to the employer'; Sir Geoffrey Howe, Chancellor of the Exchequer in the Conservative Government elected in 1979, put it in another way:

■ 'Perks are an inefficient and often wasteful way of rewarding effort – and unjust. Some perks are taxed in full, others pay no tax on identical benefits.'

'*Perk*' is the short form of the word '*perquisite*', but all the words used give rise to much confusion; other people might describe the situation like this:

■ 'Perks are what *other* people get,' and

■ 'Benefits (or "employee benefits") are what we *sometimes* get.'

It follows that some non-wage benefits are felt to be 'extras'. Certainly the vast majority of manual workers and low-paid clerical workers do *not* get cars or company mortgages, and get less good pensions, subsidised meals, sick leave and holidays – and this explains their resentment. A survey of conditions of employment carried out in 1977 by the Institute of Personnel Management was quite clear about this: the survey compared how well white-collar workers did in terms of non-wage benefits by contrast with manual workers; the survey concluded that manual workers *never* did better (although there were one or two items where they did *equally* well). Examples where white-collar workers do better were travel expenditure, housing, relocation, holidays, sick leave, subsidised meals, personal loans, maternity leave, time off for family sickness and workplace nurseries. (*Staff Status for All*, IPM 1977)

Furthermore, higher executives and management have come to *expect* a wide range of benefits (or 'perks'). The people who enjoy the more expensive benefits do not think of them as 'extras' but as part of their 'total remuneration'.

'Total remuneration'

Non-wage benefits are so widespread that the answer to the question 'How much do you earn?' is most unlikely to give much of an idea of how 'well off' the person is. This has given rise to the cumbersome phrase 'total remuneration', which means: earnings (basic + bonus, commission etc) **plus** holidays, sick leave, transport to and from work, study leave, company discount and maybe even cheap loans, relocation expenses and health insurance. **Earnings on their own no longer tell us much about somebody's conditions of employment.** These days we have to look at total remuneration.

The lack of attention to non-wage benefits is remarkable. Virtually all 'official' surveys and semi-'official' surveys by management consultants pay little or no attention to them – and when they do, they tend to have the following drawbacks:

■ they usually deal with benefits that concern relatively large numbers of workers, and not with the very generous 'perks' that top management enjoy;

■ they never deal with the *unquantifiable* aspects of benefits (e.g. how much is a loan from the employer worth when you do not have to shop around the building societies?);

■ they never touch on tax avoidance (which is legal) or tax evasion (which is illegal).

The Inland Revenue also produce figures, but they are often not helpful because:

■ a lot of benefits are not taxable anyway;

■ different people put a different value on a benefit (e.g. a company car) and the income tax they pay gives no indication of this.

The lack of official interest in non-wage benefits goes even further:

■ the *New Earnings Survey* (the annual review by the Department of Employment of terms and conditions of employment) makes no reference to them;

■ even the Clegg Commission on pay comparability for nurses and midwives found that the consultants they used (Hay/MSL) did 'not provide satisfactory information' on the benefits they wished to study.

An important exception to this rule is the Review Body on Top Salaries (chairman: Lord Boyle) which, in its 10th Report, puts a figure on non-wage benefits (see p. 8).

Employers are slowly becoming discontented with the situation: according to a recent survey, over 40 per cent of companies interviewed do not use salary surveys at all because the information supplied 'does not include the wide variety of fringe benefits'. (*Executive Remuneration and Benefits Survey Report*, John Courtis and Partners 1980)

Fortunately, there is a growing awareness among other people, too, of how inadequate earnings on their own are: a leading article in the *Guardian* on 31 March 1980 compared private sector executives' salaries of £11,000–15,000 unfavourably with Civil Service salaries of £15,000–28,500. Letters to the Editor of the *Guardian* in the next few days pointed to the 'crude distortion of the facts' caused by the omission of any reference to non-wage benefits such as cars and assisted mortgages.

Top management, certainly, know this very well; advertisements for executives' jobs are usually worded like this:

■ 'A comprehensive and competitive remuneration package' (financial analyst);

■ '£10,000 p.a. plus very interesting fringe benefits' (personnel manager).

Why have non-wage benefits become so popular?

There have been two main reasons for this.

■ The *new labour legislation* brought in during the 1970s, for example:

– the Employment Protection Act 1975 (maternity leave, time off for public duties etc);

– the Social Security Pensions Act 1975 (pensions).

The employment protection laws gave legal backing to workers who wanted to take part in public affairs – e.g. on local councils or as members of statutory bodies such as Industrial Tribunals, health authorities and water authorities; furthermore, *women* were given statutory minimum maternity leave with pay. These progressive legal moves gave rise to a large number of *locally agreed improvements*.

■ *Incomes policies* during the 1970s; when earnings were pegged to percentage increases (e.g. 5 per cent) or maximum cash increases (e.g. £2.50–4.00), union negotiators turned quickly to *other* terms and conditions of employment such as paid time off for sickness, bereavement and training.

There have also been other, only slightly less important, reasons.

■ There has been difficulty in recruiting and retaining staff (particularly certain white-collar grades).

■ It is sometimes just cheaper to give a non-wage benefit than to pay a large increase in gross earnings (because of the income tax advantages).

■ Companies have increasingly wanted to have a 'good image' in the locality.

The reasons for the remarkable spread of non-wage benefits have varied enormously from firm to firm, but they have rarely been *offered* by the employer: they have been won by negotiation backed up by *trade union organisation and pressure*.

The spread of non-wage benefits

There is no doubt that non-wage benefits have made an enormous impact in the last few years. The Government itself recognises this:

> 'Employee benefits form a large part of many employees' total earnings, and the non-cash element has been growing quite fast over the last five years.' (Eighth Report of the Royal Commission on the Distribution of Income and Wealth, 1980.)

The report then goes on to say:

> 'The cost to employers of non-cash benefits has at least kept pace with cash payments *and, at the highest levels, has grown considerably more than cash payments*.' [Emphasis added]

The management consultants Hay/MSL support this view. The following table supplied by them shows the cost to the employer of non-wage benefits (including pensions) as a percentage of average salary plus bonus and commission before tax:

	July 1974	July 1978	Average salary in 1978
superintendent	17%	18%	£7,560
works manager	23%	29%	£13,390
managing director	12%	36%	£30,240

The advance of non-wage benefits has now reached the stage where 'remuneration specialists' are now being employed to administer benefits as well as salary structures. Sometimes employers will use outside firms of 'employee benefits consultants':

■ In May 1980, a *one-day* course for top management on non-wage benefits for directors and senior executives cost £90 (exclusive of any overnight accommodation).

Employers are beginning to realise the importance of non-wage benefits in industrial relations.

■ In 1980, Commonwealth Holiday Inns of Canada, a firm owning six hotels in Britain, sent a circular to managers informing them that certain benefits to employees would henceforth have to be *negotiated* if the staff became unionised; two examples of benefits that could not be given in future were (i) 'two [cases of] mortgages obtained for personnel who would not normally have qualified' and (ii) an employee who got maternity pay although she had not been employed for the statutory minimum qualification period of two years.

Commonwealth Holiday Inns of Canada possibly had something in mind, because an IDS survey in the same year found that:

■ 'those hotels in the middle range where unions were established all had fringe benefits well above minima, or benefits not specified in the wages council schedule, like sick pay . . . The overall impact of collective bargaining has been to raise . . . fringe benefits substantially.'

The value of non-wage benefits to employees

The value varies enormously according to personal circumstances. Some non-wage benefits are good, whichever way you look at them (providing you haven't had to accept them instead of something you wanted much more):

● *season ticket loans*: there is little or no interest to pay on the loan, and you also save on the discount by paying for a whole year at once;

● *luncheon vouchers*: you can spend them at any time inside or outside the workplace;

● *company mortgages*: whether they are for relocation or not, there are the permanent advantages of a low interest rate and no hassle with the bank or building society (although there can be huge problems if you later want to leave the firm).

Other benefits are more difficult to assess:

● *company car*: would the employee have bought a car if s/he had not been given one by the firm?

There is a third category of non-wage benefits which are likely to be very valuable *only if you make use of them* – otherwise you have negotiated for nothing:

● subsidised meals in a canteen;
● sports and social facilities.

Drawbacks of non-wage benefits for employees

Probably the biggest disadvantage of *some* non-wage benefits only becomes apparent when you are thinking of changing job; for example:

■ *company mortgage*: if you can transfer it to the *new* employer's scheme, there is probably no problem; but if, on the other hand, the new employer does not have a mortgage scheme (or will not take your mortgage on):

– *either* you have to go to a building society (and therefore you need to be paid substantially more in the new job to make up for the increased costs of buying your home)

– *or* you have to decide *not to move*.

The same difficult decisions arise with tied accommodation, company cars and personal loans.

Cost of non-wage benefits to the employer

It is remarkable that a large number of employers *do not know* the cost of non-wage benefits. Many companies spoken to by IDS in preparing a survey in 1980 on non-wage benefits 'had little or no idea exactly how much staff benefits were costing them'. Occasionally, there is a reason for this:

■ it can be difficult to cost any extra administration needed;
■ some benefits are difficult to quantify anyway: for instance, it is impossible to know how much the employer gains from the better timekeeping that results from the introduction of a works canteen.

There are two organisations which have tried to estimate the cost to employers. The eighth (and final) Report of the Royal Commission on the Distribution of Income and Wealth (1980) calculated the proportion of labour costs accounted for by employee benefits as:

	1970	1977
manual workers	10%	14%
white-collar workers	17%	20%

The 10th Report of the Review Body for Top Salaries (1978) reported that the cost of non-wage benefits for senior executives in the private sector represented 24.2 per cent of their gross earnings (this included 5 per cent for the company car).

A survey published by the Alfred Marks Bureau (*Fringe Benefits for Office Staff*, 1979) estimated that all non-wage benefits (including pensions and holidays) represented an addition of 20 per cent to payroll costs. Similarly, a firm interviewed by IDS in 1980 has calculated that non-wage benefits added 28 per cent to payroll, but they had introduced a health insurance scheme in 1979 and thought that this had taken costs up to about 30 per cent; they then said that they had not included holidays, and these would have raised costs to 35 per cent. *For trade unionists, this is a very dangerous approach to most non-wage benefits*: **holidays (and other benefits such as paid sick leave, time off for public duties, pregnancy and maternity benefits, and subsistence allowances) are** *essentials* **for workers and** *must* **be included in payroll costs.**

When costs of benefits are being discussed with employers, it is most important to bear in mind two things:

■ *'double costing'*: when your employer is costing a new (or improved) agreement on such items as holidays and sick leave, ensure that he does not count the wages for these periods *twice* (once for your wages for the whole year and once for your wages while off); 'double costing' of this type can distort payroll costs (upwards) by 15 per cent;

■ *statutory duties on the employer*: employers are obliged *by law* to give you paid (or unpaid) time off for such things as court attendance (witnesses, jury service), public affairs and duties (e.g. membership of statutory bodies) and maternity benefits.

It is particularly difficult for the trade union position on these matters to be put across as the media often do not understand them, and will easily present an inflated cost unless they are carefully explained.

Income tax on non-wage benefits

First, we must distinguish between 'tax evasion' and 'tax avoidance':

■ 'tax evasion' is *tax-dodging* – i.e. tax which must be paid by law – tax evasion is illegal;

■ 'tax avoidance' is paying as little tax as possible *within* the law – tax avoidance is legal.

There are quite a few commonplace things that you must pay tax on, and which are not widely known:

■ if you are working in a pub and you receive a tip of a free drink from a customer, you must pay tax on it;

■ if you use the office phone for private calls, they are taxable.

There are other tax *concessions* which are much less common:

■ if a company *lends* an employee a Savile Row suit and after a year or so the employee *buys* it from the company, s/he pays tax on only *10 per cent of the estimated second-hand value of the suit*.

And the tax advantages to the few can have effects that are even more far-reaching:

■ *company cars*: how can a decent public transport system be built up if *most* new cars are bought for business use?

■ *private health insurance*: how can a health service for *everyone* be maintained and developed if employers find it cheaper to take out health insurance policies on behalf of some of their employees?

Income tax liability

There is a two-tier system of income tax on certain non-wage benefits. Income tax is paid on most benefits by people earning £8,500 a year or more (*including* overtime, bonus, commission and expense allowances, but *excluding* out-of-pocket expenses for food, petrol etc); for income tax purposes, these people are often referred to as '*higher-paid*' employees. Income tax is not paid on most non-wage benefits by everybody else (including company directors who (i) earn less than £8,500 p.a. and (ii) work full-time for the company and (iii) do not control more than 5 per cent of the ordinary share capital). For example:

■ if your basic wage/salary is £7,500 a year (about £144 a week) and you get £700 a year in expenses, bonus etc, your 'total remuneration' for the year comes to £8,200 – so you will *not* pay tax on a car, for instance;

■ if you get a car on top (say, taxed on a 'value' of £450 – see pages 257–58, your 'total remuneration' for the year will be £8,650 – and you *will* be liable for tax on your benefits.

In each chapter of this book there is a sub-section entitled 'Income tax', and this will tell you whether the benefit is added to your 'total remuneration' or not. The test is whether any expenses you receive are 'wholly, exclusively and necessarily in the perform-ance of [your] duties'; if you are in any doubt about your income tax liability, get your employer to check it out with the local tax inspectors – or go and see them yourself.

Although it is true that 'higher-paid' employees pay tax on certain non-wage benefits (e.g. a company car), they are also earning more money than anybody else. 'Higher-paid' workers **earn** more, are more likely to get certain non-wage benefits **and pay very little income tax** on them.

How to use this book

Each chapter of this book consists of three sections:

■ *Introduction*: some background information, including sur-veys, showing how many people – and what sort of people – have the benefit in question; there are also examples of the details of certain agreements, together with lists of employers who do (or don't) provide their employees with these benefits;

■ *Preparing for negotiations*: brief explanation of any legal rights that you may have as an employee, and your liability to pay income tax (if any); where appropriate, there is also an explanation of any *other* legislation that is relevant;

■ *Sitting down with management*: some suggestions as to what you can say to management, and how to counter their statements.

While going through each chapter, it will be useful to bear in mind certain points; for example, the 'Introductions' have a lot of information in them, and include many company and national agreements:

■ some of the lists of agreements are very long – this is to help you work out whether you can justifiably tell your employer not only that *other* employers provide a given benefit (or provide it more generously), but also that other organisations in your locality or industry or group of employers are *already* providing it;

■ these lists contain only a *selection* of company and national agreements, and are intended to give you an idea of the *range* of benefits in the country;

■ when you see a reference to a national *industrial* agreement (NJIC, JIB etc – see Glossary), this means that a very large number of workers are covered – for example, NJC for Local Authorities Manual Workers covers over one million workers;

■ the information is as up-to-date as it has been possible to achieve at the time of writing.

The 'Introductions' also give you some of your best *negotiating* points:

■ they may tell you that large numbers of workers elsewhere in the country enjoy a benefit – you can bring pressure on your employer on the grounds that *you* have a right to it as well;

■ if other workers in the same area or industry or group of employers have got something that you haven't got – or they have more of it than you – why not you? Employers are always impressed by comparisons with other firms;

■ the 'Introductions' give you *ideas*.

The second section ('Preparing for negotiations') may also give you some of your best negotiating arguments:

■ the sub-sections on labour legislation tell you what the legal *minimum* is;

■ the sub-sections on income tax tell you whether *you* may be liable (very important if you do not want to lose financially);

■ the sub-sections on income tax also tell you (where appropriate) when the *employer* will benefit from a *tax allowance*;

■ the second section is laid out in the same way in each chapter – with certain points being made each time – so that the reader who reads only some of the chapters will have *all* the information necessary.

You may also need some *legal* advice on some of the points in the second section; for matters concerning *employment* legislation: **contact your trade union;** for problems connected with *other* legal matters (e.g. setting up a sports and social club or a workplace nursery), you can use the **Green Form scheme** (£25 worth of *free* legal advice from a solicitor – but *no* repesentation in court; the £25 is means-tested). Choose your solicitor carefully. Here are some places that can help you to do so:

■ your local law centre (they are used to dealing with *groups* of people);

■ a local tenants' association (they might know a friendly and *sympathetic* lawyer);

■ the Citizens' Advice Bureau.

Before you actually sit down with management, you may also need *more information about terms and conditions of employment elsewhere*; here are some *trade union contacts* which should be able to help you:

■ union branch meetings (particularly if your branch also has members who are not employed by the same firm as you);

■ the local Trades Council;

■ delegates to regional and/or industrial conferences held by your union;

■ local trade union health and safety groups.

In the third section of each chapter ('Sitting down with management'), you will find a *summary* of negotiating arguments to put to the employer and points to help you rebut some of the things the employer might say to you.

■ Use whichever of the arguments you think will give you your best case.

■You may not like some of the points (e.g. 'company loyalty' or recruitment/retention is management's problem, not yours) – but management may buy them.

■ The points are *ideas* to help you formulate your case.

There is also a Glossary at the end of the book (see pp. 284–92) containing explanations of some terms and abbreviations, but here are a few comments on some words used in *all* the chapters.

● *Manual workers*: this phrase is used to mean all people doing manual jobs, but also sometimes includes low-paid clerical workers. In this book, 'manual workers' means people who come under manual workers' agreements (even when they include supervisory staff who are also covered); sometimes the word 'hourly-paid' is used instead.

● *White-collar workers*: this term is used to cover employees in traditional white-collar occupations (e.g. teachers, doctors – and line management) as well as those workers in supervisory grades who come under a separate company or national agreement from manual workers; sometimes the words 'weekly-paid' and 'monthly-paid' are used instead.

● *Staff*: this word means either 'white-collar workers' *or all* employees; the context makes it clear what is meant.

● *Management*: that level of management that can take *major decisions* on policy and expenditure (e.g. on higher sick pay, on better allowances or obtaining premises for a canteen); when *other* levels of management are concerned, terms such as 'middle management' or 'junior management' are used.

● *Company/firm*: for reasons of brevity, the words 'company' and 'firm' are used throughout this book to mean the organisation that employs you – this is despite the fact that most public sector employees do not, properly speaking, work for one.

● *S/he – him/his/her*: in this book, 's/he', 'his/her' and 'him/her' are used to indicate male or female *workers* – for whom this book has been written.

● *He*: the masculine pronoun reflects the fact that nearly all employers are men. It is not used neutrally.

Labour legislation

In each of the chapters, there is a sub-section dealing with the law as it affects workers. It would have interrupted the flow of these sub-sections to explain some of the laws and legal terms each time they occurred. Here is a brief explanation of them:

● *Sex Discrimination Act 1975*: it is illegal for an employer to discriminate with regard to non-wage benefits on grounds of sex: an employer must not discriminate against a woman 'in the way he affords her access to . . . benefits, facilities or services, or by refusing or deliberately omitting to afford her access to them'. (Section 6(2) of the Sex Discrimination Act 1975) This law has proved most unsuccessful in providing much legal support for working women. (For anti-discrimination laws in Northern Ireland, see 'Northern Ireland legislation' below.)

● *Race Relations Act 1976*: it is also illegal for an employer to discriminate with regard to non-wage benefits on grounds of race: an employee may not racially discriminate against a worker 'in the way he affords him access to . . . benefits, facilities or services, or by refusing or deliberately omittting to afford him access'. (Section 4(2) of the Race Relations Act 1976) Just as the Sex Discrimination Act has failed to stamp out discrimination against women, the Race Relations Act has provided little or no legal assistance in fighting racism at the workplace. (For anti-discrimination laws in Northern Ireland, see 'Northern Ireland legislation' below.)

● *Wages Councils*: these were originally set up in a number of industries where it was felt that there was insufficient trade union organisation to deal with the employees' terms and conditions of employment. Each year, the Wages Councils for the various industries publish 'Orders' setting out certain minimum conditions of employment (and some of these concern non-wage benefits of the kind discussed in this book): employers are bound to observe at least these minimum terms. If you want to find out more about Wages Councils (the industry you work in may be covered by one), contact the Office of Wages Councils, 12 St James's Square, London SW1.

● *Northern Ireland legislation*: the provisions of labour legislation are exactly the same in Northern Ireland as in England, Scotland and Wales; however, the *names* of the laws are different:
– the Employment Protection (Consolidation) Act 1978 is covered by the Industrial Relations (Northern Ireland) Orders 1 and 2 (1976 and 1977 respectively);
– the Sex Discrimination Act 1975 is covered by the Sex Discrimination (Northern Ireland) Order 1976;
– there is no Race Relations Act in Northern Ireland; instead there is the Fair Employment (Northern Ireland) Act 1976, which outlaws religious and political discrimination at work.

For further information on labour legislation in Northern Ireland, read *A guide to industrial relations legislation in Northern Ireland* and *A guide to sex and fair employment legislation in Northern Ireland* (both published by the Industrial Society, 1977).

1.

Holidays

Introduction

This chapter will discuss paid (or unpaid) holidays from work – what your contract may call your 'annual holiday entitlement'. We will look at how many days you can expect to get, how you may be able to get more holidays, when you can take the time off and how much you will be paid.

Although contracts nearly always put holidays and public holidays together, these extra days plus locally negotiated and 'industry' days are dealt with separately here in 'Public holidays' (pages 44–51). Also, paid (or unpaid) time off for other reasons – domestic reasons, court attendance, other public duties and study – is dealt with in Chapters 4–8.

Improvements in paid holiday entitlement have been rapid in the last 40 years: at the beginning of the Second World War it was unusual for working people to have any paid holidays at all but, thanks to considerable trade union pressure during and immediately after the war, the late 1940s saw approximately 55 per cent of the working population with a paid entitlement – usually one week.

Since then advances have been dramatic. Figures published in the *Department of Employment Gazette* show the following progress (1 week = 5 days): see the first table on page 16.

The *Time Rates of Wages and Hours of Work* for 1978 and 1979 (also published by the Department of Employment) show that this trend is continuing; the second table on page 16, shows the percentages of manual workers in 1978 and 1979 receiving two weeks' holiday a year, between two and three weeks a year etc: see page 16.

These statistics show that there was a decline in basic entitlements of *less* than four weeks and a considerable increase in the number of workers with a *minimum* entitlement of four weeks.

	Manual workers percentage	Paid holiday weeks
1951	28	1
	66	2
1955	96	2
1960	97	2
1965	75	2
	22	2–3
1970	41	2
	49	3
1974	37	3
	54	3–4
	7	4 and over
1978	41	3–4
	36	4 and over

Although manual workers have increased their annual holiday entitlements most impressively in the last 40 years, executive grades have succeeded in keeping well ahead: in 1977, the British Institute of Management reported that 44 per cent of top managers and 41 per cent of supporting managers had *five weeks a year or more*.

A more recent survey in *Reward*, the quarterly survey of conditions of employment, points to similar differentials: an annual entitlement of 22 days (four weeks and two days) is enjoyed by:

24.3 per cent of management;
9.9 per cent of clerical workers;
5.1 per cent of manual workers.

Number of weeks' holiday	Percentage of workers					
	2	2–3	3	3–4	4	over 4
1978	2.7	0.8	19.0	41.0	30.9	5.4
1979	1.2	0.4	18.8	36.0	39.5	4.3

This country is way behind most other European countries, as the most recent statistics of the numbers of days per year show:

	Annual basic holiday days	*Public holidays* days	*Total* days
Italy	20–24	17–18	37–42
Germany	20–30	10–13	30–43
Belgium	24	10	34
France	24	8–10	32–34
Denmark	24	9½	33½
Luxembourg	20–22	10	30–32
Netherlands	20–21	7	27–28
Britain	20–21	7	27–28

(Source: *EEC Survey of European Labour Costs*, 1976)

Since 1976, the number of public holidays in this country has gone up to eight, but at the same time holidays elsewhere have increased – for example, both Denmark and Luxembourg have now both achieved 25 days' basic holiday a year, and at least one collective agreement in the Netherlands (in the banking sector) gives five weeks from 1981. It is also true that certain public holidays were 'abolished' by law in Italy in 1977, but the majority of collective agreements (e.g. engineering and textiles) have simply increased the basic entitlement to compensate.

Germany is another EEC country to have made enormous strides in recent years; German workers' successes make their British counterparts (see page 16) look very sad by comparison.

The figures on page 18 show that, in 1979, 94 per cent of German workers had a minimum of four weeks' annual holiday and 61 per cent had at least *five* weeks.

As part of an overall strategy for decreasing the number of working hours, the European Trade Union Confederation (ETUC) launched a campaign in May 1979 aimed at achieving an annual six-week holiday for all – in addition to a 35-hour week and retirement at 60. The British TUC took this up later in the same year in its Campaign for Economic and Social Advance and, simultaneously,

	Workers percentage	Paid holiday weeks
1977	12	3–4
	49	4–5
	39	5–6
1978	9	3–4
	42	4–5
	49	5–6
1979	6	3–4
	33	4–5
	59	5–6
	2	over 6

started publishing a series of invaluable newssheets called the *Campaign for Reduced Working Time – TUC Progress Reports*; these reports provide very useful up-to-date information on advances made in the field of annual holidays, and they have been used occasionally in this chapter.

A growing awareness at shop-floor level of the widening gap between British and foreign conditions of employment can be seen in claims made by British workers employed by multinational companies. For many years, countries like Italy have had 13-month, 14-month and even 15-month years (i.e. you get paid your monthly earnings 13, 14 or 15 times a year), and the extra months' payments are often made at holiday time; in the 1980 pay round at Massey-Ferguson, part of the shop stewards' written submission of their claim deliberately highlighted the more favourable conditions obtaining in the firm's overseas operations:

'*Italy*.

Minimum annual holiday entitlement, excluding statutory holidays, is 20 days. All workers are entitled to one extra day's holiday after ten years' service with the company. Every worker receives a Christmas and a holiday bonus, each amounting to one month's normal pay.

It is significant that Massey-Ferguson employees in [France, West Germany and Italy] receive additional holiday bonuses. In the case of the Italian workers, these amount to two months' extra pay.'

How many days?

A small number of groups of workers have long enjoyed a very much longer annual leave entitlement than 20 days; two untypical examples are workers in the Merchant Navy and on offshore oil rigs:

■ Merchant Navy officers now have 127 days' holiday a year, and if shipping companies wish to improve on this minimum they have the option to give payment in lieu instead;

■ engineering construction workers on offshore oil and gas production platforms have a work/leave cycle of 27 days on the platform and eight days' holiday, with seven clear days between reaching the mainland terminal and returning to it. Their entire annual entitlement consists of:

annual holiday	4 weeks
periodic leave	10.4 weeks
statutory holidays	1.6 weeks
total	16 weeks

However, for the majority of workers, the going rate in this country is currently around four weeks (20 days), but there is a growing number of agreements giving a more generous entitlement; here are a few examples:

■ *6 weeks*: Times Newspapers (clerical, executive and administrative workers);

■ *28 days*: Jenks & Cattell (Wolverhampton);

■ *27 days*: Hosiery Trade NJIC;

■ *25 days* (sometimes the agreement says '5 weeks'): Birmingham Post & Mail (day and night composing room), British Airways (clerical and administrative staff Grades D10–11 – e.g. departmental superintendants and building service engineers), John Brown Shipbuilders (Clydebank), China Clay, China Stone and Ancillary Industries NJIC, Independent Broadcasting Authority (in 1981–82), independent shipbuilders and repairers (negotiated by the CSEU), *Daily Mail* (clerical, executive and administrative staff), *Daily Record* and *Sunday Mail* (clerical, executive and administrative staff), Deanshanger Oxide Works (Milton Keynes), Electricity Council (shift workers), engineering industry (phased in during 1979–82; extra days to be nominated by local management so to help organise Xmas/New Year shutdowns), Glacier Metals (Manchester) (phased in by 1982), Metal Box, Weir Pumps;

■ *24 days*: British Rail (management staff), British Ship-builders, Borg Warner (Letchworth), Fire Service;

■ *23 days*: H J Barlow (Wednesbury), Black & Decker (Spennymore, Co Durham), BXL Ltd (Haltwhistle, Northumberland), Cramic Engineering (Banbury), Govan Shipbuilders, Perkin-Elmer, Plessey (Nottingham), Rolls-Royce (Hillington, Glasgow), SKF (UK) (Luton).

Some of the above agreements have strings attached:

■ the increase at the *Daily Mail* was negotiated in exchange for the introduction of a new computer;

■ the extra five days under the China Clay NJIC have to be self-financing wherever possible.

In an agreement not quoted above, extra days are dependent on attendance:

■ at Hotpoint (Peterborough and Mexborough), the basic entitlement of 22 days can be increased to 27 for full attendance during the year – the extra entitlement is reduced by one day for every day absent.

Holiday arrangements normally assume that the person qualifying is a full-time employee, but NHS manual workers and people covered by the Ambulancemen's Council, no matter how many days a week they work, have an elaborate scheme detailing the basic entitlement of everyone from those in their first year of employment to those with over 10 years' service. This is what it says for those workers with the minimum *basic* holiday, showing the number of days' holiday according to the number of days' employment in a week:

Basic working week	Annual holiday entitlement
1 day	4 days
2 days	8 days
3 days	11 days
4 days	15 days
5 days	19 days
6 days	23 days

As we have seen (on page 2), white-collar workers certainly do better *on average* than manual workers, sometimes doing better for themselves when they constitute a group of their own and do *not* have a *direct* relationship (e.g. supervisory) with manual workers:

■ at the Open University, white-collar staff have six weeks;

■ at IPC, the entitlement is five weeks for everyone except for unqualified journalists (who move up from four weeks to five weeks after two years).

Other white-collar agreements giving five weeks' annual holiday include:

■ GKN Sankey (supervisory and technical staff) and The Singer Co (UK) (monthly staff).

Differentials between staff and manual workers, where they do exist, can be quite strikingly large:

■ Clark Son & Morland	monthly staff:	25 days
	weekly staff:	20 days
	manual workers:	15 days
■ Govan Shipbuilders	staff:	28 days
	manuals:	23 days
■ W & T Avery	staff:	25 days
	manuals:	20 days
■ G W Padley	staff:	20 days
	manuals:	17 days

(The agreement at Clark Son & Morland also includes four 'industry days' for *all* grades of employee; 'industry days' are extra, locally negotiated holidays (see pages 44–51).) Sometimes there are no such differentials at all – in fact, a survey conducted by IDS in 1979 found that only nine out of 77 firms questioned made any distinction, although this might have been because it was the 'better' employers that answered the questionnaire. Nonetheless, IDS were able to report two interesting patterns in holiday differentials:

1. Nearly all industrial sectors (the distributive trade and banking & insurance are exceptions) can boast a large number of agreements that have *no* differentials; companies in these sectors include Findus, Whitbread, Mobil Oil, the Calor Group, Vickers, Vauxhall, Pirelli and British Home Stores;

2. The public sector was much more likely than the private sector to maintain a differential (e.g. British Gas, British Transport Docks Board, National Bus Company and Water Service).

An intriguing characteristic of holiday differentials is that there are sometimes bigger ones *between grades of white-collar workers* themselves:

J. Sainsbury	senior management and grade 13	26 days
	middle management (grades 10–12)	23 days
	junior management (grades 6–9)	21 days
	clerical, administrative and technical staff (grades 1–5)	20 days

Some firms make provision for odd days to be taken off for *religious feasts*; this time off nearly always has to come out of annual holiday entitlement, for example at:

■ the Automobile Association, Bovril (Burton-on-Trent) and Wilkinson Match (High Wycombe).

Other arrangements for religious feasts include:

■ either you take a day out of annual holiday entitlement, or you work another day in lieu (the Littlewoods Organisation);

■ you work longer hours on other days (under the flexi-time system adopted at the Sun Alliance & London Assurance Group).

One final issue needs to be made: entitlement in the first year of employment and falling ill while on holiday. It often happens that there is *no* entitlement in the first year but the public sector, particularly, sets out the entitlement in such a way that almost any employee can take at least one day off after one month's service; in this agreement for NHS manual workers and ambulance personnel, if you work a five-day week and have been employed for only one month, you are entitled to two day's holiday; if you work a three-day week and have been employed for eleven months, you are entitled to ten days' holiday: see page 23.

Longer holidays

A well-established way of getting longer holidays is to have extra days – they might be locally negotiated over and above the national agreement, they may be 'customary' or 'industry' days of a traditional type in the industry in question; this sort of extra holiday is dealt with in 'Public holidays' (pages 44–53). There are two other common ways of extending the *basic* entitlement:

■ service-related holidays;

■ special extensions for individual circumstances.

Completed months of service	Basic working week					
	1 day	2 days	3 days	4 days	5 days	6 days
1	—	1 day	1 day	1 day	2 days	2 days
2	1 day	1 day	2 days	3 days	3 days	4 days
3	1 day	2 days	3 days	4 days	5 days	6 days
4	1 day	3 days	4 days	5 days	6 days	8 days
5	2 days	3 days	5 days	6 days	8 days	10 days
6	2 days	4 days	6 days	8 days	9 days	11 days
7	2 days	4 days	7 days	9 days	11 days	13 days
8	3 days	5 days	8 days	10 days	13 days	15 days
9	3 days	6 days	9 days	11 days	14 days	17 days
10	3 days	6 days	10 days	13 days	16 days	19 days
11	3 days	7 days	10 days	14 days	17 days	21 days

Service-rated holidays

Service-related holidays are extra days added onto the basic entitlement on completion of an agreed number of years' employment. According to the number of 'steps' that a service-related scheme consists of, an employer can attempt to 'reward' an employee who stays with the firm for a given period of time – it might also be a device for encouraging employees not to move on to another company. It is certainly very widespread. According to the Institute of Administrative Management, most of the 900 organisations interviewed give 1–2 days' extra holiday for 1–5 years' service.

Service-related holidays were long the preserve of white-collar staff, but manual workers are now catching up fast: according to the Department of Employment, more than a third of manual workers now receive service-related holidays.

The current 'going rate' for maximum holiday entitlement (i.e. including the service-related element) is about 25 days, but a few firms give more, sometimes making the extra time a lot easier to achieve:

	Maximum holiday (including service-related) days	Service qualification period years
Calor Group (all employees)	30	30
Pedigree Petfoods (all employees)	30	25
Wrigley's (all employees)	30	20
Tampax (all employees)	30	15
Commercial Union Assurance (staff only)	27	30
Crosfield Electronics (manual workers)	27	5
Rolls Royce Motors, Car Division (hourly-paid)	26	6

■ At Penguin Books, after every eight years of employment you get an *extra 20 days* which can be taken separately or together at any time during the *next* eight years.

In its survey of conditions of employment in the engineering industry, the GMWU found that workers became eligible for service-related leave *on average* as follows:

■ 1–3 days' leave; after 5 years' employment
■ 5–10 days' leave: after 20 years' employment

While there is a very large number of examples of service leave at this level – and even at less generous levels – there is also an encouraging number of more attractive arrangements; in the following examples, the number of days of *basic* holiday entitlement is in parentheses after the name of the company:

Service leave days	Qualification period years	
One element of service leave		
4	10	Osram (Birmingham) (22);
5	2	Belgrave North-Western

		Industries (Bootle) (15) – note the very low basic;
5	5	Leyland Paper & Wallpaper Co (Leyland, Lancashire) (20);
5	9	Lyons Bakery (Carlton and Wakefield) (20);
5	10	Vinatex (Chesterfield) (21); Ranalagh Gates (Malmesbury) (22), Hoover (Merthyr Tydfil) (22), Smith's Industries (South London) (22): Black & Decker (Spennymore, Co Durham) (23);

Two elements of service leave

2	2–4	Transtar (Hebburn, Tyne &
5	5+	Wear) (22);
3	5	Howard Rotavators (Halesworth,
5	10	Suffolk) (22);
3	5	Howard Rotavators (Norfolk)
4	10	(22);

Three elements of service leave

1	1	McKechnie Chemicals (Widnes)
2	2	(22);
3	3	
1	2	British Airways (engineering and
2	3	maintenance workers;
3	5	clerical and administrative staff) (20);
1	3	Suflex (Newport, Monmouth-
2	4	shire) (22);
3	5	
1	3	Pointing (Low Purdoe,
2	6	Northumberland) (20);
5	9	

2	1–5	Keyswitch Relays (Wandsworth, London) (22);
4	5–10	
7	10+	

Four elements of service leave

2	$1\frac{1}{2}$	Staedtler UK (Pontyclun, Mid-Glamorgan) (22);
3	$2\frac{1}{2}$	
4	$3\frac{1}{2}$	
5	$4\frac{1}{2}$	

Five elements of service leave

1	1	Velva Tyne Tanks (South Shields) (16);
2	2	
3	3	
4	4	
5	5	

1	2	Pistor & Kronert (Norfolk) (20), G W Wooley (Blackburn) (18);
2	3	
3	4	
4	5	
5	6	

1	2	Coles Cranes (Sunderland) (22);
2	4	
3	6	
4	8	
5	10	

1	6	Durst (UK) (Epsom) (22).
2	7	
3	8	
4	9	
5	10	

Most holiday agreements assume a 'normal' 5-day working week, but some contracts spell out arrangements for workers who spread their 40 hours over six days:

National Health Service

	5-day week		6-day week	
	after 1 year	after 10 years	after 1 year	after 10 years
Ancillary Staffs, Craftsmen and Ambulance Personnel	19 days	24 days	23 days	29 days
Ambulance Officers and Control Assistants	20–23 days	23–25 days	24–27 days	27–30 days

In periods of very heavy pressure from employers to keep earnings down, substantial improvements in holiday entitlements rapidly become a lot more important in negotiating agendas:

■ in July 1980, ICI had its first ever strike by white-collar workers; this was partly in protest against a very low offer by management on increased service-related holidays.

Pay for service-related holidays is approached from two very different points of view. One is to adopt a procedure as to payment for basic holiday entitlement (see pages 35–36):

■ at Electro Furnace Products (Hull), service leave is paid for at the average pay for the March of each year.

The other method is to give pay in lieu of holidays:

■ after 15 years, 1 week's pay (Pirelli – manual workers only; staff get 5 days' service-related holiday after 15 years);

■ this is the service-related entitlement at GEC (Bradford):

1 day after 3 years
2 days after 5 years
3 days after 7 years;

all of it is paid in lieu of time off;

■ at Thorn Electrical Industries (Enfield), the draughtsmen and tracers have a sliding scale for service leave rising to 5 days after 10 years' employment: these 5 days are accompanied by a 2 per cent salary bonus;

■ after 4 years' employment, Bush Boake Allen (Witham) give annual service pay of £24.89.

Service-related holidays made spectacular advances in the period 1978–80. Incomes Data Services have identified three major areas where companies have started making improvements:

■ some firms have introduced service-related holidays for the first time, either into certain departments or into the whole firm (e.g. Glenlivet Distillers, Leyland Paints, Mather & Platt and Tampax);

■ other companies have increased the amount of holiday entitlement: the Ford Motor Company, for example, raised the holiday from 22 and 23 days after 10 and 25 years respectively to 23 and 25 days; and at British Airways engineering and maintenance workers now climb from 20 to 23 days after only *five* years; other organisations to increase the holiday entitlement include the Electricity Supply JIC, Group 4 Total Security and Local Authorities (manual workers and craftsmen);

■ a third method of improving the service-related holiday has been to reduce the qualification period: originally, staff at Burmah Oil had to stay with the firm for 25 years to qualify for the 25 days' holiday; now they gradually increase their holiday by means of a sliding scale, starting with one extra day after 10 years, a second extra day after 15 years, and so on; under the Retail Multiple Grocery JC, the qualifying period for the full four weeks' annual holiday has been reduced from five years to two years.

There have also been some most ingenious ways of enabling workers to qualify for extra service-related leave. One very popular area where this has happened – and a most interesting one in view of the TUC's policy on the shorter working week and early retirement (see pp. 17–18) – is in the last few years of employment: companies have linked the extra days to a worker's exceptional length of service, to the worker's age or to his/her retirement age:

■ at Lucas Electrical (Four Oaks, Birmingham) and Armstrong Patents Co (York), there is an extra four weeks' holiday after 30 years' employment – at Lucas Aerospace (Liverpool) the qualification is only 25 years; at Crabtree Vickers Ltd (Leeds), there is a maximum of 10 days' extra holiday in the pre-retirement year, depending on service;

■ at Sevalco, workers in their last five years before normal retirement age receive two extra days each year – thus moving up from the basic 20 days a year to 30 days a year in the last year before retirement; long-serving employees on the wholesale side of Boots who are within five years of retirement are eligible for 25 days' holiday;

■ at J. Sainsbury, if you are over 60 years of age and have at least 10 years' continuous service with the firm, you get an extra five days' holiday (with an overall maximum of 25 days); at Berger (Newcastle and Middleton), if you have been employed by the company since your 56th birthday, you qualify for five extra days for every year of service after your 61st birthday until retirement age (65) – in other words, there are 30 extra days in the last year of employment.

Lastly, it must be said that, despite the increase in service-related holidays, it is not unknown for unions to negotiate for them to be abolished sometimes so that *everybody* gets the full entitlement:

■ an unusual feature of the 1979 settlement at the British Transport Docks Board was the *consolidation* of service-related holidays for junior clerical and technical workers into a better basic holiday;

■ the service leave entitlements were likewise 'sold' by Local Authorities craftsworkers – but the old entitlements were protected for those already receiving them and for those who qualified for them before the new scheme came into operation in April 1980;

■ sales, clerical and catering staff at Selfridges used to have three weeks and two days rising to four weeks after three years' service; since 1980, everybody has had four weeks' holiday after one year.

Special extensions for individual circumstances

A small but growing number of employers are introducing formal or informal procedures for granting longer holidays in order to fit in with individual employees' private circumstances. According to the Institute of Administrative Management's survey of 900 firms in 1980, 27 per cent allow one month to be taken in the following year, 41 per cent allow three months and 32 per cent allow more than three months.

As often as not, the matter has come to light because of the wish of migrant and immigrant workers to go back home from time to time – and because of the very complicated journeys necessary in many cases. This right has, of course, been extended to workers who simply decide to have the 'holiday of a lifetime'. The following agreement, quoted in *IDS Study 217*, from Trico-Folberth (Brentford) deals clearly with many of the organisational problems that can arise:

'1. The company policy regarding holidays is to discourage the practice of carrying forward holiday from year to year. However, it is recognised that many employees have a need or desire to visit other countries outside the UK, entailing considerable travel and expense. In an attempt to assist employees in realising this wish, the company is prepared to approve up to six weeks' . . . paid holiday providing certain conditions are met. These conditions are:

'(a) The holiday is planned and agreed with the management at the normal level for holiday approval.

'(b) The employee carries forward holiday from one holiday period to the next so that he/she has the required entitlement of holiday credits due. The credits can only be carried forward for one year.

'(c) A long holiday period is taken out of departmental peak times; this usually means the period mid-January to mid-July and mid-September to mid-December . . .

'(d) The practice of having and carrying forward holidays for a long absence does not occur more than once every four years.

'2. This concession of long holidays is open to all employees regardless of nationality. It is offered in the belief that it could be of assistance to employees regarding concessionary fares, etc.'

As can be seen from the above example, extensions of holiday arrangements sometimes involve 'carrying over' one year's entitlement into the next ('carry over' is also dealt with in the next section 'Timing of the holiday'); here are some more examples of holiday extension arrangements:

■ *Sun Alliance and London Assurance*: maximum of two months' paid *and* unpaid leave; the total length of the leave and the mix of paid and unpaid is at management discretion;

■ *Metal Box Packaging*: maximum of six weeks, to be taken between 1 November and 31 March; the company does not pay Social Security contributions during any *unpaid* leave; there is a qualification period of three years' continuous service;

■ *the Littlewoods Organisation*: maximum of four to six weeks; no formal procedure;

■ *the Automobile Association*: permission depends on grade and service: six weeks' leave would include two weeks' unpaid leave;

■ *Truman's Brewery (East London)*: carry-over from previous year, at management discretion;

■ *Wilkinson Match (High Wycombe)*: maximum of annual entitlement of 22 days + 2–3 extra days;

■ *Bovril Ltd (Burton-on-Trent)*: if as much as six weeks is taken off, it is necessary to resign;

■ *Commercial Union Assurance Co*: each individual case is judged on its merits; the company feels that this is fairer than a negotiated procedure.

Unpaid leave can sometimes lead to other problems:

■ production workers at Henry Wiggin & Co (Hereford) get paid for their *basic* holiday period according to the total number of hours worked during the year.

■ unpaid absence from work can put pension rights in jeopardy, unless it is possible to make good the contributions in a lump sum or in instalments on returning to paid employment (for a detailed explanation of this problem and how to deal with it, see *Pensions* by Sue Ward (Pluto Press 1981).

Timing of the holiday

We have already seen how 'carry-over' can be used to enable workers to take long and/or complicated holidays; in this section we shall see how 'carry-over' is sometimes conceded by the employer for different reasons. We shall discuss other ways in which the management can resist an employee's ability to choose the time when a holiday can be taken (e.g. shutdown and 'pecking orders').

First, though, let us look at the kind of agreement that sets out exactly when the holiday period is:

■ the summer two weeks between 1 April and 30 September, the winter two weeks between 1 October and 31 March (Wholesale Newspaper Distribution – Provinces (England & Wales));

■ two weeks between May and September, 'odd days' between October and April (British Gypsum);

■ 10 days in the summer, the other 10 days by mutual agreement (Black Clawson International);

■ the main summer holiday to be taken between April and September, *no* holidays during period December-January (Foster Brothers Clothing);

■ Mobil Oil and Metal Box (Speke) have an admirably flexible arrangement whereby holidays may be taken at any time so long as no more than a certain percentage of the workforce are away at any one time (at Mobil: 25 per cent; at Metal Box: 30 per cent);

■ at Shulton (GB), the five service-related days must be taken between 1 January and 30 June.

Next, there is the 'holiday year' – the 12-month period during which holiday entitlement is accumulated *and* during which the holiday has to be taken. Some contracts can be very strict about holidays which have not been taken by the end of the holiday year, while others can be much more flexible about 'carry-over':

■ The agreement at Parkinson Cowan Appliances states: '. . . ALL employees are expected to take their full holiday entitlement, and employees are reminded that a late rush for untaken holidays at the end of the year will NOT be acceptable.'

■ The NHS Whitley Council handbook, however, says: 'When an officer is prevented by his employing authority from taking his full allowance of annual leave before the end of the leave year he shall be allowed to make up the deficiency during the ensuing leave year at a time to be mutually agreed.'

One reason under this NHS agreement for carrying over one's holidays is being prevented from going on holiday by illness after being *allocated* dates on a rota. A maximum of five days' leave can be taken in the following leave year. There is a similar clause permitting carry-over because of holiday alterations at management request in the agreement covering Wholesale Newspaper Distribution – Provinces (England & Wales). Other examples include:

■ at Smith Kline & French, up to a quarter of the entitlement may be carried over into the first three months of the following year;

■ at Barclay's Bank, this right is restricted to employees who 'put the company's interests first'.

If you are unfortunate enough to be ill while you are on holiday, you *may* not be able to take your lost days later on; this is a problem faced more by manual workers than by white-collar staff, as a survey by the Institute of Personnel Management suggests: see page 33.

This is how the National Health Service deals with this problem:

■ the holiday period is converted into sick leave if you can produce a medical certificate indicating that you are incapable of work – the date on the certificate determining *when* the sick leave begins. The balance of the holiday in these circumstances can be taken after you return to work, but not later than the following 31 March.

Other employers which allow sickness during holidays to count as *sick leave* with the days lost to be taken later include the civil service, Freeman Mail Order, General Motors (Scotland),

	Manual schemes _number_	White-collar schemes _number_
Lost days _can_ be taken at a later date	7	15
Lost days _cannot_ be taken at a later date	8	9

(Alison Jago, _Sick Pay Schemes_, IPM 1979)

Imperial Tobacco, May & Baker (Norwich), Norton Abrasives (Welwyn Garden City), Victor Products.

Probably the biggest single restriction on an individual's ability to choose time off is the internal 'pecking order'; this might be based on:

■ length of service (among postmen and at Pearl Assurance);
■ grade (at the Midland Bank, for instance, _appointed_ staff have first choice, followed by other staff according to their length of service).

Another important determining factor in the timing of the annual holiday is the _annual shutdown_. In the public sector and in certain industries (e.g. soft drinks), it can be very difficult to get employers to concede holidays of any sort during parts of the summer; in most parts of manufacturing industry, however, compulsory summer shutdowns affecting manual workers are very common. Here are some examples:

	Shutdown	Remaining holiday
Ford Motor Co	three weeks in the summer	one week at Xmas
Vauxhall	three weeks in the summer	one week over the Spring Bank Holiday
Tampax	two weeks in August	one week at Xmas; one week by mutual agreement

Some firms have more than one shutdown:

Parkinson Cowan Appliances has *three* compulsory shutdowns, and the agreement is quite clear about the number – and type – of days off:

	Number of statutory days	Number of days from holiday entitlement
spring closure (end of May)	2	3
summer closure (July–August)	nil	10
September closure	1	4

It sometimes happens that part of the basic annual entitlement must be taken at the time of the Xmas shutdown (by contrast with the *extra* days for Xmas on pages 44–53):

■ three of the 22 days' annual entitlement are withheld for the Xmas shutdown (Lesney Products (Peterborough));

■ one of the 22 days must be taken at Xmas in order to bridge the gap between the Xmas holiday and the previous or following weekend (Refractory Goods Manufacture (England & Wales) NJWB).

A happier reason for a compulsory shutdown is the decision to close down in such a way as to fit in with local traditions:

■ at Weir Pumps, one of the two shutdowns (the two-week one) is always timed to coincide with the Glasgow Fair – when most industry in the city is at a standstill anyway; the shutdown is compulsory for those on the works side but staff can take this fortnight at the same time or just before or just afterwards;

■ in Lancashire, the textile industry always has a holiday to celebrate 'Wakes Week' – although it usually lasts a fortnight these days, and some firms even arrange the holiday for different times of the year.

Holiday pay

Most people's holiday pay consists of the basic rate, *possibly* with the addition of such plussages as bonus and shift pay. In theory, this means that holiday pay moves in step with normal earnings throughout the rest of the year:

■ dockers' holiday pay in 1980 increased in line with basic pay: at Southampton, it went up 15 per cent to £94 a week; at Ayr, it moved 14 per cent to £103 a week.

As most contracts of employment give only basic pay, it is a fairly satisfactory situation for white-collar workers as, for the most part, they rarely qualify for extra payments anyway; manual workers, on the other hand, can lose anything up to 50 per cent of earnings if such plussages as shift and overtime premiums and bonus payments are missed out. Varying attempts are made to bring manual workers' holiday pay up to normal pay; they include *averaging* the pay over a period of time and granting an extra sum of money in the shape of a percentage or a bonus.

There is a steadily increasing number of employers who now give *true* average earnings for holidays. A selection of these firms shows the geographical and commercial spread:

■ Bensons (Bury), BSC Chemicals (Falkirk), Commercial Plastics (Cramlington, Northumberland), Fison's (Loughborough and Stanford-le-Hope), Goodlass Wall (Liverpool and London), Harborough Rubber Co (Market Harborough), International Distillers & Vintners, International Paint Co (Felling, Tyne & Wear), Norrit (Glasgow), Synthite (West Bromwich) and the Valentine Paint and Lacquer Co (West Drayton);

■ the employers' side of the British Furniture Trade JIC has made a commitment to *phase in* average earnings.

A problem can sometimes arise when the earnings consist of a large number of items, particularly when the basic is exceptionally low:

■ in local government, manual workers' holiday pay consists of enhanced rates for *regular* standby payments, shift work, night work, split duties, rostered Saturday and Sunday work, unsocial hours payments and regularly paid plus-rates for skills, responsibilities and abnormal working conditions; their holiday pay *excludes* payments for *occasional* standby, overtime payments and payment for extra hours worked because of staff shortages.

If holiday pay is to consist of average earnings, it is important to choose the most favourable period over which to average the money: a long period may include a time before the last wage increase and a short one may exclude overtime opportunities. This is how a few very different employers go about it:

■ previous June: in local government, there are many thousands of workers who *normally* have to take their holidays during *school* holidays (e.g. school meals staffs, bus attendants, crossing patrols); their holiday pay is calculated on earnings in June;

■ previous six weeks: if overtime is *irregular* (NHS maintenance staff);

■ six weeks preceding March: Furniture Manufacture JIC;

■ previous 13 weeks: including overtime and night payments; excluding meal allowances, *ex gratia* payments and *holiday pay during the 13-week period* (Wholsesale Newspaper Distribution – Provinces (England & Wales));

■ January–March: British Bata Shoe Co (Maryport, Cumbria);

■ previous six months: including overtime (Water Service NJIC);

■ previous year: Thomas Swan & Co (Consett);

■ earnings according to the P60: and *updated to take account of wage increases* (Beecham Medicines (St Helens)).

Another method is the so-called 'rolling average' formula, as used by Black Clawson International:

■ this includes shift and nightshift allowances and individual merit rates, but excludes overtime pay and irregular payments such as productivity bonuses; total earnings for 13-week periods – but not counting weeks which include short-time working, industrial action or sickness – then form the basis for holiday pay in the *next* 13-week period:

Average pay in	*decides the holiday pay for*
weeks 1–13 1981	weeks 14–26 1981
weeks 14–26 1981	weeks 27–39 1981
weeks 27–39 1981	weeks 40–52 1981
weeks 40–52 1981	weeks 1–13 1982
weeks 1–13 1982	weeks 14–26 1982

Some employers do not try to work out what a true average might be, and are content to make a payment in addition to the basic rate; this usually takes the form of either a percentage or a holiday supplement. Some examples of percentages added to the basic rate are:

- 25 per cent: Flat Glass Industry GB (NJIC);
- 33 per cent: Tirfor (Sheffield);
- 33⅓ per cent: Darlington Insulation Co (Newcastle);
- 50 per cent: BOC.

Sometimes, a differential between groups of workers is preserved:

- pieceworkers: basic + 30 per cent; timeworkers: day rate + 12½ per cent (London Brick Co);
- dayworkers: basic + 30 per cent; shiftworkers: basic + 42½– 60 per cent (Formica, North Shields).

The additional payment is sometimes in the nature of a supplement; usually it is closely related to the existing wages structure:

- 6⅔ days' pay at General Motors;
- one week's basic pay at Shulton (GB) and at British Airways (engineering & maintenance workers and clerical & administrative staff).

Occasionally it is a straight cash payment:

- Cadbury Schweppes (Food Division):

Length of service	Holiday bonus
years	
1–2	£8
2–5	£15
5–15	£30
15–25	£40
over 25	£50

The holiday bonus *excludes* the additional profit supplement of £1.50 per week;

- paper industry: see page 38
- Laporte Industries (Widnes): £10 a week;
- Forestry Commission: £1.60 a day (also payable on public and privilege days).

Dayworkers	Holiday supplement
Grade C11	£13.92
Grade C1A	£12.25
Grade C2	£11.42
Grade C3	£11.00

So that certain groups of workers should not be unfairly discriminated against because of a rigid scheme, some employers allow a *choice* of systems, thus giving their employees the option to take the system which is financially more favourable:

■ P60 ÷ 52 or grade rate (Associated Biscuits, Reading);
■ average pay or basic salary (Parke Davis & Co);
■ average earnings minus bonus or fixed weekly earnings (Whitbread);
■ average pay or rate + 10 per cent (Carr's of Carlisle, United Biscuits (Liverpool and Toll Cross));
■ previous year's average or basic + 25 per cent (Bacon Curing (GB) NJIC).

Lastly, a word about an unusual system of holiday pay found, for example, in the building industry: holiday stamps. Stamps are now paid up to the value of £8.50 for each day of holiday (including 10p death benefit contribution), or £6.30 for workers under the age of 18; the employers' side of the Building and Civil Engineering Joint Board agreed to this rise in 1980 on condition that building workers did four full days a week in future for that week to qualify for holiday stamps.

We have seen how German workers got *longer* holidays (see page 18); they also get *paid* more. It is true that German unions have had similar difficulties in achieving 'true' average earnings, and have had to be satisfied – in the short term, at least – with the same sorts of additional payments that some British workers get; but the result is that German workers are *considerably better paid* than workers here. IDS report the following figures for 1979:

■ 93 per cent of German workers receive pay better than basic rate for their holidays;
■ 41 per cent receive a bonus of 45 per cent (*on average*) of pay;

■ 33 per cent receive a lump sum (average: DM (German marks) 455 – approximately £105 at 1979 values);

■ 19 per cent receive a daily holiday supplement (average: DM19 – approximately £4.40 at 1979 values);

■ 60 per cent receive the equivalent of an extra month's earnings as an end-of-year/holiday bonus.

This is the position in two other European countries:

■ in Belgium, workers get three weeks and two days' holiday at *double pay*;

■ in the Netherlands, there is a holiday supplement of $7\frac{1}{2}$–$8\frac{1}{3}$ per cent of annual earnings (with a *statutory minimum* of $7\frac{1}{2}$ per cent).

Preparing for negotiations

Employment legislation

Under Section 94 of the Factories Act 1961, some women workers and 'young persons' (i.e. those who have not reached the age of 16) are afforded a very modest level of protection with regard to holidays, but it applies only to Scotland and is weakened by various exemptions in Part VI of the Act. Apart from that, there is no statutory control over holidays in this country or over how much you should be paid; *there is no statutory minimum holiday in Britain*. If you work in a Wages Council industry, you *must* get at least the *minimum* entitlement laid down in the Order (see pages 13–14).

There is one small, but important, piece of legislation affecting holiday pay: the Contracts of Employment Act 1972 says that, if you get minimum notice which *includes* part of your holiday, you must be given holiday pay.

Under the Sex Discrimination Act 1975 and the Race Relations Act 1976, it is illegal for an employer to discriminate in favour of an employee on grounds of sex or race (see page 13).

Income tax

Holiday pay is taxed under PAYE in the same way as pay you receive while at work – i.e. it is deducted weekly or monthly or at whatever intervals you are normally paid at. The only exception concerns holiday stamps (as in the building and civil engineering or ventilating and domestic engineering arrangements): this holiday pay *is* taxed, but *in the following year*.

Sitting down with management

Increased holiday entitlements are one element in a *reduction in the working life* – together with study leave, the shorter working week and earlier retirement. With the onset of enormous changes in working practices thanks to technological advances and the desire of a rapidly increasing number of workers to have more leisure time, annual holidays are an important way of improving living standards – and possibly avoiding short-time working or redundancy.

As with so many of the benefits discussed in this book, one of the best pieces of ammunition you are likely to have is recruitment and retention. You should have little difficulty in finding plenty of members who will testify that: **good holidays have an immediate impact on the (potential) new employee; generous holidays go a long way to keeping employees.** Good holiday entitlements should *not* cost the employer money in the long run; you can tell him that **a worker who can have a good rest periodically and enjoy leisure time will give better productivity and a higher workrate.**

One thing that can easily turn new starters off is not being able to take any holiday – or being able to take only very little – during the first year or probationary period; you could say to the employer:

■ new recruits would be off work anyway if there was an annual shutdown or Xmas holiday in the course of the first year – so why shouldn't they be eligible for the normal entitlement, at least on a *pro rata* basis?

All the arguments about new starters also apply to temp and agency staff: good holidays are a very attractive selling point to workers who might well be encouraged to become permanent employees (this, incidentally, saves the firm money).

The biggest objection that your employer is likely to throw up is *cost*: this is a very dangerous argument because, if you do not make allowances for the higher productivity resulting from a rest (see above), longer holidays do theoretically cost money in lost production and/or replacement of workers. Try and steer the discussion clear of this and start talking about some of the positive values of holidays:

■ they make workers healthier;

■ they make workers less tired (after many months of long hours, of boring work – and of tension in certain jobs).

Your employer may not be diverted so easily – he may try and use a formula for calculating the 'cost' of an extra day's holiday. It is important not to fall into the trap of 'costing' an extra day's holiday – *it's an employer's argument* – but it is equally important to know how they work it out. The most common formula at the moment goes like this:

> 1. Add up the number of days *worked* in a year (i.e. 365 minus holidays, public holidays and other days off (e.g. weekends)) – this comes to about 233 for most workers;
> 2. Divide this number into *annual* earnings;
> 3. The result is the 'cost' of an extra day's holiday.

If this is how your employer argues, you need to oppose him on the grounds that he only sees holidays in terms of a financial charge; try and persuade him that increased holidays will result in increased productivity because:

■ the workforce is fresher;

■ there are fewer accidents because people are less tired.

This is, of course, still a 'boss's argument' but, if you're going to talk about costs – and it's very difficult not to with management – at least make *your* management talk logically about it; most employers would like to get away with the idea that longer holidays are an 'extra' which might be conceded to the unions:

■ even though you may want more holidays for other reasons, carry the argument to the employer and make it quite clear to him that the firm stands to gain substantially out of it.

You may need to use the same sort of arguments if you work in a service industry and the employer says that increased holidays will cause a lower standard of service;

■ the answer is that the service had been surviving in the past on *inadequate* holiday entitlements, and there is now therefore a need for higher staffing levels.

Your employer may say that he is prepared to concede on holidays – but only if the increase is service-related. First you need to do a survey amongst the members to establish whether:

■ they want service-related holidays;

■ they agree with the idea of some people getting better holidays because they have been employed for longer;

■ a reasonable number of people stay that long with the firm.

It may be that the members will oppose the idea on the grounds that
service leave discriminates against workers who have not built up
service *in the right places* over the years through no fault of their own
– perhaps by being made redundant. If the members are *opposed* to
the idea:

■ hold your employer to his offer of an improvement;

■ get him to share the offer throughout the workforce.

If the members are *in agreement*, make it a condition of the scheme
that:

■ the increases go in *big* steps that start *early* during the period
of employment (otherwise hardly anyone will be around to benefit).

If your employer says he will give you more holidays – but in
the form of an annual shutdown – you first need to carry out
another survey of the members to find out if:

■ they object to not having the freedom to go away when *they*
choose;

■ they object to having to be off at what could be the most
expensive time of the year;

■ their friends and relatives *can* get time off *their* jobs at that
time (so that people can go away on holiday at the same time).

If the members do not reject the idea outright, it is worth trying to
find out exactly *why* the management are offering a shutdown; if
your employer is *that* keen to close down for a fortnight or so, you
may be able to push for better holiday pay.

One way of having an extended holiday, as we have seen, is to
carry over holiday credits from one year to the next; a reason that
will apply in *all* workplaces is:

■ employees may want to have the 'holiday of a lifetime';

a slightly less common, but socially extremely important, reason is:

■ employees may have relatives living overseas.

It is true that there is no legislation obliging employers to organise
extra time off for migrant or immigrant workers, but what you can
do instead is:

■ quote the Commission for Racial Equality, who say that it is
best to have a laid-down procedure for extended leave because it can
look unfair if every case is judged on its merits.

At the end of the day, your employer might be quite adamant
in refusing, and he may only offer you unpaid leave; in the
circumstances, you may have to accept *for the time being* – but make
sure that, during unpaid leave:

■ the job is *kept open*;

■ all employment rights depending on continuity and seniority (e.g. sick leave, pension, long-service awards) are *preserved*.

Also, if the boss is happy to allow people to take odd afternoons off (e.g. the afternoon before the Xmas break) to go shopping etc, you may need to hold him to it from time to time. These 'grace and favour' days, as they are often called, are *not* part of the written contract and are supported only by *custom and practice*:

■ keep your eyes open to any attempts by management to eliminate them.

2.
Public holidays

Introduction

This chapter is concerned with arrangements (including payment) for public holidays *and* for locally agreed days sometimes known as 'customary days'. It is true that 'customary days' are, properly speaking, part of the annual holiday entitlement (see chapter 1.) but they are being dealt with here, as pay and time off in lieu are very often the same as for the public holidays, and they are frequently attached to Xmas and Easter. This chapter will also refer to illness on a public holiday and what happens if it coincides with a rest day.

There is no single term to cover these public holidays – in addition to 'bank holidays', the terms 'special holidays' and 'nominated days' are also to be found in a number of contracts, and the phrase 'public and customary holidays' is being increasingly used – but we shall say 'public holidays' throughout this book.

If there is no single way of describing these holidays, there is also no single list of days covering the country as a whole; the public holidays you are entitled to according to where you happen to be are on page 45.

This country compares very badly with the rest of Europe in terms of the number of public holidays (see the table below), and it is only by the addition of 'customary days' that this part of a contract often gains any respectability. Here are a few examples of above-average agreements for public and customary holidays:

- *12 Days:* Staveley Chemicals (Chesterfield);
- *11 days:* Tirfor (Sheffield);
- *10 days:* Dia-Prosim (Talbot Green, Pontyclun);
- *9½ days:* Bush Boake Allen (Witham);
- *9 days:* Alpha Automotive Productions (Dudley), Automotive Products (Birmingham), Dowty Seals Plastics Division

England & Wales (8)	Scotland (8)	Northern Ireland (10)
New Year's Day	New Year's Day	New Year's Day
—	2 January	—
—	—	St Patrick's Day
Good Friday	Good Friday	Good Friday
Easter Monday	—	Easter Monday
May Day	May Day	May Day
—	First Monday in May	—
Last Monday in May	—	Last Monday in May
—	—	12 July
—	First Monday in August	—
Last Monday in August	—	Last Monday in August
Xmas Day	Xmas Day	Xmas Day
Boxing Day	Boxing Day	Boxing Day

(Cheltenham), ICI, London & Scandinavia Met Co (Rotherham), Peterson Livingston (Lothian), Wites Chemicals (Droitwich);

■ *8½ days:* Armstrong Patents Co (York), MO Valve Co (Hammersmith, London), Thermal Syndicate (Wallsend, Tyne & Wear), Vickers Elswick Works (Newcastle).

You are more likely to get an extra day or two added to your basic annual entitlement if you work for a large firm. Sometimes, these days can be taken more or less 'by mutual agreement' (just like the basic holiday); sometimes, these days are meant for a particular time of the year. Here are some examples of companies in which days can be taken at any time 'by mutual agreement':

■ *4 days:* British Transport Docks Board (4 'nominated days' for staff only);

■ *3 days:* Gas Supply GB (NJIC) (manual workers);

■ *2½ days:* Post Office (2½ 'nominated days');

■ *2 days:* British Gas (2 'nominated days' for manual workers, 3 for everybody else);

■ *1 day:* BBC (1 'corporation day'), Bryant & May.

An example of customary days being transferred to another part of the year is:

■ at Leyland Paint & Wallpaper, where the August holiday is used to make the September shutdown into a full week (no premium payment is made).

■ at Shulton (GB), you get the Friday before the annual holiday begins as an extra day off; furthermore, any other Friday that occurs during a holiday period counts as a half-day when the annual entitlement is worked out.

However, a more common fate for these additional days is to be attached to either Easter or Xmas, for example:

■ 4 days: Clark Son & Morland (4 'industry days'), MCIF (Aldridge) (1 day at Easter, 3 at Xmas);

■ 3 days: Imperial Tobacco, Molins;

■ 2 days: Glacier Metal;

■ 1 day: Manns Brewery (Xmas Eve only), Sun Life Assurance Co.

Occasionally, the intention of these arrangements is to suit local circumstances:

■ at Edward Curran Ltd, the August holiday is moved to Easter so as to make this holiday longer;

■ in the London Borough of Hackney, the negotiators of the three 'Hackney days' agreed they should be taken over Xmas so as to fit in with Xmas holiday arrangements of *other* manual workers in the area.

Other negotiators have been less successful: USDAW's policy for shop workers over Xmas 1979 was that shops should close on both Xmas Eve and New Year's Eve (which fell on Mondays) so that members could have a four-day Xmas break and a three-day New Year's break – in the end, Debenham's had to offer *treble* pay to get enough staff in for New Year's Day. Similar demands are regularly made in banking to allow for four- or five-day holidays over Xmas (including any weekend days) – and are consistently greeted in the media as yet further examples of 'lazy British workers', or even of 'union power'; this impression is *not* confirmed by at least one management survey carried out by Churchill Personnel: over Xmas/New Year 1979, they estimated that *most* workers in the country had 12 days off – for instance, in most engineering firms and in motor car manufacture there was an official shutdown from 21 December to New Year's Day inclusive. They also considered that such a break is not necessarily harmful to the economy and, furthermore, the Engineering Employers' Federation (EEF) was not at all worried as the extra days *all came out of annual holiday entitlements* – if they had been taken at any other time, production might have been seriously disrupted.

As far as *pay* for working on public and customary holidays is concerned, there are two distinct ways of doing it:

■ normal pay + special extra payments + time off in lieu;

■ a multiple of the basic rate + time off in lieu.

Here are some examples of the first type:

■ for work done on Xmas Day and on one other holiday in the Xmas/New Year period: an additional hourly payment of £2.52; for work done on other public holidays: an additional hourly payment of £1.36 (weekly-paid staff at ICI);

■ for work done on Xmas Day and on one other holiday in the Xmas/New Year period: an additional hourly payment of £2.11; for work done on other public holidays: an additional hourly payment of £1.14 (all staff groups at ICI);

■ a payment of £32.50 + one day off in lieu for all public holidays (assistant managers and sales personnel at Birds Eye Foods);

■ a holiday supplement of £1.60 a day (Forestry Commission).

An interesting variant on the above scheme is:

■ basic rate + double disturbance money (i.e. 73p × 2) for each hour worked (Associated Octel).

With regard to the *second* method, (T means basic rate, $2T$ means double time, $2\frac{1}{2}T$ means double time and a half etc), it would appear that the 'going rate' at the moment is about $2T$ (double time) + one day off in lieu; in fact, a survey of GMWU membership in chemicals in 1980 found that close to half (30 out of 70) of the agreements studied gave this as the entitlement; here are some examples of this from some other industries:

■ Associated Biscuits (Reading), Birds Eye Foods, Burmah Oil, Gillette Industries and United Biscuits (Toll Cross).

The financial side can be better – for example:

■ non-management grades at Woolworth's get $3T$, but this is unusual; something that is growing in popularity is the *choice* between schemes:

■ *either* $2\frac{1}{2}T$ *or* $T+\frac{1}{2}$ + one day off in lieu (Post Office and Burton Gold Medal Biscuits (Edinburgh)).

It is assumed in all the above agreements that *all* public (and customary) holidays are being paid at the same rate; this is not always the case, for example:

■ in motor car manufacture, it is common for only Xmas Day and Good Friday to qualify for 2T, if worked;

■ at Vauxhall, the other days qualify for only $T+\frac{1}{2}$.

A problem can arise when an *off-duty* period coincides with a public holiday:

■ ancillary workers in the NHS, for example, qualify for an *alternative* off-duty period with pay in these circumstances.

When a public holiday coincides with a *rest day*, agreements again vary – with the public sector doing less well:

■ manual workers in local government simply get a substitute rest day;

■ craftsmen and operatives at Unigate Dairies get three days' basic pay (instead of two) + one day off in lieu;

■ hourly- and weekly-paid workers at Asda Stores also qualify for 3T + one day off in lieu.

Whereas there can sometimes be a qualification period for the annual holiday entitlement (see chapter 1.), it is somewhat less common when it comes to public holidays. Nonetheless, problems have arisen in the Water Service, for instance, owing to the relevant clause not making it clear enough that payments and days off are an entitlement from the first day at work:

■ an *unambiguous* contract will state to the effect that the benefits will accrue to 'all employees on the payroll at the time when a public holiday occurs' (British Gypsum).

With regard to sickness on a public holiday, manual workers in local government automatically transfer to holiday pay *for that day*; even if the employee is excluded from the sick pay scheme on medical grounds, s/he qualifies for holiday pay on that day.

Where there are differentials between manual and staff workers, it is usual for manual workers to do better. Sometimes the differential is absolute:

■ at Black Clawson, William Blythe and G. W. Padley, manual workers get 2T and *either* time off *or* a bonus – and staff get *nothing at all*.

Sometimes, the differential is one of degree; here are three examples, including a really elaborate one:

Vickers	manual workers	2T
	staff (earning below a locally specified salary level)	2T

	other staff	time off in lieu
Bovril	manual workers	2T + day off in lieu
	staff	T + day off in lieu
Findus Ltd	process workers	2T + day off (at T + ½)
	engineering employees	2T + day off (at T + ⅓)
	security officers	2T + day off (at basic)
		or 3T
	technical and clerical	2T + day off (at basic)
	engineering supervisors	2T + day off (at T + ⅓)
	management	2T + day off (at basic)

Pay and time off for public and customary holidays has for some time been an area where manual workers did better than staff, but white-collar workers now seem to be catching up fast:

■ the growing number of companies which make no distinction include Ciba-Geigy, Courage, Glacier Metal, Kimberley-Clark, London Brick and TAC Construction Materials.

An interesting and important point to make is that this closing of differentials does *not* have the effect of 'averaging down':

■ all employees at Perkin Elmer have 3T, although they are obliged to take three days' holiday at Xmas to allow for a week-long shutdown.

Finally, there can be strings attached to payment and time off for public holidays – for example, you may *have* to be at work the day before and the day after; here are two instances:

■ in local government, manual workers do not get paid if they fail to report for duty the day before and after (there is nothing about this for white-collar staff);

■ the Parkinson Cowan announcement to manual workers states: 'Employees are further reminded of the consequences of losing odd days before and after holiday closures.'

This mistrustful attitude of managements has sometimes been successfully challenged by unions:

■ at Metal Box in 1977, the management agreed to withdraw the qualification on the understanding that it would be reintroduced only if there were abuses.

At Massey-Ferguson, the hourly-paid workers' contract currently states that they will not be paid for public holidays if they:

■ fail to work the full normal working shift immediately preceding and the full working shift immediately following the statutory [i.e. public] holiday unless they can produce evidence that their absence was due to causes beyond their control.

This book can do no better than quote in full from the trade unions' written submission to Massey-Ferguson in support of their 1980 wage claims:

> 'The Massey-Ferguson holiday agreement for manual employees is outdated and discriminatory. It imposes unnecessary obligations on manual employees and implies that our members are untrustworthy and unreliable. The requirement to work the "full normal shift", both before and after statutory holidays, should therefore be recognised for the anachronism it is and should be abolished. The Engineering Employers' Federation has already accepted the logic of our argument and qualifying days have been deleted in the current engineering agreement. Massey-Ferguson should now accept this principle and cease its petty discrimination between staff and manual employees.'

Preparing for negotiations

Employment legislation

There is *no* legal right to time off (paid or unpaid) for public holidays, although women and 'young persons' have to be given days off under Section 94 of the 1961 Factories Act. If you work in a Wages Council industry, any clause relating to minimum holidays is binding on the employer (see pages 13–14).

If the employer were to discriminate against any employees on grounds of sex or race, this would be illegal under the Sex Discrimination Act 1975 and the Race Relations Act 1976 respectively (see page 13).

Income tax

All pay for public and customary holidays, whether at premium rates or not, is taxed in the usual way under PAYE. Similarly, whatever pay is received on days off in lieu is taxed in the same way.

Sitting down with management

As there is no legal protection for paid time off on public and customary holidays, one of the most persuasive arguments is likely to be entitlements at other workplaces in the locality:

■ if you can show that another local employer pays better and/or gives more time off in lieu, you can suggest that members might be attracted to *move*;

you can try to find information of this sort from the local trade union sources mentioned on page 12. If you suggest that your employer is having difficulty in recruiting and retaining workers, you might say that:

■ an attractive arrangement for public holidays has an *immediate impact* on employees – this is particularly true of temps and agency workers.

It can sometimes be quite easy to tell if the company is experiencing difficulties in attracting certain categories of workers: it may be, for example, that the management is consistently going to outside contractors for certain types of work to be done. If your employer denies that there is any difficulty in this area, it may be advisable to ask straight out if he has any intentions of *reducing* the workforce; if he can demonstrate *to your satisfaction* that this is *not* the case:

■ you can start arguing along the lines that he could have a more *stable* workforce if the terms of employment were more *appealing*.

Depending on how the members think about better pay and time off arrangements for public holidays, you could also say that:

■ the members *may* put up with poor treatment over public holidays a little longer – after all, they've been doing so for years – but in the long run it will alienate the workforce and build up a lot of resentment: is this the sort of atmosphere the management wants? Do they want to be known in the locality as penny-pinchers?

The last line of attack – and often the most effective – is *humanitarian considerations*:

■ at traditional holiday periods like Xmas and Easter, most people are keen to spend time with their families and friends.

In many industries – such as service industries and public utilities – it is essential for the work to continue, but you can point out that:

■ the members realised this when they started the job, and they are prepared to *continue* providing the service, but they need to be able to afford to make up for it at another time *convenient to them*.

3.
Sick leave

Introduction

This chapter is concerned with employers' arrangements for paid (or unpaid) absence from work caused by your *own* sickness or incapacity; paid release to look after relatives who are ill is dealt with in 'Time off for family sickness' (pages 90–95) and membership of *private* health schemes is discussed in 'Health insurance' (pages 277–83). It is also not the purpose of this chapter to deal with sickness benefits under the State scheme in any detail: this is explained in a new Labour Research Department pamphlet (*A Negotiator's Guide to Sick Pay*, LRD 1980). After a general introduction, which includes an examination of the Government's Green Paper on changes in the state scheme and an explanation of insured schemes, this first part is divided into sub-sections covering:

- establishing that you are ill and how ill you are;
- qualifying period;
- waiting days;
- certification;
- pay and length of entitlement;
- medical appointments;
- exclusions from the scheme.

Much of the information in this chapter is drawn from two important sources:

- the GMWU's surveys of 521 local agreements in the engineering, rubber, paint, biscuit, cocoa and chocolate, sugar and confectionary industries;
- *A Negotiator's Guide to Sick Pay* (Labour Research Department 1980) – a survey of sick-pay arrangements in 302 manual and 161 white-collar schemes.

The most recent nationwide, official examination of sick pay schemes was carried out in 1974 by the DHSS (*Report on a Survey of*

Occupational Sick-Pay Schemes, Department of Health and Social Security, HMSO 1977); it shows some improvement in employer provision over the previous 10 years:

	Workers covered by occupational sick-pay schemes
1964	57 per cent (men and women)
1970	73 per cent (men and women)
1974	80 per cent (men)
	78 per cent (women)

It was noted that, in 1974, there were considerable differences in provision from one part of the country to the other:

■ the South-East, the South-West and East Anglia were the best for both men and women;

■ the West Midlands were worst for men;

■ Wales was worst for women.

There were also certain industries and jobs that did better than others; the best-off industries were:

■ public administration and defence (98.9 per cent of men and 96.9 per cent of women covered);

■ public utilities (gas, electricity, water) (97.4 per cent of men and 95.5 per cent of women covered);

and the best-off jobs were:

■ management (90–95 per cent of men and 100 per cent of women covered);

■ professional workers in education, welfare and health (98.7 per cent of men and 100 per cent of women covered).

The DHSS commented that the higher people were paid, the more likely they were to be covered by an employer's schemes. A few other features of sick-pay schemes were also analysed:

■ nearly everybody had to have their sickness or incapacity certified (i.e. by a doctor);

■ qualifying periods (i.e. how long you need to have been employed before qualifying for the scheme) varied considerably:

– no qualifying period: 42 per cent of men and 52 per cent of women;

– 6 months: 20 per cent of men and women;

    – 12 months: 19 per cent of men;

    ■ most people who were in schemes *started* on basic pay at least (66 per cent of men and 85 per cent of women), but there was an enormous variation with regard to *continuing* on the same pay (this was usually at management discretion).

The above statistics on pay are, however, sharply contradicted by the GMWU's survey of manual workers in 212 engineering firms:

Amount paid per week	Agreements number	percentage
up to £5	7	3.5
up to £10	24	11.9
£10–15	20	9.9
£15–20	17	8.4
£20–25	5	2.4
£25 plus	2	0.9
percentage of basic pay	15	7.5
percentage of average pay	20	9.9
100 per cent of basic for half the period, 50 per cent of basic for the other half	72	35.7
100 per cent of average for half the period, 50 per cent of average for the other half	20	9.9
Total	212	100.0

And from a totally different quarter comes another indication that eligibility for membership of occupational schemes is not as common as is often supposed: a survey in 1980 by the Research Institute for Consumer Affairs (part of the Consumers' Association) looking into the effects of accidents to pedestrians and pedal cyclists found that as many as 25 of the 31 casualties who were employed at the time of the accident were not paid while recovering. There is also considerable evidence to support the view that there is a high discrepancy between white-collar and manual schemes:

    ■ The British Institute of Management reports that over 60 per cent of the 336 firms interviewed had different schemes for white-collar and manual workers and, of this 60 per cent, 36 per cent of skilled manual workers and 40 per cent of semi-skilled and unskilled manual workers *received State sickness benefits only*. (*Towards Single Status*, BIM 1976);

■ the Institute of Personnel Management discovered that only one of the 31 firms they surveyed had the same agreements for all employees. (Alison Jago, *Sick-Pay Schemes*, IPM 1979).

At all events, there can be no doubt that a lot of sick leave (whether paid for by the employer or not) is taken. The DHSS says that claims for State sickness benefits are running at the rate of 10 million a year, and in all about £600m is claimed (including £375m in flat-rate benefit) annually; average individual claims are about £30 a week. Also, approximately 390m days are lost every year through sickness and invalidity (compared with 5–10m days lost through industrial action).

It is not known how much sickness absence is attributable to people coming into work carrying an infection and making *other* workers ill.

A common myth, often elevated into a 'fact' by certain employers during negotiations, is that the introduction of – or improvement to – an occupational sick-pay scheme will result in increased absenteeism.

There is no evidence anyway to support this view; in fact, Government figures suggest that the opposite may often be the case. The statistics from the *General Household Survey* 1976 show the percentages of full-time workers aged 16 and over who had sick-pay schemes, together with their absence rates are on page 56.

Objections to the theory that sick pay schemes contribute to absenteeism may be summarised as follows:

■ *if* there were a direct link, one would expect the industry groups with the best provision to have the highest absenteeism rates, but this is not the case: in fact, the industry group with the *worst* provision (leather, clothing and footwear) has the *same* absenteeism rate as the industry group with the *best* provision (public administration and defence), and there are several other groups near the bottom of the list which have *lower* rates of absenteeism;

■ it is noticeable that the industry groups with the highest absenteeism rates are the most dangerous (mining and quarrying) or those suffering from extremely low provision of sick-pay schemes. The official TUC model agreement for sick-pay schemes is

■ *qualifying period::* 6 months;

| Industry group | Full-time workers aged 16 or over | |
	paid when sick percentage	absence rate percentage
1 public administration, defence	98	8
2 professional scientific workers	97	5
3 gas, electricity, water	96	9
4 insurance, banking, finance	95	5
5 coal & petroleum products, chemicals	92	—
6 transport & communication	88	6
7 distributive trades	83	6
8 agriculture, forestry fishing	80	4
9 mining & quarrying	80	16
10 food, drink & tobacco	79	9
11 miscellaneous services	77	6
12 paper, printing & publishing	74	6
13 mechanical, electrical instrument engineering, vehicles & metal goods	67	7
14 construction	64	8
15 metal manufacture	59	9
16 other manufacturing industries	57	6
17 timber, furniture	55	7
18 shipbuilding	54	11
19 bricks, pottery & glass	52	6
20 textiles	42	11
21 leather, clothing & footwear	33	8

■ *pay and length of entitlement*: 26 weeks on full pay and 26 weeks on half pay (+ National Insurance payments, tax rebates etc);
■ *waiting days:* none.

Regrettably, very few firms have approached this standard, although it should be said that some companies have come a long way and, in one or two cases, have even surpassed it (e.g. on qualifying periods). When assessing schemes, it is important to take *all* the elements into account. When *negotiating*, much depends on one's bargaining power *and* on the wishes of the members, and it is vital not to be taken in by *one* relatively impressive element; for example:

■ if Company A has six months on full pay and six months on half pay, it is much less generous than it looks if you have to wait 25 years to get there;

■ if Company B has a qualifying period of only three months and no waiting days, it's not quite so good if you get only six weeks' pay at basic rates.

Use the list of elements on page 52 as a checklist to make sure you get as good a deal as possible on *all* of them.

The Government's Green Paper

There are four kinds of occupational sick-pay scheme:

● schemes financed by workers' contributions only (these are unusual);

● schemes financed jointly by workers' *and* employers' contributions (slightly more common);

● insured schemes (see pages 61–64);

● schemes financed solely by the employer (this type is by far the most common).

However, *all* occupational schemes have to be seen against the background of the State sickness scheme, as there is nearly always a *link* between the two (i.e. a sum of money or a percentage of earnings offset against National Insurance payments); workers invariably have to fall back on the State scheme at one time or another (e.g. sickness benefit, invalidity benefit, industrial injury benefit), no matter how generous the employer's scheme may be. The implementation of the Green Paper and the abolition of earnings-related supplement will inevitably lead to a distinct lowering in many people's standard of living: 'A two-child family on £75 a week, for example, would be £13.67 a week worse off. Even if they claimed supplementary benefit to top up their income, they would still be £7.62 worse off.' (Jean Coussins, deputy director of the Child Poverty Action Group, writing in the *Morning Star*, 29 August 1980). Any radical change in this link between the occupational scheme (if any) and the State scheme needs to be examined very closely. The Conservative Government elected in 1979 produced a policy document for just such a change: a Green

Paper entitled *Incomes During Initial Sickness: A New Strategy* (Cmnd 7864, HMSO 1980). Planned to be introduced by law in 1982, the Green Paper's *political* strategy is outlined in the following statement: 'The State should, wherever possible, disengage itself from activities which firms and individuals perform perfectly well for themselves.' (Green Paper §5). The *practical* implications, in general terms, are that the responsibility for the first eight weeks of sick pay in any tax year (beginning in April every year) is *transferred from the State to the employer*; sickness benefit will then be paid by National Insurance for the next 20 weeks.

Here is a summary of the *proposed* new scheme (sometimes called 'Employers' Statutory Sick Pay' (ESSP)):

- *eligibility:* all employees, except married women and widows paying the lower-rate National Insurance (NI) contributions of 2 per cent;
- *qualifying period:* one day – but if you have been employed for less than eight weeks, the employer will be able to claim back from the DHSS half of the *statutory* minimum sickness benefit paid to you; the qualifying period may *exclude* part-timers;
- *waiting days:* three days;
- *establishing you are ill:* this will be on the basis of the advice of your doctor and according to any rules negotiated between your union and the employer; disputes might be settled by the DHSS Regional Medical Service and appeals could be heard by industrial tribunals or National Insurance Local Tribunals;
- *length of entitlement:* eight weeks in each tax year (which starts in April);
- *pay:* a minimum of £30 a week (pre-November 1980 prices) or 75 per cent of 'normal earnings', whichever is the *lower* – and 'normal earnings' could be the basic rate (particularly low in industries like hotels and catering); this money will be *taxable*;
- employers may be 'compensated' for having to administer the scheme by having to pay 0.5 per cent less in *their* NI contributions (employees will *not* pay lower rates).

The response from bodies of very different political persuasions was critical:

■ *Child Poverty Action Group (CPAG):* 'the first wave of a general rolling back of State responsibility for income maintenance'; the CPAG has also pointed out that the DHSS would need to be informed in good time of employees who are going to be off for more than eight weeks, but 'small businesses . . . are simply not geared up for this kind of bureaucratic paper work.' (*No way to treat the sick*, CPAG 1980).

■ *Civil and Public Servants' Association (CPSA):* a 'half-baked' scheme that would produce an 'administrative nightmare' for both workers *and* employers; the CPSA also called the Green Paper proposals 'a tax on ill health'.

■ *Society of Civil and Public Servants (SCPS):* the SCPS has stressed that the Government has proposed no real safeguards to take account of unscrupulous employers who sack people rather than pay sick pay, or who keep no individual records, thereby making it impossible to check that the right amounts of money are being paid; furthermore, the Green Paper does not define 'incapacity': under the original NI scheme, local insurance officers are bound by decisions taken by the Commissioner, but under the new proposals 'the absurd situation could be reached of two people working for different employers falling sick with the same illness and one being paid and the other one not'. (*Your Sickness Benefit under Attack*, SCPS 1980)

■ *National Chamber of Trade:* this employers' body representing 250,000 companies in Britain criticised the financial and administrative burden that would face small firms; the Government estimates that the cost to *all* employers will be about £500m a year at 1980 prices, and the National Chamber of Trade warns that the proposed legislation may well make small employers less willing to take on workers in poor health.

■ *Engineering Employers' Federation (EEF):* this organisation, representing 6,500 companies in the engineering sector, also found fault with the proposed scheme on the grounds that it would be too expensive, particularly for firms already badly hit by the world recession; the EEF recognised that 'firms were also expecting pressure from workers to make up the difference in their earnings-related benefits due to be reduced by 10 per cent in January [1981]'. (*Guardian*, 18 August 1980)

■ *British Medical Association (BMA):* the BMA is the professional organisation of all doctors in this country and was reported as saying: 'It will take away the patient's right to decide whether to reveal the confidential information in his National Insurance certificate to his employer and will undermine the confidential doctor-patient relationship.' (*The Times*, 3 April 1980) The BMA's General Medical Services Committee is disturbed that employers will, according to the Green Paper, have to be given a statement about the patient's incapacity; this is confidential and doctors will not disclose it.

There are also a number of points made either in the Green Paper itself or by Government ministers since, and these points need to be refuted:

■ *'The State should, wherever possible, disengage itself from activities which firms and individuals perform perfectly well for themselves.' (Green Paper §5)* 'Perfectly well'? The fact is that a large number of workers are doing extremely badly at the moment – see the various tables in the sub-sections on pages 66–79.

■ *'In 1974, the DHSS reported that 80 per cent of full-time workers were already covered by occupational sick-pay schemes, so we don't need NI so much any more.' (Green Paper §5).* But a *large* proportion of the 80 per cent have very poor schemes (as Annex A of the Green Paper itself shows), and there are still 20 per cent *not* covered (mostly low-paid and not in unions); there is also a much higher percentage of *part-timers* not covered;

■ *'£30 or 75 per cent of 'normal earnings' is fair and nobody is going to starve.'* The people who will lose more than others if the Government's proposals get through are:
  – the low-paid;
  – people whose 'normal earnings' are their *basic rate* (perhaps because they can usually expect to make up their earnings by tips, bonuses, allowances and other plus-payments).

■ *'Nobody will lose out.'* A combination of ESSP and the abolition of earnings-related supplement (ERS) in 1982 would mean that anyone not covered by an occupational scheme will be worse off after two weeks' absence than originally; furthermore, the Green Paper proposals accompanied by the cut of 45p *in real terms* in Child Benefit (autumn 1980) means that workers with *no* children are favoured at the expense of sick workers *with* children – as the Green Paper says, 'Individuals with dependants may lose relative to single workers.' (*Green Paper* §7)

■ *'The fact that* **many** *employees receive full pay during sickness, but do not pay tax on part of it, means that they are actually better off financially in sickness than in health.' (Green Paper §4)* [Emphasis added] Employers have added their weight to this criticism, but it is difficult to see why as it is *they* who agreed/negotiated the system in the first place; however, there is no indication that it is widespread:
  – a recent survey of *900* firms employing approximately 1,060,000

workers found that only 12 made no deductions. (*Office Holidays, Sickness Entitlements and Other Benefits*, Institute of Administrative Management 1980)

■ *'For many people, National Insurance is no longer a major element in their income during short-term sickness.' (Green Paper §2)* For a large number of workers, National Insurance is a major element – possibly the only element (i.e. those with poor or non-existent *occupational* schemes).

It should be said that the policies set out in the Green Paper bear a certain similarity to procedures found in other European countries but, in the words of *IDS Report 327*, 'the size of their social security payments and the level of the employees' statutory entitlements dwarf the British proposals.' The Government has tried to give the impression that sick-pay schemes abroad are little better than the Green Paper proposals but, in fact, the differences are enormous; this is what happens in four European countries:

■ *Belgium:* a sick non-salaried worker must receive from the employer 29 per cent of a proportion of previous earnings and 91.5 per cent of the remainder (both parts have a maximum); on top of this, the State pays 60 per cent of previous earnings (up to a certain maximum). A salaried worker who is sick must receive from the employer 100 per cent for the first 30 days of sickness absence.

■ *Denmark:* with a qualification period of 40 hours' employment in the previous four weeks, workers who are sick must receive 90 per cent of earnings from the employer (up to a maximum for the first three weeks); thereafter, the State pays.

■ *West Germany:* as long as there is a medical certificate handed in within three days, sick workers must receive 100 per cent of earnings from the employer (up to a maximum) for the first six weeks of sick leave.

■ *Norway:* with a qualification period of two weeks' employment, sick workers must receive 100 per cent of earnings from the employer (up to a maximum) for the first two weeks of absence.

Insured sick schemes

If the Green Paper goes through, insured schemes are likely to be on *employers'* negotiating agendas before long. Insured schemes (sometimes called 'cost-plus schemes') are not at all the same as insuring a normal sick-pay scheme against loss of production resulting from, say, a flu epidemic; insuring a normal sick-pay scheme in this way is something to which trade unionists will have no objection.

On the surface, there are apparent advantages to workers in insured schemes, but it is necessary to examine them closely to see what the *longer-term tactical and financial consequences* are. This is how an insured scheme works in simple terms:

   ▣ the employer pays a sum of money (a premium) into an insurance company, which then pays sickness benefit direct to the employee;

and the financial effects are:

   ▣ the employer pays the insurance company *less* than he would have paid out by paying gross sick pay, *and* he does not pay *his* National Insurance (NI) contributions of 13½ per cent;

   ▣ the employees receive direct from the insurance company a tax-free sum of money on a weekly or monthly basis (tax-free as long as you are not earning more than £8,500 a year).

The sickness payments to the employee are tax-free (in technical terms, the Inland Revenue will treat this sick pay as annual payments within Case 3 of Schedule E) as long as:

   ▣ the money comes direct from the insurance company and not from the employer;

   ▣ the payments are not made for more than 52 weeks;

   ▣ you do not receive any other sick pay from the employer.

There are certainly advantages so far, but they all belong to the employer – mainly because *he* avoids paying tax and National Insurance:

   ▣ he does *not* pay his NI contributions (of 13½ per cent);

   ▣ he pays out less (to you via the insurance company): he only pays you your net earnings instead of your gross earnings (including income tax and NI);

   ▣ he can claim all sickness payments *and* the management charge to the insurance company as a trading expense for tax purposes;

   ▣ furthermore, there is no certainty that he will pay you true average earnings – to quote a manual giving advice to employers thinking of setting up insured schemes, 'If the total net income of the employee while sick is already a high proportion of net pay while at work, then an increase in the benefit should not be conceded.' (*Short- and Long-Term Sickness Benefits and Private Medical Arrangements*, Metropolitan Pensions Association Ltd)

Above all, the employer will *save money*: figures produced by the employee benefits consultants firm of Wyatt Harris Graham show that an employer can make *a saving of 31 per cent each week* on an employee off sick *and* receiving average net earnings. The fact that the payments to you are tax-free is not such an *advantage* as it might appear: you will **not** be receiving your gross earnings tax-free, just a percentage of them – say 50 or 60 per cent – and it is on this smaller percentage that you won't have to pay any tax.

Employers know well that there are problems in negotiating an insured scheme; for example, the Metropolitan Pensions Association booklet quoted above states: 'The first difficulty is concerned with putting the new arrangements over to the employees.'

In fact, *the drawbacks of an insured scheme for workers are enormous*:

■ Negotiations on improvements to the scheme are taken out of the industrial relations area – i.e. they are carried out behind closed doors between the employer and the insurance company – and you cannot bring *any* trade union clout to bear on the terms of the agreement eventually reached (e.g. how much money you are going to get).

■ What are you going to do if your illness or incapacity lasts more than 52 weeks and if the employer has no long-term insured scheme for your grade? Will you simply be sacked (indirectly by the insurance company)?

■ You can more easily be sacked *while you are off sick* because, during this type of absence, you may not be protected against unfair dismissal by the Employment Protection (Consolidation) Act 1978.

■ As you are not earning in the normal way (i.e. you are not paying income tax), you will not be paying NI contributions either; if you are not claiming State sickness benefit, the effects of this will be:

– you will not be eligible for State sickness and unemployment benefits in the *next* year because you won't have paid, or been credited with, enough NI contributions;

– you may be ineligible for State sickness and unemployment benefits for the year after that as well because you won't have been credited with enough NI contributions;

– you will be ineligible for earnings-related supplement – if you qualify for it in the first place (this is due to be abolished by the Conservative Government in 1982);

– even if you *are* claiming State sickness benefit during this time, you will not be credited for the earnings-related addition to your State pension (for the full implications of this, see *Pensions* by Sue Ward (Pluto Press 1981)).

A lot of employers have already shown particular interest in insured schemes, even when the unions have indicated their opposition. This is what has happened in two cases:

■ When Chief Executives of all Local Authorities in the country were circularised early in 1980 with proposals to introduce insured schemes for white-collar staff, the response from the trade unions was immediate: they informed the employers that they would oppose any proposals on the grounds that:

– they would be contrary to the basic principles of trade unions regarding private health schemes;

– any current tax advantages could not be guaranteed;

– they would have harmful implications for local authority staffing.

■ When Cow Industrial Polymers (London) proposed the introduction of an insured scheme in the autumn of 1980, the union did its sums carefully. It found that:

– the current *company-funded* scheme was costing approximately £35,000 a year;

– the proposed *insured* scheme would cost them several thousand pounds *less* (despite an improvement in payments to a minority of the employees);

– the company would also be paying the insurance company a charge of *£3,500 a year*.

The union had no difficulty in recommending that the offer be *rejected* on the grounds that the only people to gain were the employer and the insurance company.

Establishing that you are ill and how ill you are

In the vast majority of cases, you can establish both that you are ill *and* how ill you are by handing your employer a doctor's certificate (the doctor's certificate is explained in 'Certification' (pages 71–73)). However, there will be times when the employer will query this. Here is a list of things that need to be done – they are 'good practice' *and* they are the things that an industrial tribunal is *likely* to look at if you found it necessary to claim unfair dismissal:

■ A doctor's statement from your GP – perhaps several

statements – or from a hospital doctor or from any other medically qualified person (see 'Certification' (pages 71–73)).

■ The employer may ask the company doctor (or medical adviser) or any other doctor or specialist to examine you as to your ability to return to work.

■ If *your* doctor and the *company's* doctor disagree (and it can go either way: the company doctor may say you are fit for work *or* s/he may say you should not return to work), get your trade union to negotiate for an *independent* medical opinion; this means that a *third* doctor will be asked to give his/her opinion. Make sure that the employer pays for this service:

■ If the employer is considering sacking you because of your illness/incapacity, insist that he discusses the matter with you and your union representative(s) (employers usually call this 'consulting').

■ *At any stage*, use the Grievance Procedure if you feel that your case is not being properly considered.

This is the Greater London Whitley Council's advice to employers in the London boroughs with regard to problems about returning to work after a period of sickness leave:

> 'In this instance the Authority's doctor might claim the officer is fit to return to work, whereas his own doctor feels that he is not yet fit. Again, the reverse situation could apply. This is . . . a straight conflict which could benefit from the involvement of a medical referee.'

And this is the advice when there is disagreement about the possibility of retirement for ill health:

> 'His [the employee's] own doctor may disagree with the medical adviser to the Local Authority, suggesting that his sickness is not permanent and that he will recover in a reasonable time. Equally, the difference of medical opinion may exist in a reverse manner. This is a straight conflict of medical opinion where reference to a medical referee, *jointly agreed by the authority and the trade union*, can be usefully made.' [Emphasis added]

Qualifying period

The qualifying period is the amount of time you need to have been working for your employer before you are eligible for benefits under the sick-pay scheme. Most workers have to be employed quite a time before qualifying; in its surveys of six major industries, the

GMWU found the situation was as follows *where an occupational sick pay scheme was in operation*:

Qualifying period	Agreements	
	number	percentage
none	25	7.4
up to 6 months	131	38.9
6 months–1 year	126	37.4
over 1 year	55	16.3
Total	337	100.0

There were also large divergencies between industries: 61.2 per cent of agreements in the rubber industry had a qualifying period of *over* six months while 62 per cent in chemicals demanded *less* than six months.

It is common practice for service-related schemes (see page 71 to involve a long wait before eligibility to maximum length of entitlement, and the picture changes for the worse if we look at qualifying periods for this:

Service required before maximum entitlement	Manual workers' schemes percentage	White-collar schemes percentage
on qualifying	6.3	11.2
at 5 years or less	34.1	37.9
over 5 years	56.0	42.2
discretionary	3.6	8.7

Some firms to stipulate *no qualifying period at all* are:
■ Art Reprographic (London), Aveling Barford (Newbourne), BBC, British Aerospace (Brough), BSC Chemicals (Southampton), Butlins, Civil Air Transport, Clark Chapman NEI (Gateshead), Crompton-Parkinson (Leeds), Durst (UK) (Epsom), F J Edwards (Chard), EMI (Hayes), Fisons (Loughborough), John

Hastie (Greenock), Leyland Vehicles (Chorley), Howard Rotavators (Norfolk), ICL, Henry Williams (Darlington).

In the majority of occupational schemes, the qualifying periods before maximum sick *pay* is achieved are service-related; for examples of this type of arrangement, see page 75 in the sub-section entitled 'Pay and length of entitlement'.

Another very common feature of qualifying periods – and of sick-pay schemes in general – is a more favourable treatment of white-collar workers; two recent surveys bear this out:

Qualifying period	Manual workers' schemes percentage	White-collar schemes percentage
none	13.9	65.8
0–6 months	15.9	18.0
6 months	31.8	11.2
1 year	28.5	3.1
over 1 year	5.6	—

(*A Negotiator's Guide to Sick Pay*, LRD 1980)

Qualifying period	Manual workers' schemes number	White-collar schemes number
none	2	22
less than 6 months	8	9
6 months–1 year	5	3
over 1 year	4	1

(Alison Jago, *Sick Pay Schemes*, Institute of Personnel Management 1979)

Lastly, since people will often reserve the right to move jobs – but do not want to lose sickness benefit entitlements – a useful device for maintaining eligibility to the scheme is for *previous employment* to count. Three examples of this system are:

■ *National Health Service:* any previous employment with an authority covered by the NHS Whitley Council;

■ *Road Passenger Transport NJIC:* employment with any public authority with transferable superannuation (i.e. pension) rights;

■ *Rolls-Royce:* employment in any Rolls-Royce firm as long as you were made redundant.

Waiting days

These are the days you have to wait *after* going off sick *before* qualifying for *paid* sick leave. (If your sick leave extends beyond the number of waiting days, the waiting days are then paid.) The following two surveys, from the LRD and the IPM respectively, give a good idea of the sort of provision in the country as a whole, and also give a good indication of how much better white-collar workers do:

Number of waiting days	Manual workers' schemes percentage	White-collar schemes percentage
none	30.8	67.7
1–2 days	7.6	0.6
3 days	32.8	6.2
4 days or more	13.6	0.6

Waiting days number	Manual workers' schemes number	White-collar schemes number
none	6	30
1–2 days	3	3
3–5 days	8	2
over 5 days	2	—

The GMWU's surveys shows a similar picture:

| Waiting days | Agreements | |
number	number	percentage
none	121	36.2
1–3 days	128	38.3
4–5 days	48	14.4
over 5 days	37	11.1

As with qualifying periods, there are considerable variations between industries: 59.5 per cent of agreements in the chemical industry have *no* waiting days.

Among the companies in all industries to have *no* waiting days are the following:

■ Abbey Chemicals (Livingstone), Albright & Wilson (Barton, Oldbury, South Humberside, Stratford (London), Whitehaven (Widnes), Belgrave North-Western Industries (Bootle), BOC Gases Division, British Gas Corporation, Burmah Castrol (Ellesmere Port), Caterpiller Tractor Co (Birtley), Civil Service, Croda Hydrocarbons (Rotherham), Dutton & Reinisch (Maryport), E Elliott Ltd Group (Walsall), Electricity Council, Eschmann Bros & Walsh (Sussex), Eyelure (Cwmbran), Ford Motor Co, Hoover (Merthyr Tydfil), ICI, Jeyes (Cheltenham, Thetford), Laporte Industries (Rotherham), Lloyds Industries (Croydon), Local Authorities, M O Valve (London), RHP (Stonehouse), Robinson Bros (West Bromwich), Shell Chemicals (Carrington), Smiths Industries (South London), Synthite (West Bromwich), Torday Electro-Foils (North Shields), Trebor (Maidstone), Trox Bros (Thetford), United Biscuits (Liverpool), W R Wilkinson (Pontefract).

As can be seen from the tables on pages 68–69, the majority of workers' schemes do not provide for immediate eligibility for sickness benefit. However, some company agreements have been negotiated that allow for getting round the waiting days in certain circumstances:

1. date of the doctor's statement;
2. longer-term sickness;

3. recurrence of illness;
4. service-related.

Date of the doctor's statement

Some agreements state that benefit will be paid from the *date* of the doctor's statement (what used to be called a 'medical certificate'); this practice is growing: LRD found that 30 per cent of manual schemes and nearly 7 per cent of white-collar schemes operated in this way. The organisations paying for *all* certified absence include:

■ Cement Manufacture NJIC, Hoover, MGD Graphic Systems, Petters (Staines), Phillips Industries, Pilkington Bros (St Helens), Rolls-Royce Motors (Shrewsbury), Ross Foods, Francis Shaw (Manchester), Seddon Atkinson Vehicles, Tallent Engineering (Aycliffe), United Biscuits, A Wheaton, Weir Pumps.

Longer-term sickness

A somewhat more common way of waiving waiting days is when you have been off sick for more than an agreed number of days; this is to give proper financial protection to workers who are rather more seriously ill, although many managements also believe it discourages people from taking the occasional day off when not really sick. The following is a list of some companies with agreements which trigger sick pay for the entire period of absence after a certain number of days off (the *smaller* the number of days, the better):

■ after 3 days: Air Products, Anchor Motors (Chester), Dewrance Dresser (Skelmersdale), Livermead Hotels, Peterson Livingston (Lothian), Tufnol;

■ after 4 days: Parsons Peebles;

■ after 5 days: M A Craven & Sons (York), Foseco (Tamworth), Newton Chambers Engineering;

■ after 8 days: TI Tubes;

■ after 10 days: Barker & Dobson (Liverpool), Geo Bassetts (Sheffield), Ferro (GB) (Wombourn), Joseph Terry & Sons (York).

Recurrence of illness

Another way in which waiting days can be waived is when you need to go off work *again* within an agreed number of days or weeks of returning from the previous sickness absence. It is to the advantage of workers with seriously recurring illnesses to have *as long a period as possible* under this heading, or else they will probably have to be unpaid for the waiting days on each occasion they are ill again. The LRD quotes the following firms with a 13-week period of grace:

■ Walter Alexander & Co, Asda Superstores, Montague Burton, Dunlop, Duport Steel Works (South Wales), Electrical Contracting JIB, P J Evans, Express Dairies, International Harvester, International Paints, Massey-Ferguson Holdings, Plumbing JIB, Rolls-Royce (Parkside), Talbot Motor Co, Turner Spicer (Wolverhampton), Van Leer (UK), York-Borg Warner (Basildon).

Service-related

A much smaller group of firms cancel the waiting days after you have been employed for an agreed number of years. The major problem with this system is that, unless the period is very short, it is likely to discriminate against those workers who have so far been unable – or who are rarely able (e.g. women workers) – to notch up enough 'service'. Four firms with better agreements than most (the period of employment needed before the waiting days are waived is shown in brackets) are:

■ Cadbury Schweppes (6 months);
■ Morganite Electroheat (Perth) ($2\frac{1}{2}$ years);
■ Hepworth & Grandage (Bradford) (3 years);
■ Mardon Son & Small (4 years).

Certification

This sub-section deals with your need to provide your employer with a doctor's statement saying that you are ill and cannot go to work; when you get such a statement, you will be on what is normally called 'certificated sick leave'. However, GPs no longer *have* to give doctor's statements for absences of up to three days and therefore may ask you to pay for them if they are required for your employer.

Usually, the doctor's statement has to be handed (or posted) to your employer within a certain number of days; this is how matters stand according to two recent surveys by the LRD and the IPM:

	Manual schemes percentage	White-collar schemes percentage
within no special period, but needed if you are going to be paid	30.8	6.8
after 1–2 days	19.9	26.7
after 3 days	25.5	42.2
after 4 days or more	3.3	1.2
other	20.5	23.0

	Manual schemes number	White-collar schemes number
after 1 day	3	1
after 2 days	5	9
after 3 days	11	22
after 3 days or more	—	3

One of the better agreements on certification is to be found in the National Health Service: 'A first certificate is submitted within six days (*excluding Sundays*) from the first day of absence.' (NHS Ancillary Staffs Council) [Emphasis added]

While trade union negotiators are always likely to try and argue for a period of uncertificated sickness, this view is also backed up by medical opinion:

■ the British Medical Association (BMA) believes that workers should be allowed short periods of *paid* time off because of illness or other incapacity *and* without the need to get a doctor's statement.

Among recent improvements in *non-certification* are:

■ the first two days at National Cash Register (manual workers now have the same conditions as white-collar staff);

■ the first three days for sales, clerical and catering staff at Selfridges (Oxford Street, London);

■ the first three days due to an accident at work (under the Bacon Curing NJIC and at Boots);

■ *self-certification* (i.e. you simply *inform* management that you are ill) for an absence of up to five days at Rowntree Mackintosh (Edinburgh, York) and at the British Medical Association;

If the employer *disputes* the doctor's statement, this should be a matter between the employer and the *doctor*, *not* between the employer and the employee.

Pay and length of entitlement

These two elements of a sick-pay scheme are being dealt with together as they are always very closely linked:

● the *length of entitlement* is *how long* you are going to get any sort of money from your employer;

● *pay* is *how much money*.

We shall return to length of entitlement soon, but first we need to look at *what pay consists of*; it is *either*:

■ a *flat-rate payment* (according to the DHSS, in 1977 about 10 per cent of workers received their occupational sick pay in this way – an example in 1980 is £5.25 a day under the Timber Container NJIC); or

■ *basic or average earnings – or a percentage of basic or a percentage of average* (almost invariably, NI payments will be subtracted by the employer).

It is extremely common, as we have seen on page 54, for workers (nearly always manual workers) to receive less than true average earnings while off sick; this is because a lot of agreements stipulate that certain plus-payments are excluded (e.g. bonus, overtime, shift allowances etc). Here are three agreements that go a long way towards full pay:

■ *British Gypsum:* basic hourly rate + job grade rate, shift allowance and underground allowance, multiplied by the basic working week of 40 hours;

■ *National Health Service (ancillary workers):* pay includes London allowances, service supplement and protected first-aid qualification payments; bonus is averaged over the previous three months; the following allowances are also included if the employee regularly receives them: instructional pay, shift duty, night duty, care of patients, split day, standby duty, unsocial hours payments, handling foul linen and stoving;

■ *Local Authorities (manual workers):* payment includes rates for shift work, night work, split duty, rostered Saturday and Sunday work, unsocial hours pay, skill and responsibility allowances, and rostered standby pay.

Increasingly, companies are including shift pay in their sick-pay schemes; here are a few that do:

■ Crown Paints, Flour Milling JIC, Kent Messenger Group, Monsanto, Phillips Industries, Pilkington Bros (St Helens), Ready Mixed Concrete NJC, Road Passenger Transport NJIC, Turner Spicer (Wolverhampton), United Glass.

Examples of true average earnings (i.e. including *all* payments) will be found on pages 77–79.

The *length of entitlement* to sick pay varies enormously from one firm to another, and white-collar workers do a lot better, as this table supplied by LRD shows:

Maximum entitlement	*Manual schemes* percentage	*White-collar schemes* percentage
under 13 weeks	17.5	3.7
13–26 weeks	50.0	29.2
over 26 weeks	27.5	56.5
discretionary	5.0	10.6

However, the GMWU's survey of the engineering industry shows a much bleaker picture there:

Weeks paid number	*Agreements* number	percentage
0–4 weeks	41	18.8
4–13 weeks	113	51.8
13–26 weeks	46	21.1
26–52 weeks	18	8.3
over 52 weeks	0	0.0

The length of entitlement must be *as long as possible*; this makes it much more difficult for the employer to sack a worker who is very seriously ill or incapable of working.

Sickness payments are not always a right from your first day of employment, as we have seen in 'Qualifying period' (pages 65–68); however, among those firms that do pay from the beginning, there is still considerable variation in how much they actually give you. These are the findings of the LRD survey:

Payment at the start of entitlement	Manual schemes percentage
full pay	59.3
51–99 per cent of full pay	10.6
50 per cent of full pay or less	8.3
flat-rate payment	20.9
discretionary	1.0

Here is a selection of employers paying true average earnings (offset against NI payments):

■ Agma Chemicals Co (Hexham), Angloplas Polythene (North Shields), Baird Tatlock Hopkins & Williams (Romford), Beechams Medicines (St Helens), Berger Paints (Middleton), Bush Boake Allen (Barking, Stratford (London), Witham), Commercial Plastics (Cramlington), Dorman Diesels (Stafford), Francis Searchlights (Bolton), Formica (North Shields), Harborough Rubber Co (Market Harborough), David Howard (Steele), ICI, International Paint Co (Felling), W R Jacob (Aintree), James Keiller (Dundee), Bob Martin (Southport), Mather & Platt (Parks Works, Newton Heath), MK Electric (Eastwood, Shoeburyness), Procer (UK) (Wakefield), Rolls-Royce (Hillington), Squirrel Horn (Stockport), Tirfor (Sheffield), Williams (Bootle).

Because of the common practice of dividing paid sick leave into two parts (the first half on full pay, the second half on half pay), employers usually offset NI payments on the second term of sick pay as well as the first. The TUC is opposed to this, and a number of employers do pay the full 50 per cent of earnings during the second period, allowing the sick worker to claim State benefits on top; here are a few that do so:

■ *manual schemes:* British Gas Corporation, Flexible Ducting (Glasgow), Gardner Merchant, NHS, Tallent Engineering (Aycliffe);

■ *white-collar schemes:* British Steel Corporation, Fisher Controls (London);

■ *manual and white-collar schemes:* Electricity Council, Oxford University Press, Plessey.

Some employers cut down on the amount of money paid out by relating the reduced payments to either absence or service. *Absence-related sick pay* is mercifully rare. It discriminates against workers who are frequently ill and/or who are away from work for a variety of other legitimate reasons; an example will suffice to demonstrate how the system works:

■ Fibreglass have a sliding scale of absence levels corresponding to a sliding scale of payment: for example, if you have been off work for up to 5 per cent of the time, you are eligible for only 75 per cent of pay in your first two weeks' sickness and 90 per cent for subsequent weeks; with an 8 per cent absence record, you receive only 35 per cent of sick pay for the first two weeks and 50 per cent after that.

Service-related sick-pay schemes are a lot more common: according to the Institute of Administrative Management, 62 per cent of firms grant paid sick leave under a service-related formula (*Office Holidays, Sickness Entitlements and Other Benefits*, IAM 1980). These service-related schemes may not be quite as unacceptable to managements as is sometimes thought; here is some advice to management negotiators on extending sick-pay entitlement:

> 'The organisation can show that it is rewarding loyalty to the firm, yet in actual fact it is a cheap concession for any organisation to make, as few employees are going to qualify and even fewer are likely to use their maximum entitlement.' (*Guide to Sick Pay & Absence*, Incomes Data Services 1979) The authors then go on to quote the British Sugar Corporation agreement.

Service-related schemes are certainly less objectionable to trade unionists than absence-related ones, although they still discriminate against people who have just started work or who are unable to accumulate enough service. Here is a selection of service-related agreements – some of which reach the TUC objective of six months on full pay and six months on half pay, some of which do not:

Service qualification period	Sick leave entitlement	

Beans Engineering (Tipton)

3 months–1 year	20 days (per quarter)	
1–5 years	45 days (per quarter)	
over 5 years	1 year	

Blackie (London)

	months on full pay	months on half pay
up to 1 year	2	1
1–2 years	3	2
2–3 years	4	3
3–5 years	5	5
over 5 years	6	6

Collins (London)

	months on full pay	months on half pay
up to 1 year	2	1
1–3 years	4	3
3–5 years	5	5
over 5 years	6	6

FT Business Publications and IPC

up to 1 year	13 weeks	
1–5 years	30 weeks	
over 5 years	1 year (in every 18 months)	

National Health Service (ancillary workers)

	months on full pay	months on half pay
up to 4 months	1	
4–12 months	1	2
1–2 years	2	2
2–3 years	4	4
3–5 years	5	5
over 5 years	6	6

Dowty Electrics (Staverton) and Dowty Rotol (Gloucester)

1–4 years	12 weeks
5–9 years	20 weeks
over 10 years	1 year

GEC Witton Kramer (Birmingham)

4–26 weeks	8 weeks
26 weeks–1 year	3 months
1–5 years	6 months
5–10 years	9 months
over 10 years	12 months

MT Chemicals (Tividale)

1–5 years	20 weeks
5–10 years	34 weeks
over 10 years	1 year

Wallman Alloys (Stourbridge)

2–5 years	13 weeks
5–10 years	26 weeks
10–12 years	40 weeks
over 12 years	1 year

BP Chemicals (Stroud)

6 months–1 year	6 weeks on full pay, 6 weeks on half
over 1 year	26 weeks on full pay

May & Baker (Norwich)

up to 1 year	8 weeks
1–2 years	10 weeks
2–10 years	26 weeks

ICI

6 months–1 year	4 weeks
1–2 years	8 weeks
2–3 years	13 weeks
over 3 years	26 weeks

Leyland Vehicles (Chorley)

up to 5 years	13 weeks
over 5 years	26 weeks

McEvoy Oilfield Equipment (Stroud)

26 weeks–5 years	13 weeks
over 5 years	26 weeks

Painter Bros (Hereford)

1–3 years	12 weeks
3–5 years	18 weeks
over 5 years	26 weeks

GEC (Kirkcaldy)

1–2 years	6 weeks
2–3 years	10 weeks
3–4 years	14 weeks
4–5 years	18 weeks
5–6 years	22 weeks
over 6 years	26 weeks

There are often problems about the sick-leave entitlement of workers not doing a 'normal' five-day, 40-hour week. Appalling discrimination against part-time workers is still to be found in many firms; for example:

■ sales assistants at British Home Stores doing *less than 34 hours a week* are not entitled to any paid sick leave at all (quoted by *IDS Report 330*).

This is how two other employers deal with this situation:

■ at ICI, part-time manual workers now qualify for the same amount of paid leave as part-time white-collar staff;

■ in the National Health Service, the sick pay entitlement for ancillary workers is calculated according to the number of days normally worked in a week:

4 days: 18 working days;

5 days: 22 working days (all public holidays being counted as full working days);

6 days: 26 working days (all Saturdays and public holidays being counted as full working days).

Other problems of a *medical* nature can also arise, of course, at work; here are some examples of how some of them are dealt with by the employer:

■ Three companies out of 35 interviewed by the Institute of Personnel Management give paid sick leave to any employees who are in contact with an infectious disease (and not directly affected by it); the time off has to be supported by medical or management advice. (Alison Jago, *Sick-Pay Schemes*, IPM 1979). This is *not* the same as 'medical suspension' (see 'Employment legislation' (pages 85–86)).

■ At Porvair, there is a company doctor who can be contacted on health matters connected with *work*.

■ At Pedigree Petfoods, too, there is a company doctor who can be consulted on work-related health matters, and the company also provides chiropody, physiotherapy and eye testing *free of charge*.

We have so far looked at firms that give true average earnings and at others with long periods of entitlement. Here are a few more firms which give a whole year's paid sick leave on high percentages of pay, followed by a handful of others which give approximately six months:

■ *1 year on full pay:* Cadbury Schweppes, Index Printers;

■ *39 weeks on full pay, 15 weeks on half:* Plessey Controls;

■ *6 months on full pay, 6 months on half:* Altrincham Laboratories (Broadheath) (staff only), British Airports Authority, British Gas Corporation, British Petroleum, Burrage & Boyde (Northampton) (staff only), Electricity Council, National Freight Corporation, National Health Service, *Time Out*, UK Atomic Energy Authority;

■ *6 months on full pay, 12 months on half (maximum of 12 months in a period of 4 years):* Forestry Commision;

■ *6 months on full pay, 6 months on half (maximum of 12 months in a period of 4 years):* Civil Service, Post Office;

■ *26 weeks on 90 per cent, 26 weeks on half:* Plessey (Nottingham);

■ *26 weeks on full pay:* BBC, Burmah Castrol, workers in Civil Air Transport, ICI, Ross Foods;

■ *20 weeks on full pay, 6 weeks on half:* Thomson Books, Thomson Magazines;

■ *16 weeks on full pay, 16 weeks on half*: Morgan Grampian, technical, general & clerical staff in film processing laboratories;

■ *13 weeks on full pay, 13 weeks on half*: Crane Fruehauf Trailers (East Dereham), National Cash Register.

Schemes of the type mentioned so far in this chapter do not necessarily cope with the worker who is seriously ill for a long time (i.e. beyond the entitlement period of the scheme). There are two main solutions: one is Permanent Health Insurance, the other is to write extra clauses into the company's sick pay scheme:

■ Permanent Health Insurance (PHI) is a system whereby the employer pays a proportion of earnings for as long as you are unable to work *or* up to retirement age (for a full explanation of this, see *Pensions* by Sue Ward (Pluto Press 1981).

■ At Monsanto, if the sickness benefit is exhausted and the illness continues for six months after the last sickness payment, some of the *next* year's paid leave can be used. It is a service-related system, and the benefits range from:
- service of 6 months to 1 year: 4 weeks to
- service of over 15 years: 26 weeks.

An interesting variant on this covers workers who have been made redundant:

■ *Cadbury Schweppes:* non-managerial employees with one year's service before being made redundant, who have found a new job *or* who are registered as unemployed, and who have a certificated illness or accident disability qualify for this scheme; pay is related to the weekly wages used in calculating redundancy payments and will be offset against NI benefits or earnings from a new employer, as appropriate. Payment will be made under this scheme for the number of weeks that the employee was entitled to under the company's normal sick-pay arrangements, up to a maximum of 13 weeks.

Medical appointments

After a good number of illnesses and periods of incapacity, it is often necessary to go for further treatment; sometimes, such a visit will avoid the need to take any extra time off at all. These facts are recognised in agreements by some employers, although some-times there is no separate agreement:

■ at Avon Cosmetics, for instance, hospital visits are taken out of the basic sick leave entitlement.

Hospital visits at management request are, of course, a different matter and a few firms give paid time off for this:

■ Sketchley Cleaning (white-collar only);
■ Calor Group (including travelling time).

Several other companies allow time off for medical appointments that the *employee* decides to keep; they prefer the visits to take place during free time if possible, but are otherwise prepared to give paid time off work on production of an appointment card or letter and at about 24 hours' notice. Here are a few companies, with some of the details of their arrangements:

■ Anderson Strathclyde (Glasgow): 1 day at 60 per cent for hospital visits;

■ Associated Octel: half a day or half a shift;

■ G Blair (Bishop Auckland): 1 day on average pay for hospital visits;

■ British Aluminium (Invergordon): 1 day;

■ Calor Group: basic pay;

■ Civil Service: employees are encouraged to have X-rays, cervical screening and breast cancer screenings in working time without loss of pay;

■ Chubb Fire Security: $3\frac{1}{2}$ hours paid time off;

■ Dunlop: 12 hours a year for dental appointments and for other medical treatment (including hospital visits);

■ Rolls-Royce (Hillington): average pay for hospital visits;

■ SKF (UK) (Luton): approximately average pay for dental and hospital appointments.

Other firms giving paid time off for visits to the GP, the hospital or dentist include:

■ Bakelite (UK), Crittall Windows, Imperial Tobacco, Laporte Industries, Litra Machine Plates, McKechnie Metals (Aldridge), Monsanto, Smiths Industries, Vickers.

Exclusions to the scheme

We have already seen how workers can be excluded from some, or even all, of the benefits of the company's sick-pay scheme (e.g. by being a part-timer, by not having worked long enough with the firm etc). There are other reasons for exclusion, which we will divide into:

1. certain illnesses/incapacities;
2. industrial action and layoffs.

Certain illnesses/incapacities

A lot of agreements will automatically pay for sickness that is totally unconnected with work (e.g. colds, appendicitis etc), but will somewhat arbitrarily draw the line at illnesses or incapacities caused by certain activities. Some examples of these are:

- any other paid employment;
- anything illegal;
- part-time service with the police, armed forces etc;
- professional sport.

In fact, there are several sports (some of them currently becoming very popular) that are expressly excluded from certain occupational schemes:

- 'winter sports abroad, ice hockey, polo, hunting, mountaineering, racing (except on foot) or professional football' (Cutlery & Silverware Manufacture NJIC);
- motorcycling, parachuting, pot-holing and hang gliding (Chrysler).

There are a few agreements that go even further, for example:

- Lesney Products will not pay for any 'illness or injury, either mainly or in part, attributable to recreational activities'; employees are encouraged to take out insurance policies to cover against any loss of earnings.

A different sort of hazard is an injury caused by criminal assault:

- no sick pay for any absence 'due to injury resulting from a crime of violence not sustained on duty but connected with or arising from the officer's employment where the injury has been the subject of payment by the Criminal Injuries Compensation Board' (National Health Service PTA 'B' Council).

In schemes like this, there is a need to ensure that there is no loss of earnings should the Criminal Injuries Compensation Board award *less* than the *total* amount of earnings lost.

While it can sometimes be difficult to dissuade managements from excluding such activities as mountaineering, parachuting and hang gliding, there are far greater dangers to trade unionists in other more vaguely-worded exclusions; examples of this are:

- self-inflicted injury;
- injury arising out of carelessness.

This sort of exclusion is dangerous because some employers may try and 'stretch' them so as to encompass almost any injury, particularly one that happens at work. Another dangerous and loose exclusion is:

- any accident occurring outside the UK;

there is the problem here that you could find yourself ineligible for sick pay if you were to fall ill, or have an accident, while on holiday.

Another, and rather different, exclusion is illness or injury occurring while under the influence of alcohol or of drugs other than those prescribed by a doctor. This can be a dangerous catch-all clause: for instance, if you take pills to cure a headache and then have an accident at work, you could find the management refusing to pay you. The DHSS estimate that about 4 per cent of the population of England and Wales and 10 per cent of the population of Scotland and Northern Ireland have severe alcohol-related problems – and undoubtedly a large proportion of them are at work.

The Government is pressing for 'a major drive among employers and trade unions to develop more effective personnel policies and so help with both detection and early treatment' (the Secretary of State for Social Services, quoted in *The Times*, 10 June 1980). While alcohol dependence is often caused or exacerbated by the boring, repetitive nature of so many jobs, most trade unionists would want to keep all information regarding any 'alcohol problem' away from the employer. However, there are attempts currently in North America to deal with the situation *head-on and in a totally confidential way*. In spite of the problems of invasion of privacy and confidentiality, union negotiators in this country *might* like to consider looking at a model agreement produced by the Canadian Union of Public Employees (CUPE) for a 'Labour-Management Addiction and Rehabilitation Committee', part of which states:

'The Committee shall concern itself with the following general matters:
a) an educational campaign against alcohol and drug abuse;
b) the study of the incidence of alcohol and drug abuse among the workforce;
c) the establishment of a viable rehabilitation program in conjunction with the appropriate social welfare and medical authorities;
d) encouragement of medical treatment and/or counseling;
e) recommendations of policy with regard to discipline, discharge and *sick-leave coverage* where an employee's work performance has been impaired by such addiction.' [Emphasis added]

Industrial action and layoffs

Eligibility for sickness benefit is sometimes temporarily cancelled as a result of industrial action (i.e.. not necessarily a strike) and/or layoffs; one agreement is very explicit about this:

'The hourly sick-pay plan will be suspended during any industrial action, by any union, as described here:

– strike;
– work to rule;
– go-slow;
– employees who are laid off as a result of industrial action in this or any other establishment.' (Caterpillar Tractors)

Sometimes the benefit is less restricted:

■ under the Heating, Ventilating and Domestic Engineering Industry NJIC, sickness benefit already being paid is continued until the end of the calendar month following the commencement of the strike.

Under both of these types of agreement, sick workers are being directly discriminated against at a time when they may well be in need of extra heating, special food etc. By far the majority of agreements that have a clause covering this sort of thing say that employees who are receiving sick pay at the time the industrial action begins will continue to be paid, although anyone going sick *during* the period of industrial action will not be eligible. Employers using this type of scheme include:

■ Applied Chemicals, Electrical Contracting JIB, Hepworth & Grandage (Bradford), International Harvester, London Brick Co, Plumbing JIB, Seddon Atkinson Vehicles, TI Desford Tubes, Yarrow Shipbuilders.

Preparing for negotiations

Employment legislation

There is *no* legal obligation on employers to grant sick leave (*paid or unpaid*) unless you work in a Wages Council industry, in which case your employer will be obliged to give you at least the minimum laid down in the Order (see pages 13–14). (If the proposals set out in the Government's Green Paper (see page 57) become law, there will then be statutory obligations on the employer.) Your employer *is* obliged, however, to inform you what the conditions of the sick scheme are (Section 1 of the Employment Protection (Consolidation) Act 1978). Any sex or race discrimination is illegal under the Sex Discrimination Act 1975 and the Race Relations Act 1976 (see page 13).

There is some other legislation which can affect sickness absence:

■ If you are off sick during your period of notice, you are

legally entitled to be *paid* as long as the period of notice is no more than one week above the statutory minimum period of notice (Section 50 of the Employment Protection (Consolidation) Act 1978).

■ If you are suspended from work on medical grounds *either under any statute law or under any recommendation in a statutory code of practice* (and for no other reason), you are legally entitled to what is called *medical suspension pay*, but you will not be eligible if you refuse an offer of 'suitable alternative employment'. There is a qualification period of four weeks' service, and medical suspension pay lasts for a maximum of 26 weeks (Sections 19–22 of the Employment Protection (Consolidation) Act 1978).

■ Be careful of what lawyers call 'frustration of contract': if you are off sick and the employer can show that he has to replace you 'for the smooth running of the organisation' *and* sacks you, you may have great difficulty in winning an unfair dismissal claim at an industrial tribunal. This particular problem underlines the absolute necessity of using procedures agreed between your union and the employer.

■ If you are off sick, usually for a long time, and the employer believes that you will not be able to do the job again (or soon enough), you can legally be sacked under what is called 'capability'; for a full explanation of this, read a companion volume (Jeremy McMullen, *Rights at Work*, Pluto Press 1978, pages 144–184).

Income tax

You pay income tax on any pay your employer gives you *after National Insurance benefits have been deducted*.

Sitting down with management

The most important things about occupational sick-pay schemes are that:

■ they are not 'an extra cost' – the employer would be paying you your wages if you *were* at work;

■ you are not being paid 'for not working': you are being paid in order to be able to get *back* to work.

Managements are usually worried about sick-pay schemes on grounds of *cost*, and *may* be thinking about asking for a total or part contribution from the workers:

■ you should resist this on the grounds that the employer still reserves the right to control *how much* time off you have – despite the fact that you would be paying for part, or all, of it yourselves;

■ you could also say that you believe that workers should not have to pay for their earnings when they are ill.

Alternatively, the employer might want to have a special way of paying you:

■ flat-rate payments: you could remind him that sick pay would then have to be a permanent item on the negotiating agenda; does he really want to have to renegotiate the scheme again and again?

■ an insured scheme: see pages 61–64 for the enormous drawbacks for workers.

If your employer agrees to have a scheme whereby he pays a sum of money for every day/week you are off (or if you already have such a scheme), your *aim* should be:

■ 'true average earnings' – i.e. *exactly* what you would have earned if you had been at work (*including* all allowances for shift, overtime, dirty money etc and *all* bonuses).

If the employer says that he will offset the sick-pay money against National Insurance, you can try and persuade him to:

■ offset *only* the allowances that are *yours*, and *not* those that are given to other members of your family (e.g. Child Allowances for your children).

Your employer may also wish to talk about waiting days. *Any* number of waiting days is bad because:

■ they discriminate against the huge majority of illnesses which usually last only a day or two and which can rarely be avoided (e.g. colds and flu).

Perhaps the boss will say that he accepts that longer illnesses or periods of incapacity need proper provision; you could suggest that:

■ waiting days *could* be waived in these circumstances after a certain number of days.

If you already have this system and the management say that they think some workers wait for that number of days to pass before returning to work, you could say that:

■ it appears to be a good reason for abolishing the system altogether.

Managements are often keen to establish 'company loyalty', so you could suggest that:

■ all waiting days are waived after a period of employment –

say, after six months or one year (people can wait for only so long to show their loyalty);

it would also be useful here if you can:

■ point to other grades in the firm who do *not* have waiting days.

If the employer is prepared to move at all on waiting days, he will certainly want 'proof' of some sort that the system is not being abused; this is where certification comes in. If he insists on a doctor's statement, you can say that you have no particular objection, but:

■ What will happen if a GP won't give them?

■ Will the company pay if the GP *charges* for giving a doctor's statement?

Managements are always worried about 'malingerers', and *your* employer might say that he wants certification from the *first day* of absence; you could point out that:

■ If the employer wants the workers back at work as soon as possible, is it sensible to make him/her venture out to the doctor's surgery on the first day, just at the time when s/he should be taking most care? Might this condition not lengthen the period of absence?

■ Furthermore, the DHSS sometimes asks people *not* to get certificates for the first day (during flu epidemics, for example).

Some companies refuse to pay any sick pay at all until the doctor's certificate has been received *and* processed by the wages department; if the illness is certified, it is certain that payment will be made, so:

■ why not pay at least a percentage of earnings until such time as the wages department has been able to process the claim?

In the unhappy event of the employer proposing an absence-related scheme, you could firstly say that:

■ such a scheme penalises workers who happen to be seriously ill themselves and/or who happen to have relatives, for example, who need a lot of looking after.

In order to deter the employer from pursuing the idea, you can also say that:

■ you will insist on a status quo arrangement (whereby no money is stopped until it is conclusively established that the worker is not entitled to full benefit);

■ you will *not* consider the scheme being operated on a departmental basis (this can easily discriminate against any departments that have a larger percentage of older workers, or of other workers who may *need* rather a lot of time off; it also makes it easier for the boss to 'divide and rule').

You may well find that, when a new or improved scheme is being considered, the management starts 'costing' it – and publicising, perhaps via the media, how much they are going to have to spend. You should consider this, also in the media if necessary, *not* by coming up with alternative figures but by saying that:

■ workers have a *right* to a decent standard of living while sick and, until such time as the State decides to take over the payment of adequate sickness benefits, it is the duty of employers to look after their employers while they are ill;

■ workers who can recover from illnesses without having to worry about returning to work too early are much more likely to recuperate completely and be able to work well when eventually they come back.

You can also use the recruitment/retention argument:

■ older workers, particularly, are certain to look at the sick-pay scheme – perhaps more carefully than they did when they were younger;

it is also worth pointing out that:

■ part-timers are just as likely to move on if they find they are discriminated against.

But the most vital ingredient in any sick scheme, no matter how generous it may be, is to be able to:

■ make use of the Grievance Procedure *at all stages* – not just for negotiating changes in pay or waiting days, but for negotiating each and every stage of a member's absence. This also applies when there are changes in Social Security legislation (e.g. the abolition of earnings-related supplement (ERS) or the introduction of the Green Paper proposals (see pages 57–61)).

Even if your bargaining position is powerful now, it can easily and quickly deteriorate as a result of shutdowns, short time and reductions in union membership.

4.

Time off for family sickness

Introduction

In this chapter we look at paid or unpaid time off work because of sickness in the family. Time off for sickness to the *employee* is dealt with in 'Sick leave' (pages 52–89) and a *death* in the family is covered in 'Bereavement leave' (pages 96–103).

Until the last 10–15 years, it was the norm for employers to grant this type of compassionate leave *on a discretionary basis*, but the trend now is for companies to move towards formalised agreements: a survey in 1979 by IDS estimated that just under half of employers have a policy of some sort, leaving a significant minority (about a third) that still operate a discretionary system; there is a small number of firms that give no leave whatsoever. This contrasts substantially with practices in some other European countries:

■ in Germany, workers are entitled to five days on social security if their children are ill;

■ in Italy, mothers qualify for two one-hour breaks on account of a sick child – with no loss of pay;

■ in Sweden, workers are legally entitled to benefits under the Swedish parental insurance scheme for up to 60 days a year to look after a child under the age of 12.

A lot of negotiated agreements in this country grant leave for the illness of 'close relative', giving little or no indication as to precisely who is covered. By contrast, a clear and fairly comprehensive agreement is to be found at the Greater London Council:

'Serious illness of husband, wife, parent, child, brother or sister, grandparent or grandchild or of a person standing in loco parentis to the employee or to whom the employee stands in that direction. (In the case of an employee having no husband, or wife, parent or child,

serious illness of a person whom the employee maintains or with
whom the employee shares a home.)'

Other agreements have a slightly more extended list, including a
large number of relatives:

■ relatives living in the same household (Smith Kline &
French, TAP Portuguese Airways);

■ 'other persons for whom members [i.e. employees] have a
responsibility' (Penguin Books);

■ fosterparents (British Aluminium);

■ elderly and infirm relatives (Civil Service) – this right also
exists at the UK Atomic Energy Authority, but there the leave is
unpaid.

There is an enormous variety in entitlements to time off for
family sickness, ranging from relatively generous terms (principally
in the publishing sector) to discretionary leave. Here is a selection of
agreements giving paid time off over and above any sick leave:

■ *20 days:* Batiste Publications;

■ *15 days:* Penguin Books, *Time Out*;

■ *5 days:* Independent Broadcasting Authority, Imperial
Tobacco;

■ *4 days:* Shell (UK) Ltd;

■ *3 days:* Abbey Life (dangerous illnesses only), Amoco,
Avon Cosmetics, British Aluminium, GLC, Pedigree Petfoods, UK
Atomic Energy Authority;

■ *2 days:* Associated Octel, IMI Marston;

■ *1 day:* Smith Kline & French.

These periods of leave can be extended in a variety of ways:

■ at Associated Octel, any leave over and above the initial two
days comes out of annual holidays or unpaid leave;

■ Avon Cosmetics give up to 30 days' additional unpaid leave
at the discretion of a director.

At a number of other firms, time off to look after a sick
relative has to come from other sources:

■ *sick leave:* Clark, Son & Morland, Foster Brothers Clothing
Co, Imperial Tobacco (maximum: 5 days in any 52-week period),
Mobil Oil, National Westminster Bank, Parke Davis & Co
(maximum: 3 days), Sandvik;

■ *holidays:* Porvair, Sun Life, TAC Construction.

At Parke Davis & Co, when sick leave has been exhausted, extra
time off can be taken out of annual holidays; at Porvair and TAC

Construction, the opposite applies. However, there are some firms that do not give any *paid* leave at all for family sickness:

■ *Unpaid* leave only is available at Bovril and Commercial Union (both unspecified periods), Ciba-Geigy, Lesney Products (maximum: 3 days) and Vauxhall.

■ In the Post Office, an employee taking compassionate leave for family sickness receives full pay but must pay the costs of employing a replacement worker. The effect of this is that lower-paid workers in the Post Office get no payment at all – although higher-paid staff might make a small sum of money.

A feature of a number of company agreements is a 'differential' between white-collar and manual worker entitlements, with the manual workers always doing less well:

	Staff	*Manual workers*
Findus	3 days paid	no entitlement
Firestone	1 week paid + 1 month unpaid	unpaid leave
Ford Motor Co	paid leave at management discretion	unpaid leave
Pirelli	'an occasional day'	unpaid leave or holiday
Tucker Fasteners	holidays	unpaid leave
H Wiggin	'as needed'	3 days paid

However, one condition for getting time off in a wide variety of firms is the production of medical certification; doctor's notes are required at:

■ Associated Octel, Avon Cosmetics, British Aluminium, Foster Bros Clothing, Hymatic Engineering, Imperial Tobacco, Mobil Oil, National Westminster Bank, Parke Davis & Co, Vauxhall Motors, UK Atomic Energy Authority.

Most agreements confine themselves to fixing periods of time for looking after relatives at home, but there are many other circumstances where illness in the family requires the presence of a working relative; for instance, to visit a sick relative in hospital you might get:

■ five days' paid leave a year (Independent Broadcasting Authority);

■ time off taken out of sick leave entitlement (Sandvik).

On the other hand, there might be other unexpected pressures on you arising out of the relative's illness:

■ if the illness of a close relative gives rise 'to serious domestic difficulties which are certified by a doctor to require the presence of the employee', the GLC/ILEA will grant one day's paid leave, in addition to other time off for family sickness.

Finally, some agreements cater specifically for the problems faced by parents with sick children:

■ at Avon Cosmetics, if you decide to accompany a child of yours to the doctor, to the dentist or to the hospital, you qualify for one day's paid leave per child per occasion – up to a maximum of two days' paid leave a year per child (at management discretion, there are also available an extra three days' unpaid leave a year per child). For school medical examinations, the company grants one day off – this is unpaid if you, the parent, choose to accompany the child, but it is paid if you *have* to go with your child.

Preparing for negotiations

Employment legislation

You have no legally enforceable right to have time off work to look after sick relatives. The only employment laws that affect us here are the Sex Discrimination Act 1975 and the Race Relations Act 1976 which make it an offence for the *employer* to favour or discriminate against any of his employees on the grounds of sex or race (see page 13).

Income tax

There are no special income tax provisions for any time off work spent looking after members of your family. If you are paid during your absence from work, you will be taxed on the money just as if you were at work.

Sitting down with management

Depending on what sort of person your employer is, you may need to remind him of certain basic facts about family sickness; for instance:

▨ sickness in the family is *not* the fault of the employee;

▨ when an employee feels it necessary to stay home for a day or two to look after a sick relative, s/he should not be penalised. Indeed, if you do not have a scheme at all, you may need to go over these points with the members as well. Your employer may say that 'management discretion' has worked perfectly well for years and that he sees no reason for change: it is important to establish from the outset that you disagree with this, perhaps by saying:

▨ there *could* be some favouritism going on;

▨ even if there isn't any, a lot of people think there might be. If your employer is still unhappy about committing any policy to paper, you could say that:

▨ *any* scheme concerning time off should be *seen to be fair to everybody*;

▨ any scheme should be easily understood by all workers.

The management is likely to be worried about abuse of the scheme, and it might therefore be a good idea to get in with the point first: you could say that:

▨ you don't *think* it would happen, but that in your opinion any abuse would be minute compared with the overwhelming majority of workers who would use the scheme honestly.

If he continues to be worried about people taking time off without a valid reason, it would be reasonable to accept that employees must produce appointment cards, medical certificates and doctor's notes. You could suggest at a later point that, if enough evidence can be found to show that there is little or no abuse, perhaps the handing over of this documentation could be dropped. You could remind the employer that getting hold of these letters can be very time-consuming just when you are hard put to it looking after your sick relative.

Even if the management can be persuaded that there will not be too much abuse, they will undoubtedly be worried about any loss of production. Your arguments against this will vary considerably according to the sort of people employed, but you might say, for example, that:

▨ neither the employer nor you can predict exactly how it will work out;

▨ almost invariably the amount of time taken off is going to be minute;

▨ perhaps there could be a trial run lasting, say, 12 or 24 months;

■ parents will always be anxious if their children are ill and *will take the time off anyway*.

There are also some 'commercial' arguments: again, depending on what sort of people the management wants to employ, you might be able to say that, if there are not suitable arrangements for family sickness leave:

■ the company may not be able to recruit staff;

■ the company may not be able to retain staff.

You might also be able to play on the employer's wish to have a good, progressive image in the area: you could say that it is essential for there to be a procedure which processes every request for time off *quickly and without embarrassment* –

■ it will do the firm's name no good if its employees have to wait for hours or even days to have a request for leave granted.

Finally, you can point out that illnesses can sometimes turn out to be a lot more complicated than first thought, and you would therefore like an option on further leave; if it looks as if the employer is quite unsympathetic to the idea, it would be all right to concede that this leave was:

■ unpaid, and

■ at management discretion;

the reason is that once you *do* have extra time for those who badly need it, you can go back to the employer the following year (or even later) and try and get it consolidated into a better deal.

5.

Bereavement leave

Introduction

This chapter deals with paid or unpaid leave granted on the death of a member of your family, although the definition may sometimes be extended to include a person who has acted *in loco parentis* (i.e. someone who has acted as one of your parents) and a person with whom you shared a home. Leave for family bereavements is sometimes called 'compassionate leave', and other types of compassionate leave are dealt with in other chapters, mainly 'Time off for family sickness' (pages 90–95).

The provision of bereavement leave is far from universal: a survey by IDS in 1979 found that 70 per cent of companies gave paid bereavement leave as of right, and a further 25 per cent granted time off 'at management discretion'. By contrast, a series of surveys carried out by the GMWU in 1979/80 give a much less favourable picture; the table opposite is a summary of three of the GMWU surveys showing the level of provision in three industries (the percentage figures in brackets represent the proportion of agreements in each industry).

The GMWU felt sufficiently disturbed by the findings of their surveys to circulate a model agreement for bereavement leave; it is as follows:

■ '(a) Employees who are absent from work because of family bereavement will continue to be paid their average wage for their normal job for a period of three days.

'(b) Family bereavement in (a) above covers wife or husband, including common-law spouse, sons and daughters, mother and father, mother and father-in-law, brothers and sisters. In circumstances where the employee is required to make the funeral arrangements for a member of the family not covered above, the entitlement to paid leave under (a) above will apply.

'(c) At the discretion of the company, employees may be allowed a longer period and consideration will be given to exceptional circumstances.

'(d) By 'average earnings for their normal job' is meant all the elements that make up the worker's weekly wage. As such it will include the basic rate, job rate, bonuses, shift pay, together with any disturbance payment or working conditions payment associated with the job. It will also include a figure for average overtime pay.'

	Agreements giving paid bereavement leave		Agreements giving paid bereavement leave 'at management discretion'		Agreements giving unpaid bereavement leave	
	number	%	number	%	number	%
engineering	129	39	22	7	175	54
chemicals	47	53	16	18	25	29
rubber	21	37	2	3	34	60

Some employers continue to leave open the question of precisely who is covered by the agreements, but it is rapidly becoming the practice to lay down a set number of days for family bereavement *and* specify *which* members of the family are covered:

■ the hourly-paid workers' agreement at Massey-Ferguson says: ' "Close relative" shall be defined as follows: spouse, parent, spouse's parent, child, son-in-law, daughter-in-law, sister, brother, grandparent, grandchild [or] any person who has been recognised as taking the place of a parent'.

Other close relatives covered in other agreements include:

■ parents-in-law (Avon Cosmetics);
■ fosterparents and step-parents (Vickers Ltd).

In order to get over the problem of who is a 'close relative' and who is not, some agreements have a separate category of 'non-immediate relative':

■ the British Airports Authority and Scholl (UK) give only

one day's paid leave (instead of three) for a 'non-immediate relative';

■ the three-day entitlement at the Singer Company (UK) for immediate family or guardian is reduced to one day for in-laws and grandparents;

■ Glenlivet Distillers give three days' paid leave for close family and one day for less immediate family.

Very rarely, an agreement will go outside the family:

■ at Pergamon Press, 'sympathetic consideration' is given on the occasion of the death of a *friend*.

As to the amount of paid time off, arrangements vary enormously even among those companies that do give paid release:

■ one of the most striking examples is Penguin Books where the entitlement is 15 days a year, but this also has to cover looking after relatives who are *sick* (see 'Time off for family sickness' (pages 90–95).

And it is still possible to find firms that do not lay down exact numbers of days:

■ Commercial Union Assurance Co give paid leave 'of no specified duration' and make up their minds according to 'individual circumstances'.

More conventional arrangements for paid bereavement leave specify a number of days for each bereavement – together with the rate of pay; the following examples are of days off *on average pay*:

■ *seven days:* Berger (Newcastle);

one week: National Magazine Co;

five days: Baird Tatlock Hopkins & Williams (Romford), Bush Boake Allen (Witham), Dawson (Sheffield), EMI, Independent Broadcasting Authority, McKechnie Metals (Aldridge), TAP Portuguese Airways, TI Metscc (Oldbury), Trianco Redfyre (Sheffield);

four days: Brian Donkin Co (Chesterfield), Nettle Accessories (Chadderton);

three days: George Angus (Newcastle), Anderson Strathclyde (Glasgow), Baker Perkins (Tyne & Wear), Beans Engineering (Tipton), BICC, Black & Decker (Spennymore), Blundell Permoglaze (Hull), Cranes Screw Fasteners (Birmingham), Goodlass Wall (Speke), Jeyes (Cheltenham), Plessey (Beeston), Rolls-Royce (Glasgow), Ruston Diesels (Merseyside), Joseph Terry (York), sawmilling industry.

Many workers are not fortunate enough to receive average pay when on bereavement leave – in the GMWU's survey of the engineering industry, only half of the agreements studied gave average pay; here are some examples of agreements giving *basic pay*:

  ■ *one week:* Birds Eye Foods;
  five days: Crane Fruehauf Trailers (East Dereham);
  three days: British Timber (Daventry).

Most national agreements make a reference of some sort to bereavement leave; some actually lay down the terms of the leave:

  ■ three days for the death of a close relative at basic rate of pay (Flat Glass Industry – GB (NJC)).

Other national agreements play an enabling role in that they ask for leave to be negotiated locally:

  ■ 'Leave of absence in cases of family bereavement is a matter for local arrangement.' (NJC for Local Authorities Manual Workers).

An example of a locally negotiated agreement for bereavement leave, which includes time off for the person you share a home with, is to be found in the GLC/ILEA:

  ■ '*Purpose:* death of husband, wife, parent, child, brother, sister, grandparent or grandchild or of a person standing in loco parentis to the employee or to whom the employee stands in that relation. (In the case of an employee having no husband or wife, parent or child, death of a person whom the employee maintains or with whom the employee shares the home.)

  Entitlement: period reasonably necessary but not more than two days with pay.

It seems to be standard practice for employees to qualify for these entitlements as soon as they start work – in other words, there is no 'service qualification'; however, there are instances occasionally of a 'service-related' element:

  ■ at Staedtler UK in Mid-Glamorgan, the agreement for bereavement leave is as follows:

0–5 years' employment	$2\frac{1}{2}$ days;
over 5 years' employment	5 days

  Leave is taken at basic rate.

In fact, it is relatively unusual these days for there to be any distinctions among the workforce; the most likely area for differentials is between white-collar and manual workers but, according to IDS, most employers now give identical entitlements to both groups:

■ examples which they quote of firms making no distinctions include Tucker Fasteners, Beckman Instruments, Shell (UK) Oil and the IBA;

■ they also give details of a few companies where differentials survive:

Findus: management, engineering supervisors, technical and clerical staff and security officers are eligible for three days' paid leave; engineering employees and process workers get three days on *basic* pay for immediate family and parents-in-law;

Ford Motor Co: white-collar workers get five days, manual workers get three days.

It is recognised in many agreements that the amount of leave will sometimes not be sufficient, and special provision is made for extensions:

■ Workers covered by the General Whitley Council handbook (NHS) get three days' paid leave, but the agreement goes on to say: 'Since much may depend on individual circumstances the period may, on general and humanitarian grounds, be extended in cases of special hardship up to a further three days, i.e. up to a maximum of six days in all.'

■ At the British Airports Authority, the three days' paid leave can be extended by two days' *paid* leave on humanitarian grounds, and further days of *unpaid* leave can be negotiated, but *they can affect continuity of employment.*

■ The three-day entitlement at Avon Cosmetics can be extended by a maximum of 37 days' unpaid leave because of exceptional circumstances arising out of the bereavement – all at management discretion.

Other reasons for extending bereavement leave are certain particular problems caused by the death:

■ The National Freight Corporation and BDH Chemicals give one day's paid leave for the funeral and three days' paid leave if the employee is *responsible* for the funeral arrangements (all of this is on a non-discretionary basis).

■ At the GLC there is a three-day allowance depending on whether there is a long journey involved.

■ J Sainsbury give up to a week's leave with pay if the employee is put in charge of the deceased's private affairs (e.g. the will); McDermott Scotland and the UK Atomic Energy Authority also give time off for this purpose, but it is unpaid and at management discretion.

■ The NUJ agreement at Cassell's gives 10 days' paid leave if you are the sole surviving relative; Rolls-Royce Motors (Car Division) give three days at basic rate for the same reason, although it is discretionary.

In most agreements, extensions to the basic entitlement to bereavement leave are *paid*; sometimes the agreement will specify an alternative system:

■ when the entitlement has been exhausted, employees can make use of annual holidays and unpaid leave (Burmah Oil, Lesney Products and Parke Davis & Co).

Although most of the above agreements refer to *paid* leave, considerable care needs to be taken to ensure that the amount of money received is what you would have received if you had been working – it is important to try and avoid the sort of deal that says that 'payment for bereavement leave shall exclude premiums' (Massey-Ferguson). Sometimes normal earnings are guaranteed – for example:

■ full pay (National Health Service);

■ 'current average earnings' (Plessey (Beeston));

■ full shift pay (Burton Gold Medal Biscuits, Edinburgh).

Sometimes premium payments are specifically included:

■ the good timekeeping bonus (10 per cent of salary) at Pedigree Petfoods is paid to employees absent on bereavement leave;

■ at Vaux Breweries, bereavement leave does not constitute a break in entitlement to the company's good attendance prize.

At all events, it is important to try and avoid having to take bereavement leave out of sick leave (Smiths Industries, Putney Vale, London). Lastly, there are other rights which depend on *length of employment* and which can be jeopardised by bereavement leave; one of these, at least, is protected by the Nurses' and Midwives' Council handbook which states that such leave 'shall count as service for incremental purposes'.

Preparing for negotiations

Employment legislation

There are no laws in this country giving workers the legal right to time off (paid or unpaid) on the death of a relative. However, the Sex Discrimination Act 1975 and the Race Relations Act 1976 make it illegal for your employer to discriminate on grounds of sex or race (see page 13).

Income tax

Any pay received from the employer while you are absent on bereavement leave is taxed in the normal way.

Sitting down with management

If you find that your employer is unenthusiastic about granting bereavement leave, you may have to point out from the outset of your negotiations that:

■ when relatives die, *people HAVE to take time off* – if only because of the shock, although an equally important reason is the considerable family disruption that is inevitably caused.

You could also say that:

■ *some people will take the time off anyway*;

you might tell your employer that he should accept this as a fact, and so:

■ he might just as well agree with a good grace to a decent scheme – and perhaps gain a little prestige out of it.

If you work for a large organisation, you can argue further for *a company-wide scheme* on the grounds that:

■ the small (or big) differences in practice from one location to the next are unfair.

Of course, your employer might not mind about differentials between locations, so:

■ you can ask if the head office is happy about any disparities (and you will quite possibly have the personnel department on your side when you say this, as they have a natural preference for *standardising* what goes on).

On the other hand, if you work for a small company you may find that the employer resists the idea of a written agreement because he prefers to treat each request for leave 'on its merits'; depending on what the members have said to you, you can answer this point by saying that:

■ this sort of system is too paternalistic these days;

■ the members fear that there could be too many examples of discrimination and favouritism.

The management may well be worried about loss of production and abuse; you can say that:

■ it is quite possible to get confirmation of somebody's death;

■ the amount of time away from work every year is extremely small (see if the management are prepared to give you the figures for the previous year or two – if they haven't been keeping records, they are in no position to argue that large numbers of days have been 'lost').

You can also point out that the death of a relative cannot really be foreseen:

■ the company's image can be seriously damaged in the locality if there is no procedure which can be brought into operation immediately to deal with the crisis;

■ the employer can get a (worse) reputation for penny-pinching if the pay is poor, or delayed.

Whatever the final agreement on paid leave is, see if you can get a discretionary extension – that is to say, an option to take extra time off, at management discretion. This is not a position of weakness: in *all* negotiations, there is a point beyond which you are not going to proceed – and extra discretionary days give you the possibility to come back next year and ask for more. Finally, try and get an assurance from the employer that:

■ line management are made *fully conversant* with *both the spirit and the letter* of the agreement, so that extensions can be negotiated without embarrassment to the members requesting them.

6.

Time off for court attendance

Introduction

You may be required – or requested – to take part in court proceedings for several reasons:

- as a juror;
- as a witness;
- as a plaintiff, defendant, petitioner or respondent (see Glossary).

This chapter deals with your employment rights if you are seeking to get time off work in order to perform one of these duties or activities in court. For the position regarding members who are magistrates (i.e. JPs), see 'Time off for public affairs and duties' (pages 109–117).

Jury service

Company agreements vary a great deal as to whether wages are paid in full or not – this is mainly because of the existence of certain allowances that can be paid to jurors out of public funds (see page 107):

■ some employers pay normal wages (e.g. Birds Eye Foods, British Airports Authority, the Civil Service, the UK Atomic Energy Authority and the Water Service);

■ occasionally, the contract is very clear that the employer undertakes to pay all wages: under the Local Authorities agreements for both manual workers and craftsworkers, for example, 'no deduction shall be made from wages and the employee shall be instructed not to claim compensation for loss of earnings.'

Other employers tell their staff to take advantage of the loss-of-earnings compensation:

■ at BICC the instruction is to claim the compensation and that the company will make it up to normal salary;

■ under the Whitley Council for the Health Services, the agreement is slightly different: 'Employees who are called for jury service shall be granted special leave with pay for the purpose in the understanding that any court fees received (as distinct from allowances for travelling and subsistence expenses) are handed over by the employee to his employing authority.'

The employers quoted above give normal (or *true* average) pay – i.e. the money you would have received if you had been working:

■ at Pedigree Petfoods, the good timekeeping bonus of ten per cent of earnings is paid to workers serving as jurors.

This practice of paying full wages is not universal, however:

■ at Ilford, the entitlement is to 'holiday pay' only.

There can also be other restrictions on one's freedom to serve on juries – for example, a maximum period of time:

■ special leave for jury service is limited to three months at Ilford;

■ local government APT&C (white-collar) grades have as little as 30 days after which their pension contributions are no longer payable and 'the service thereafter does not reckon for superannuation benefits, unless the officer elects to continue paying contributions based on full pay.' The APT&C agreement goes on to say that officers are 'strongly advised' to do just that.

Some workers in other parts of Europe are better protected than here: in the Netherlands, for example, paid time off is automatic when there is a *legal* obligation to perform a function (e.g. jury service); the same applies in Belgium under the civil code.

Other court attendance

As far as paid release from work is concerned, the role of witness is the most important after that of juror – and a lot depends on the kind of court case you are appearing in, and on whether you are appearing voluntarily or not. For example, if you appear as a *voluntary* witness in *criminal* proceedings (e.g. theft, burglary), a lot of employers have similar arrangements as for jury services:

■ normal wages are paid at Birds Eye Foods, the Civil Service and the UK Atomic Energy Authority;

■ at BICC and British Rail you claim the loss of earnings compensation and the employer tops it up to normal earnings.

■ in the NHS you claim the compensation and hand it over to the employer, who pays full earnings.

However, if you are *subpoenaed* as a witness in criminal proceedings, the situation can be very different:

■ the loss-of-earnings compensation is topped up to normal wages (Co-op Bank);

■ the loss-of-earnings compensation is handed over to the employer (NHS);

■ you don't get paid at all – you have to try and get the money from whoever has subpoenaed you (British Rail).

If you are subpoenaed in a *civil* case (e.g. concerning the Rent Act), agreements again vary:

■ sometimes employees are paid in full (British Airports Authority, the Co-op Bank and the NHS);

■ sometimes there is no pay at all (UK Atomic Energy Authority);

■ sometimes there is no pay but there is an option on taking annual holidays (Civil Service).

When it comes to litigation (see Glossary), the situation is no less varied:

■ at the Co-op Bank, loss of earnings compensation is topped up to normal wages;

■ at the UK Atomic Energy Authority, normal wages are paid if the case is connected with work – otherwise it is holidays or unpaid leave.

It sometimes happens that employers *require* members of their staff to appear in court; this might be in an official capacity:

■ in these circumstances, the Civil Service and the NHS pay wages in full.

When there is any other reason for appearing in court at the request of management, it is usual for there to be no financial loss:

■ at British Rail, staff receive full pay, including any night enhancements;

■ under the same British Rail agreement, release is on full pay if the court attendance is the result of assault in the course of employment (this applies even if the court appearance is not at the request of management).

If you are *directly* involved in court proceedings, (i.e. not as a witness), for example, as a plaintiff (e.g. tenant versus landlord), defendant, petitioner or respondent (e.g. divorce), it is unusual to get paid time off:

■ British Rail, for instance, say quite simply 'no pay'.

Preparing for negotiations

Employment legislation

There are no laws protecting your *employment rights* if you appear in court as a witness, juror etc; in other words, you have no legally protected right to *time off with pay*. This is not to say, however, that you can necessarily ignore a request to take part in a trial (see 'Legislation for witnesses and jurors' below). Except when your appearance in court is a statutory duty, you will have to *negotiate* the time off – *and* the pay.

Legislation for jurors and witnesses

If you are called for *jury service*, you've got to go – although there are a number of exemptions; you can claim that you cannot attend, for example:

■ if you are ill, blind, deaf or pregnant, if you are abroad or on family holiday, if you are studying for exams or if you have 'heavy business commitments'.

If you do go, you are legally entitled to certain payments under the Jurors' Allowances Regulations; these payments are:

● loss-of-earnings compensation;
● travel and subsistence allowances.

If you are called as a *witness*, it depends on what sort of witness you are:

■ if you are *subpoenaed*, you are legally obliged to attend; and your employer must release you to go;

■ if you are a *voluntary* witness you are *not* obliged to attend, but if your employer wants 'proof' that you have been asked to give evidence you should ask the solicitor to send a confirmatory letter to the company.

Income tax

You do *not* have to pay income tax on travelling and subsistence allowances, but you *do* pay tax on the loss-of-earnings compensation. However, two groups of workers could lose financially if the tax were deducted *by the court*: they are very low-paid workers who do not normally pay income tax and people who receive a lot of money in Social Security benfits. These workers need an agreement whereby the loss-of-earnings compensation is paid direct to the employer who then deducts any tax.

Sitting down with management

As jury service is compulsory (with certain exemptions outlined above on page 107, you should have little difficulty in getting the necessary release for those members who do act as jurors.

The same applies in the case of *subpoenaed* witnesses, who are legally obliged to attend. When it comes to *voluntary* witnesses, your employer may balk at paid release on the grounds of disruption to the firm's operations – and cost; you can point out that:

■ the amount of time off is likely to minimal; in the vast majority of court cases, witnesses give their evidence well inside a day.

If your employer says he won't pay normal net earnings (offset against loss-of-earnings compensation), you can say that:

■ it is no fault of the member that s/he is appearing in court (whether as a juror *or* as a witness), and that therefore s/he should not be penalised financially.

You can also argue that:

■ the 'due process of law' can scarcely be upheld if people can't *afford* to participate in proceedings;

■ the periods of absence are going to be extremely short in nearly every case, and the employer could easily be seen as discriminating against those who, through no fault of their own, appear in court.

If you are told that the person *issuing* the subpoena should pay the wages, you can say that:

■ most people issuing subpoenas can in no way afford to pay their witnesses' wages, and the employer would therefore be directly influencing the outcome of a court case.

7.

Time off for public affairs and duties

Introduction

This chapter deals with paid or unpaid time off for membership of statutory bodies. These range from Parliament to local government, the education system, prisons, statutory tribunals and water authorities.

Parliamentary elections

Usually the first employment problem facing a member considering whether to stand for Parliament is whether s/he is going to be given time off to *fight* the election. Where agreements do exist, practice varies as to whether the leave is paid or not:

■ ICI gives paid leave from nomination day to election day;

■ the Civil Service and the UK Atomic Energy Authority both give one month's paid leave;

■ the Water Service and the NHS gives *unpaid* leave;

■ the Co-op Bank gives three weeks' unpaid leave, but a negotiable sum may be given if the political party concerned gives no financial assistance.

ICI agreed to its relatively generous arrangements for employees who are Parliamentary candidates (and MPs) because they feel that *industry is not adequately represented in the House of Commons.*

A later problem arises for those who actually win the election: where do they stand with respect to their *present* employment?

■ the NHS and the Water Service insist that you must resign;

■ at ICI you are guaranteed continuity of your pension rights;

■ at the Co-op Bank you qualify for up to 10 years' unpaid leave of absence and your pension rights are guaranteed on condition that you pay both *your own and the employer's* contribution to the company's **Pension** and Death Benefit Scheme.

Of course, MPs have no more job security than most other workers, and a union member of yours may well worry about employment prospects when his/her time at Westminster is over:

■ workers in the NHS have no special rights at all: 'Resignation must be unconditional and the employee, if he should seek reemployment on ceasing to be a Member of Parliament, shall have *no claim to reinstatement* either in his old post or in any other post in the National Health Service.' [Emphasis added]

Two other employers, however, are considerably more enlightened:

■ the Co-op Bank undertake to look for a job at least as good as the old job;

■ ICI guarantee the old job back for 10 years, on condition that you had at least five years' pensionable service *before* becoming an MP.

This contrasts sharply with Italian practice, where workers who are elected members of parliament are legally guaranteed their jobs back *with no loss of seniority*.

Finally, on the question of 'agents' – people who act as personal assistants to parliamentary candidates and who are technically in charge of the election campaign: these agents, who often do the job on a part-time, voluntary basis, are also sometimes granted time off in the period leading up to an election:

■ the Co-op Bank gives three weeks' unpaid leave;

■ the Civil Service gives six weeks – if the agent is assisting a 'bona fide' candidate.

Other public bodies

The areas of public life dealt with under this heading are local government, the health service, the water and sewage industries, education, prisons, the law and statutory tribunals. We have already noted that at least one firm (ICI) regrets the lack of representation of industry in the House of Commons, but industry is not the only section of the community to feel underrepresented in public life: the Equal Opportunities Commission has expressed great anxiety about the small number of *women* on almost every type of public body – a point taken up by many women's organisations; the TUC General Council has added the significant rider that 'in responding, governments were, in general, appointing middle-class and professional women', with working-class women being even more underrepresented than ever.

Practice varies widely among employers as to whether an application to take time off for membership of public bodies should be judged 'on its merits' or whether a set number of days is allotted:

■ *no maximum* time off (BL Cars – staff and manual workers; Rolls-Royce Motors – Diesel Engine Division manual workers);

■ 'reasonable' paid time off (UK Atomic Energy Authority);

■ paid time off as long as the operational requirements of the firm are not impaired (BP Chemicals and Dow Corning).

A somewhat more progressive attitude towards the problems facing lay members of public bodies is to be found in the agreement at the UK Atomic Energy Authority: their management is quoted in *IDS Study 155* as saying that they give special leave:

'for attendance at meetings and in connection with other essential business of bodies where *voluntary unpaid public service is relied upon for the fulfilment of statutory duties, and where the work cannot be carried out in leisure time*, e.g. regional hospital boards, river authorities and parole boards'. [Emphasis added]

Increasingly, employers are fixing set amounts of paid time off in a year and there is a trend – particularly in the public sector – for highly detailed agreements to be drawn up between the employers and the unions. An example of this (quoted from a survey carried out in 1980 by IDS) concerns non-industrial staff in the Civil Service:

■ 24 days: Mayors;

18 days: Justices of the Peace, local government councillors, members of children's panels (Scotland);

6 days: Regional Health Authorities, Area Health Authorities, local review panels, local valuation panels, National Insurance tribunals, prison visiting committees, river authorities, Local Authority committees, reinstatement in civil employment committees, supplementary benefit appeal tribunals, war pensions committees;

3 days: Community Health Councils, Internal Drainage Boards, school governors and managers.

The agreement covering staff and manual workers in the Post Office also includes the following items:

■ 6 days: NHS Regional Boards, Executive Councils, Boards of Governors and Hospital Management Committees, local parole review committees, boards of prison visitors, National Insurance local tribunals.

An interesting agreement covers those employed in the school meals service of the ILEA:

■ unlimited time off: Mayors and chairpersons of local councils;

20 days: Justices of the Peace, leaders of councils and political groups, chairpersons of council committees;

15 days: everybody else.

Time off in all examples given in this chapter is *paid*, but there are companies where there is only *unpaid* leave – e.g. GKN Sankey (Hadley Castle Works); probably the most common way of organising payment is:

■ by topping up any loss-of-earnings compensation to normal earnings.

This frequently involves manual workers losing overtime payments (e.g. at Metal Box).

It is also worth pointing out that the National Union of Seamen has given the lie to the theory that the nature of some jobs makes it impracticable to take part in public affairs:

■ there is a ship's rating on seagoing duty who is a local councillor – and special arrangements are made for him to fulfil this role.

Employers with agreements closely modelled on that outlined above for the Civil Service include the British Airports Authority, the National Health Service and Shell Oil, although the latter company has a few entitlements that are somewhat better:

■ 18 days for membership of Regional and Area Health Authorities, Regional Hospital Boards and Water Authorities;

■ 18 days for sitting on statutory tribunals;

■ 18 days for school governors and managers.

Employees of the NHS who become Justices of the Peace (JPs) may take their annual entitlement of 18 days 'in days or half days as required', but those who go into local government face unusual restrictions:

'There need be no objection as a general rule to National Health Service employees contesting local elections or taking part in local government activities, provided always that in the discharge of any local authority functions which impinge on the functions for which their Health Service employing authorities are responsible, *due regard is had by the employees to the circumstances of their dual position.* (General Whitley Council Handbook, Section XXVIII) [Emphasis added]

Elsewhere in Europe, workers tend to have much better *legal* protection than workers here: in Belgium, for instance, workers are legally entitled to a maximum of five days' paid leave a year for *each* 'public duty', and that includes those occasions when they happen to be in court on a charge; if a Belgian worker stands for election to the local council, there is also paid leave – but the state foots the bill. In France, workers are legally entitled to paid time off for a wide variety of public and voluntary activities, and they do not have to specify the reason.

Totting up

Where agreements specify a set number of days off for membership of this or that public body, they also usually lay down a maximum for those employees who qualify for paid release under more than one heading (e.g. an employee who is a local councillor *and* a member of an Area Health Authority):

- industrial workers at the Post Office have an overall maximum of 24 days a year;
- at Shell Oil the maximum is 18 days;
- the maximum at the British Airports Authority is also 18 days unless you happen to be a Mayor, in which case you qualify for 24 days *for that year*.

Other annual maximum entitlements include:

- 2 days a month: Birds Eye Foods;
- 18 days a year: National Bus Co;
- 12 days a year: Allied Breweries.

Going over the limit

Membership of a large number of public bodies (particularly in local government and the Health Service) puts very severe demands on time: for example, reorganistion of the NHS gives huge amounts of work to members of the Area Health Authorities and Community Health Councils, while high levels of local unemployment are likely to keep members of National Insurance tribunals very busy indeed. It often happens that the maximum amount of paid release agreed with the union(s) is not enough, and some employers have recognised the validity of a claim for an option on extra time off:

- the Post Office gives up to 60 days' unpaid leave;

■ Shell Oil gives 10 days' holiday or unpaid leave;
■ Lloyds Bank says holidays should be used up, although unpaid leave *may* be granted;
■ the Civil Service gives unpaid leave in exceptional circumstances;
■ BICC, Metal Box and Allied Breweries give unspecified unpaid leave.

Preparing for negotiations

Employment legislation

Under Section 29 of the Employment Protection (Consolidation) Act 1978 you can demand time off for *some* public duties, and your union does *not* have to be recognised by the employer (see page 287).

You are legally entitled to time off work (the law does not talk about payment) if you hold certain positions on public bodies:
■ a Justice of the Peace (JP);
■ a member of the Local Authority (i.e. the local council);
■ a member of any statutory tribunal (e.g. an industrial tribunal);
■ a member of a Regional Health Authority or Area Health Authority (England and Wales) or a Health Board (Scotland);
■ a member of a governing body of a Local Authority school;
■ a member of a Water Authority (England and Wales) or River Purification Board (Scotland).
What you can get time off to *do* is:
■ to attend 'a meeting of the body or any of its committees or sub-committees';
■ to carry out anything 'approved by the body' which is to do with 'the functions of the body or of any of its committees or sub-committees'.
However, your employer may try and impose certain restrictions (see Section 29 (4) of the Act): he can say that the time off must be 'reasonable in all the circumstances', and can take into account:
■ how much time is required;
■ how much time off you have already had for trade union duties and activities (see Section 27 of the Act);
■ 'the circumstances of the employer's business and the effect of the employee's absence on the running of that business'.

If you are not given time off *as required by Section 29 of the Act*, you can go to an Industrial Tribunal; you must do so within three months of your employer not giving you the time off and, if the Tribunal finds in your favour, you can get compensation (i.e. *not* the time off).

Under the Sex Discrimination Act 1975 and the Race Relations Act 1976, any discrimination by your employer on the grounds of sex or race in the granting of time off is illegal (see page 13).

Income tax

Allowances for travel and subsistence are not taxable, but the loss-of-earnings compensation (or fee) is. A serious problem can arise for two groups of employees: very low-paid workers and those who receive a lot of money in Social Security benefits; if *their* loss-of-earnings compensation (or fee) is taxed at source (i.e. by the local council, tribunal, Water Authority etc), they could find that their net earnings for the period are *reduced*. In these cases, it is important to negotiate with the employer an agreement whereby the compensation (or fee) is handed direct to the employer who then makes the appropriate deductions.

Sitting down with management

If you are negotiating a new (or improved) scheme, possibly the first thing you will need to do will be to bring to your employer's attention the provisions of the Employment Protection (Consolidation) Act. Particularly if you work for a small organisation, it may be that your employer is not aware of some – or any – of this legislation (see pages 114–115).

Your job as a negotiator, of course, is to try and *improve* on the legal minimum requirements: for instance, you may decide to go for *paid* release, whereupon your employer is likely to complain about the cost – you could say that:

- relatively short periods of time are involved;
- *very* few employees are ever likely to be affected.

Your employer may not be convinced about 'what's in it for him', and you might consider saying that:

- it could do the company's image no harm if an employee

occupied a prominent position in public life in the neighbourhood (e.g. as Mayor);

■ the industry in which you work is underrepresented in public life.

It can be very helpful if you are in a position to say that:

■ there is (or has been) an employee who has been given time off for such activities (e.g. a higher executive, perhaps, who is a councillor or a JP);

you can quote this as a precedent that should be applied to *all* employees – i.e. that nobody should be discriminated against on the grounds of their lower position in the company. Try and persuade your employer that:

■ time off for public affairs and duties should be equally available to all employees *irrespective of grade*;

if you can hold the management to this, you should be able to defend a member who is *promoted* and his/her time off reduced because of the firm's 'operational requirements'.

Your employer may be generally sympathetic to the idea of paid release – in which case, you can:

■ remind him that the Act makes no mention of time off for *training* for school governors and for membership of public bodies such as Supplementary Benefit appeal tribunals and other statutory tribunals; you can point out that participation on these bodies will be less effective without such training, and that therefore the firm should grant short periods of time off for this purpose.

If your employer is worried about abuse of the scheme, you can say that:

■ it is very easy to provide written confirmation for each meeting,

but also try and ensure that the agreement is *open-ended*: you could say:

■ as participation in some public duties is protected by law, it should be possible to take part in all *extra* activities of the body concerned.

Your employer might agree to this – but only on *unpaid* leave: the best response might be to:

■ accept the proposal and

■ bear it in mind for future negotiations when you can try and extend the period of *paid* release.

It is important to establish this flexibility wherever possible, as this will make it a lot easier to *negotiate locally in individual cases.*

If your employer later includes time off for public affairs and duties in '*the cost of the union claim*', make it very clear to him (and the Press, if necessary) that:

■ time off work for membership of public bodies is *a legal obligation on the employer*, and must not be included therefore in the cost of any package agreement between the company and the union.

8.

Time off for study

Introduction

In this chapter we look at paid or unpaid time off work to do courses, whether they are connected with your job or not; this is sometimes called 'study leave'. Subsistence allowances on courses are dealt with in 'Subsistence' (pages 182–95). This chapter is not concerned with the training of shop stewards nor with courses for union safety representatives. By far the majority of agreements negotiated by trade unions concern job-related time off (i.e. for courses or other educational/training activities directly related to your work); very occasionally, and never for manual workers, there are arrangements for sabbatical leave.

Employers have long been notorious for having little or no sympathy for workers who wish to undergo training courses – and this in the face of strong pressure from unions, the TUC, the Government of the day and international bodies. The 1974–79 Labour Government proposed introducing by 1983 a scheme whereby vocational training would be extended to cover at least one-third of all school leavers going into jobs below craft level. These proposals, overall, were very well received in most quarters – unions, business and the Civil Service:

■ The TUC General Council welcomed them, and also supported the suggestion from the Business Education Council (BEC) to set up short courses for adults already in employment. The BEC have estimated that 80 per cent of school leavers going into business undergo no further business education or training.

■ The Department of Industry (DoI), too, recognises that promotion to positions of high responsibility should not be limited to those who have gone straight from school into higher education.

The DoI therefore believes that there is a need for a scheme of part-time and full-time courses aimed at people already working.

■ The National Association of Teachers in Further and Higher Education (NATFHE) now have a policy urging the introduction of bridging courses for young women to make up for the almost total absence of technical education in secondary schools – *and* to prepare them for specialist training in certain skills that have traditionally been the preserve of men.

The Government's Advisory Council for Adult and Continuing Education is pressing for paid educational leave from work and for study grants for adults, and the Tory Government elected in 1979 has been urging employers to devise a new type of training scheme that is relevant to people in mid-career who already have valuable experience in the factory or office. The Government says it is not satisfied with job-related courses in this country:

> 'Training in this country leaves a lot to be desired, the whole of the apprenticeship system, the retraining of unemployed people and the uptraining of people at work.' (Government spokesperson in a House of Commons debate, 22 July 1980)

The TUC has been similarly anxious:

> 'The General Council believe that the new Government [the Conservative Government elected in 1979] now has a responsibility to consolidate and build up on the steps that have already been taken to create new education and training opportunities for 16–18 year olds. There is *a responsibility also on the people in industry*, in training and in education, as well as on the young people themselves. The stakes are high. We cannot expect to accomplish the industrial changes that are necessary, and to cope with the challenges presented by the new technology of microelectronics unless, at the same time, the nation invests in its future manpower.' (*TUC Policy Statement on Education and Training for 16–18 year olds*, 1979) [Emphasis added]

A major obstacle to a satisfactory solution to these problems is the present Government's cutbacks in public expenditure: as the TUC has pointed out, in the June 1979 Budget alone £120m was cut from the Manpower Services Commission's funding for adult retraining, support for apprenticeship training by Industry Training Boards (ITBs), and special courses for unemployed adults and school leavers. More recently, in the summer of 1980, the Government proposed to transfer the taxpayers' contribution to the running of ITBs (approximately £51m a year) entirely over to the employers; it is thought this might lead to the disbanding of most of them. An example of the work that some ITBs undertake is as follows:

■ in July 1980, the Engineering ITB organised a week's course for 36 16- to 17-year-old female students to encourage them to look for a job in engineering (in engineering currently, women only account for 6 per cent of managers, scientists and technologists, technicians, administrative and professional staff, and supervisors – figures supplied by the Engineering ITB).

The TUC has also criticised the way the Government has failed to make full use of the EEC Social Fund to help women *back* into employment, and there have been threats from Brussels that Britain's entitlement to draw on the EEC Social Fund could be reduced if cuts in industrial training continued. Some of this money is available via the Government's in-plant training schemes administered by the Manpower Services Commission (MSC):

■ in England, Scotland and Wales, free training courses are run by the Training Service Agency (part of the MSC);

■ in Northern Ireland, free training courses are organised at Government Training Centres and grants are also available for training courses on company premises.

The performance of successive British Governments compares sadly with that of governments elsewhere in Europe; here are two examples:

■ *West Germany:* under *federal* legislation introduced in 1976, if the supply of training places in any one year is not at least 12½ per cent higher than the demand for them, the government can impose a training levy of 0.25 per cent of payroll on all public and private sector industrial and commercial organisations employing over 20 people. The money raised by means of this levy is used to subsidise companies that train school leavers for certain trades specified by the Ministry of Education and Science. The 12½ per cent minimum has yet to be achieved, but 1979 at least saw a small surplus (2½ per cent) of places over applicants for the first time since 1974 – and the federal government decided, as a gesture of goodwill, not to impose the levy. A number of German *states* have also introduced the legal right to time off for *private* study: this usually means up to 10 days a year and is limited to workers who are under the age of 25.

■ *Italy*: one of the less generous schemes (outside Britain) is to be found in Italy where the legal entitlement is only 150 hours in three years (250 hours in the engineering industry), and there is an obligation to attend courses which last at least double that length;

the only courses, to which the provisions apply are those jointly approved by employers *and trade unions*.

Job-related time off

It is the firm policy of large employers, particularly, to arrange training schemes for employees; firms doing this include:

■ Cadbury Schweppes, Lesney Products, May & Baker, Wilkinson Match (High Wycombe).

Other firms tend to put more emphasis on training schemes for special purposes:

■ Ford Motor Co (managers);

■ London Borough of Lambeth (employees who are involved in training others);

■ courses for managers in new technology are regularly booked up, despite the fact that many of them cost as much as £70–100 for a two-day course *plus* the cost of travel (frequently abroad), food, accommodation and other expenses.

The question of *which* courses and qualifications are 'approved' is sometimes laid down by outside bodies (e.g. in law and accountancy), but the employer will sometimes take a hand in deciding what is approved and what is not:

■ the local government APT&C agreement has a 'list of examinations recognised for promotion and appointment purposes' containing over 65 institutions and approximately double that number of examinations;

■ in the NHS there are 14 'approved' cookery institutions offering 31 'approved' qualifications;

■ in Local Authorities parks and gardens, there is an 'in-house' scheme and an external one (City & Guilds).

Sometimes there can be a doubt as to whether a course will be suitable for a given job; this needs to be clarified by your employer – perhaps with the appropriate Industry Training Board – but it is much easier to have your agreement endorsed:

■ local government plumbers have their training service agreement endorsed in this way: 'It is agreed by the parties hereto that the conditions of service of the apprentice shall be in accordance with the conditions of service prescribed from time to time by the Joint Negotiating Committee for Local Authorities' Services (Building and Civil Engineering).'

However, time off to go on a course will ultimately be of little use if you are unable to *practise* what you learn on the course. Taking the local government agreement as an example again, if you are serving an apprenticeship as a motor vehicle service mechanic your employers must make sure that they have the facilities available for the apprentice to receive practical workshop training or that they can make arrangements for some part of that practical training.

Contracts vary enormously with regard to time off for courses; here are two examples of detailed, but clear, schemes as quoted by IDS:

Birds Eye Foods

Examination	Study by day release	Study by evening class or other course
ONC or City & Guilds	½ day + exam time	2 days per part + exam time
HNC	2 days per part + exam time	4 days per part + exam time
degree or HND	4 days per part + exam time	8 days + exam time

Birds Eye also give paid release for day classes (usually eight hours a week) and for sandwich courses – and will pay you if you have to leave work early in order to get to evening class.

Civil Service

Examination	Paid release	Extra days
GCE 'O' levels or equivalent (e.g. ONC)	5 days	If *exams* take up over 2½ days a year, another 4 days' leave a year
GCE 'A' levels or similar	10 days (maximum of 5 in any one year)	If *exams* take up over 2½ days a year, another 4 days' leave a year
Degree	20 days (maximum of 10 in last year of course)	If course could not otherwise be completed 10 days

The Civil Service also give you one day's paid leave if you are taking a GCE exam which qualifies you for promotion.
Other arrangements include:

■ five days' paid leave for study in the month preceding a public examination (GLC);

■ paid release for day classes (Eagle Star – staff only);

■ two days off for an exam (Lesney Products);

■ one day off for an exam, but if the exam is in the morning you get the *previous* day off on full pay (Co-op Bank);

■ 'The working week should be inclusive of lectures and tutorial classes.' (nurses).

Here is another example of job-related study leave from the travel business:

■ at the Pontinental head office in Bournemouth, the women who sell trips over the phone and the sales administrative staff decided they wanted to know what they were selling. They eventually negotiated with management an undertaking that *all* staff at head office would spend one week each year on full pay as training at one of Pontinental's sites abroad. The venues are chosen by management, and spouses travel at concessionary rates.

Correspondence courses continue to be a popular way of passing 'professional' exams, and a good number of firms – particularly in the finance sector – strongly encourage their employees to make use of them:

■ at Eagle Star, an employee who is obliged to follow a correspondence course because there is no suitable classroom course in the locality is entitled to study time *during working hours*.
In recent years, one of the most successful external courses has been the Open University (OU); the Conservative Government elected in 1979 has strongly recommended employers to give more financial assistance to workers on OU courses by paying the fees, to grant leave to attend OU Summer Schools – and to recognise achievement through promotion. Some employers have made formal arrangements for their employees to have time off for these Summer Schools:

■ in the Civil Service, the entitlement is the same as for other degree courses (see page 122);

■ staff at British Rail and Shell Oil (UK) may take one week a year (the rest coming out of annual holiday).

Although employers will sometimes grant time off, they will

not always pay full wages – and there is also the matter of plus-payments that must not be forgotten. Some of the better agreements are:

■ Local government manual workers get normal wages (including plus-payments) and reimbursement of course and exam fees.

■ Local government APT&C staff get the same *and* qualify for paid release for revising before an exam.

■ Staff at Hambro Life Assurance have their exam fees and text books paid for.

■ At Brooke Bond Liebig, attendance on courses must first gain the approval of the manager; then: 'When the course is approved, day or part-day release may be granted if necessary. Entrance fees paid in full and initially, half the cost of tuiton, approved books and examination fees. The second half of the cost of tuition etc., may be paid following successful examinations, or, if no examination is held, satisfactory reports on attendance, progress and completion are received from the college concerned.'

■ Pedigree Petfoods pay the good timekeeping bonus to workers on approved courses.

Some employers produce highly detailed statements of what they will pay:

■ *Greater London Council:* 'Compulsory part-time day release: full cost of all text books reasonably necessary for the course and in any event not less than £14;

'Personal study, sponsored study (day release) and recruitment training: 75 per cent of the cost of text books or related course materials as reasonably necessary for the course and in any event not less than £28.'

Financial inducements – or encouragement – to follow job-related courses have been common in the banking and insurance world for many years; this kind of financial assistance, which is almost unheard of amongst manual workers, is *over and above* whatever arrangement there may be for the payment of salaries:

■ Staff at Prudential Assurance qualify for an interest-free loan to cover expenses during the first year of the course; a small amount of interest is charged in the second year, and the money is paid back over 12 months.

■ Examination awards at the Royal Liver Friendly Society range from £25 to £250.

■ Staff at Sun Alliance receive £300 for:

- associateship of the Chartered Insurance Institute;
- fellowship of the Chartered Insurance Institute;
- associate membership of the Association of Certified Accountants, the Institute of Personnel Management and the Institute of Data Processing.

■ Teachers, too, qualify for similar increments: teachers at primary and secondary schools in England and Wales who have already completed four years of full-time study, training or research are paid one increment for each year in excess of three (with a maximum of three increments altogether); Local Authorities also have the discretion to pay up to two more increments for any full-time study lasting more than six years.

Recognition of comparable success by manual workers is somewhat less generous:

■ in the NHS, successful completion of the cookery courses *may* qualify those workers for placement on a higher rate of pay within their grades.

Sabbatical leave

Sabbatical leave is time off – usually designated for study purposes – given to non-manual workers who have generally been employed for a good number of years: according to a recent survey, sabbatical leave is limited to 4 per cent of directors and heads of department and to 7 per cent of employees in general (*Executive Remuneration and Benefits Survey Report*, John Courtis and Partners 1980). There is a small number of jobs where there is a tradition of sabbatical leave – for example, publishing and education. Where there is *no* tradition, the employees who become eligible seem to be exclusively in top management. There seem to be no examples in this country of sabbaticals being given to manual workers.

Most firms do not appear to have any formal arrangements for granting sabbatical leave, but this has not prevented some of them from releasing employees from time to time:

■ the BBC, Birds Eye Foods, Bovril, Molins and Selfridges occasionally grant sabbatical leave, but on a totally discretionary basis;

■ Burmah Oil has no policy at all, but has nonetheless released two employees (one paid, the other unpaid) – without undertaking to keep their jobs open for them.

Those organisations that do have a policy clearly favour employees in senior management grades:

■ in the Civil Service the leave is limited to high-ranking officers who are *likely to go even higher*, and will usually be granted only once in a career;

■ permanent staff at the GLC are eligible for three months' leave for work connected with the Council's activities – the GLC are quoted by IDS as awarding this time off 'to alleviate "the stress of office" '; *senior* staff can put in for leave 'to undertake work or study projects *of their own choice* not necessarily related to the work of the Council' [Emphasis added];

■ the three months' leave at British Home Stores has a qualification period of 25 years – except for senior management, who qualify after 10 years.

A job with a long tradition of sabbatical leave is journalism, and here it is unusual to find this sort of management favouritism:

■ at Thames & Hudson, journalists qualify for leave after seven years' continuous employment;

■ journalists, photographers and artists with Mirror Group Newspapers qualify for one week's leave every four years.

Very slowly, though, sabbaticals are gaining in popularity in other jobs; banking is an example:

■ at Barclays Bank, the qualification period is as high as 15 years, but the three months' leave can be accumulated by 'banking' up to five days' holiday every year.

This method at Barclays is similar to a new scheme in France whereby:

■ service-related holiday can be either taken at will *or* 'banked' and taken as a sabbatical – 'banking' all service-related days for 13 years will produce a *five-month sabbatical* (Peugeot-Citroën).

In this country, management and white-collar workers seem to have an absolute exclusive on sabbatical leave; however, in 1979 manual workers in Australia made a major breakthrough:

■ Australian metal workers have negotiated the right to 13 weeks' paid sabbatical leave after 15 years' employment.

Non-job-related study

This sub-section is concerned with time off to pursue studies which are *not* connected directly with your work. Here are three agreements worded in general terms:

■ An employee at Brooke Bond Liebig is eligible for a course if it is 'likely to assist him/her either to do his/her present job better or *to prepare for a future job*'. [Emphasis added]

■ 'Staff except apprentices and trainees in recruitment training schemes shall be required to continue with their education until the end of the academic year in which they reach the age of 18 years.' (GLC)

■ The national agreement for APT&C staff in local government goes even further: 'The local government service should . . . afford adequate opportunities for serving officers to obtain university degrees.'

The GLC agreement also states that:

> 'It is the Council/authority's policy to encourage and assist staff who wish to study in their own time for qualifications and examinations in subjects . . . which provide individual development for their future career.'

Two other very important areas of non-job-related study are reading and writing, and English as a second or foreign language. Courses for people who have difficulty in reading and writing (often called 'literacy classes') are available in a large number of adult institutes up and down the country; increasingly, employers are granting time off for employees who wish to take advantage of them.

■ The London Borough of Hackney gives time off during working hours to any employee who wishes to attend courses locally; these courses, which were negotiated by the manual workers' trade unions in the borough and organised by Centerprise, consist of one four-hour lesson each week.

A growing number of employers who take on workers from overseas are also negotiating for these employees to have time off for lessons in English:

■ at the Hilton Hotel in London, there have been two courses during working hours with no loss of pay;

■ at the New Southgate site of Standard Telephones, there has been a 13-week course consisting of three $1\frac{1}{2}$-hour lessons a week; each course has places for 12 students.

Other courses have taken place at Elco Plastics (High Wycombe) for the Asian supervisors, and there is provision for setting up more courses under the national agreement for the textile industry.

Time off work for courses unconnected with your job always has to be negotiated at local level in Britain; but this type of study has been *legally protected* in several other countries since the early 1960s, although the takeup has not been quite as great as had been expected. Under French legislation (which dates back to the late 1950s), certain workers are entitled to a year's paid leave for full-time courses and to 1,200 hours for part-time courses; there is a minimum service qualification of two years and you are not eligible if you have gained a similar diploma or certificate in the previous three years. The employer can legally refuse to release you if a specified level of absenteeism has been reached, but he otherwise shares with the state the payment of the worker's wages.

There are two systems in Belgium: the first goes back to 1963 when 10 days were granted by law to go on any non-job-related course that was run by recognised organisations (these include trade unions and adult education bodies); participants, who must be under 40, are paid a 'study wage' by the state. In 1973 a further law was passed entitling workers (again up to the age of 40) to paid release which increased with each course completed – for example, on the third course Belgian workers qualify for the *whole* time to be paid. The system, as in France, is funded jointly by employers and the state.

Preparing for negotiations

Employment legislation

There is no law in this country obliging your employer to give you time off for study leave of any description. However, as long as an apprentice's contract of employment expressly states that time off will be granted to follow a suitable course, the employer is *obliged* to grant him/her that time off. If the employer were to discriminate against any employees on the grounds of sex or race, this would be illegal under the Sex Discrimination Act 1975 and the Race Relations Act 1976 respectively (see page 13).

Income tax

Any expenditure *you* may incur in going on a job-related course or in gaining a qualification is *not* tax-deductible, but if your employer pays for the course and exam fees the Inland Revenue will *not usually* make *you* liable.

For tax payable on any travelling and subsistence expenses you may run up on a course, see 'Using your own transport' (pages 222–35), 'Travelling by public transport' (pages 236–40) and 'Subsistence' (pages 182–95).

Sitting down with management

Study leave can be – or should be – quite easy to obtain in certain circumstances:
- where it is custom and practice in the industry (e.g. the finance sector);
- where apprentices are concerned;
- where the job or industry is covered by an Industry Training Board (ITB).

Apprentices are likely to be reasonably well protected because:
- their original contract of employment *should* spell out their rights to pay, time off etc.

If the employer refuses to go along with the recommendations of the ITB, say that you may:
- take the matter up immediately with the trade union representatives on the appropriate ITB (all committees and sub-committees of ITBs have at least one-third union representation).

Your employer is bound to be worried about money. He might say that he does not think it is his job to organise – or pay for – his employees' education and training, and that it is the Government's duty to do this, in which case:
- remind him that the 1979 Tory Government *encourages* employers to set up training schemes (see page 119).

If the employer says that training must be *cost-effective* (i.e. he wants to see a financial return on the money spent on training), you can say that a good scheme will:
- help in recruiting new workers;
- help to keep existing staff;
- encourage company loyalty.

The management may say that there are no particular problems in these areas, in which case you could try persuading them that *individual* workers will help the company by being:
- better educated;
- better trained;

- more skilled;
- better placed to aim for promotion and/or a career.

It would be a mistake, though, to play the employer's game throughout and pander to his need to run a 'successful' business; you could also try arguing that study leave will be welcomed by workers who:

- had an inadequate full-time education;
- left school very early;
- have now decided that they want to improve their lives.

Beware of any attempt by the employer to 'cost' your claim for study leave, particularly when he is talking to the Press. What a lot of employers do is to add up the money likely to be earned by workers when they are off on study leave, and then describe the total as the 'cost of the union claim'. This completely fails to take into account:

- any advantages accruing to the firm from a better trained workforce;
- any advantages accruing to the *workers themselves* from any further education;
- any contractual requirements (e.g. apprentices).

Your employer may be worried that the right to time off work for study purposes may be abused; in this case you can say that:

- arrangements can always be made with the college concerned to keep the employer informed about the member's attendance – and progress.

But what the management may be really thinking about is the fact that the firm already spends a lot of money on its own training department. Depending on what *sort* of subjects the members may want to do, you may not want the company to have a say in the course content, so you can:

- tell the employer that the training department cannot reasonably be expected to handle *all* training needs;
- recommend that the study leave scheme (non-job-related as well as job-related) is made one of the day-to-day responsibilities of the training department.

Your employer may object to workers going *outside* the workplace for study purposes on the grounds that there is no suitable establishment in the locality; you can remind him of the existence of:

- correspondence courses;
- the Open University;

■ free training schemes organised by the Government.

But the employer may be more concerned that he may pay for an employee to train in a subject, after which s/he goes off to another firm. If the employer says he will agree to a scheme as long as all participants undertake to stay on for a minimum period afterwards, you may find you have to agree *in the short term* – but you can always point out that:

■ for people to stay with the firm longer than they want to is not necessarily *good* for the firm.

Finally, beware of an employer agreeing too abruptly to a study leave scheme:

■ a prolonged *unpaid* absence from work could adversely affect your pension rights (see Sue Ward, *Pensions*, Pluto Press 1981).

As far as sabbatical leave is concerned there is no doubt that, where there is custom and practice (e.g. in journalism, publishing and university education), great advantages accrue to both the employer and the individual. These benefits are:

■ a fresh look at the problems of the job;
■ an opportunity to do special research;
■ a chance to spend a few weeks abroad;
■ a chance to report back to colleagues who stayed at work.

If you find that other grades in your firm *do* go on sabbaticals (but you also think that the members you represent would not want them), you could suggest to management that this is unfair and that:

■ manual workers could, instead, build up a number of lieu days and later on take an extra week's holiday; this might be taken at management discretion with, say, four weeks' notice – perhaps during a time of slack business.

9.

Pregnancy, maternity and paternity

Introduction

This chapter deals with paid or unpaid time off for having a baby. It will discuss arrangements for time off before the birth (antenatal or pregnancy leave), the significance of the date of the birth, arrangements for time off after the birth (maternity leave) and the mother's right to her job back. There will also be a brief look at paternity leave. Negotiations for workplace nurseries are dealt with in 'Child care for working parents' (pages 157–66).

Statutory maternity rights in this country are among the worst in the industrialised world; a study by the Labour Research Department of legal rights in member countries of the European Economic Community (EEC) concluded that 'the UK is at or near the bottom of the league in almost every aspect of maternity benefits' (*Bargaining Report No 8*, Labour Research Department 1980):

■ Britain is the only EEC country to insist on a minimum period of employment before you are entitled to maternity leave *or* maternity pay;

■ only one other country (Ireland) has a lower rate of maternity pay;

■ only one other country (Belgium) gives maternity pay for a shorter period of time.

If we look outside the EEC, the picture is the same: in Western Europe, Austria gives legal protection which is superior *in every respect*; in Eastern Europe, Hungary grants a monthly child-care allowance for three years during which time the job is *guaranteed*.

It is often said that the statutory rights in this country – let alone locally negotiated improvements – are an obstacle to economic progress. With capitalism in crisis and the world economy in recession, improvements in maternity rights will remain difficult to achieve for some time, but the customary arguments against improvement must be challenged just the same:

■ *Employers spend long and unnecessary hours trying to understand the legislation*: a lot of employers seem to spend very little time indeed on it: a Department of Employment survey carried out in 1978 of 301 firms employing fewer than 50 people found that only 11 per cent of them knew about the qualifying conditions of maternity leave under the Employment Protection (Consolidation) Act 1978.

■ *Protective legislation of this type impedes the smooth running of the firm*: the Department of Employment survey referred to above – it was carried out by the Opinion Research Centre (ORC) – found that this was not generally true. No fewer than 213 of the small firms questioned by the ORC employed under 10 people but only *one* of them thought that, of Government measures currently in force, maternity leave was a problem. Also, among the welter of labour law introduced by the 1974–79 Labour Government, maternity leave was considered to be a problem by only *two* of the employers in the survey. Four per cent of the sample had kept a worker's job open for 40 weeks and 2 per cent had given maternity pay – but none had experienced any difficulty. (This may have been because very few women were exercising their legal rights.) Furthermore, a survey carried out in 1980 by *Industrial Relations Review and Report* (IRRR) of 261 firms found that 83 per cent considered that the *original* maternity provisions (i.e. under the Employment Protection (Consolidation) Act – see pages 150–54) were working well; IRRR also discovered that most of the remaining 17 per cent had had no experience in dealing with the legal provisions regarding maternity.

■ *Most working women qualify for maternity pay AND for their jobs back, and this is an intolerable burden on employers:* a Department of Employment survey – carried out by the Policy Studies Institute in 1980 – shows that only half of the women working while pregnant actually qualify for the statutory rights, and 26 per cent said they would be returning to work after maternity leave – but only 10 per cent did. The same study also found that the nine large firms in the banking and insurance sector which they looked at coped with any problems 'by taking commonsense precautions': by finding out informally whether the women *really* wanted to return or whether they probably would not if all went well.

■ *It costs far too much money:* the *Industrial Relations Review and Report* quoted above found that few companies in their sample (18 per cent) gave pay and leave over the statutory minimum – and even fewer (16 per cent) granted any special concessions after the return to work (e.g. crêches, a reduction of working hours or time off for postnatal care); moreover, the takeup by working women of maternity pay is estimated at only about 2 per cent, and IRRR discovered that no more than 0.3 per cent took maternity leave *and* returned to work! There are certainly huge differences between employers in this respect – for example, Rochdale Metropolitan Borough Council reports a return rate of 58 per cent – but one reason might be high unemployment amongst men: BAT's return rate at their Liverpool plant is approximately 71 per cent, whereas at their London head office nobody returned at all. Another reason could be that many women do not know their rights: many employers could take a leaf out of the books of Arthur Guinness and the London & Manchester Assurance Co where all pregnant employees are called in for an explanatory interview as soon as it is known that they are pregnant.

The weakening of statutory rights in 1980 (see pages 150–54) was hailed as 'good for women': for instance, the Government said in the House of Commons that they thought some of the new laws 'should encourage employers to employ more women'; this was immediately rejected by the Equal Opportunities Commission on the grounds that women who might have children will shy away from small firms – which in turn will find it increasingly difficult to recruit. It is worth adding that, in the view of the DHSS, there would be three times as many families claiming Family Incomes Supplement (FIS) but for the fact that women earn.

However, it is not just certain official bodies that call for better protective legislation for women workers: a survey carried out by APEX (*Workplace Attitudes to Maternity & Nursery Facilities: A Case Study*, APEX 1980) came to very similar conclusions: this took the form of a lengthy questionnaire sent to over 2,000 women workers at Lucas factories, and a summary of their answers is set out below:

■ 40 per cent thought that maternity leave should be a year or more (over 80 per cent of them were under 35);

■ 75 per cent thought that part-timers should have the same leave entitlement as full-timers;

■ 74 per cent felt that part-timers should have pro rata payment;

■ 78 per cent believed that they should be able to hang onto such rights as seniority and promotion;

■ 85 per cent felt that maternity leave should not count as a break in service;

■ 90 per cent wanted to keep their pension rights;

■ 52 per cent were in favour of a shorter working week after returning to work and, of those who specified a period, 70 per cent suggested that this should last for up to 12 weeks;

■ 87 per cent felt that it should be possible to have paid leave of absence or a transfer in the event of exposure to such illnesses as German measles;

■ 81 per cent were in favour of paid leave of absence in order to attend antenatal clinics;

■ 93 per cent thought that, if the child were to die, there should be an extension of leave (53 per cent were of the opinion that it should be up to three months);

■ 31 per cent thought there should be no qualification period for maternity leave.

Over the years, trade unions – in a more 'official' capacity – have occasionally taken a stand on women's maternity rights. Some unions have also had policies on maternity rights that have always been in advance of the terms of the legislation. Here are some of the better policies:

	Paid leave	Total leave + guaranteed job back
NATFHE	52 weeks (26 on full pay, 26 on half pay)	2 years
NALGO	38 weeks	1 year
GMWU	30 weeks	1 year
ACTSS	26 weeks	—
APEX	24 weeks (16 on full pay, 8 on half pay)	1 year
ASTMS	18 weeks	1 year

The TUC, in their Model Maternity and Paternity Agreement, have also gone for 18 weeks' paid leave for mothers with the job guaranteed back after a total absence of a year. Much of the official TUC policy comes out of a Working Party set up in 1976 to examine State and other provisions of facilities for looking after children of preschool age; the Working Party's report (*The Under-Fives*, TUC) and subsequent TUC General Council amendments have now produced an impressive shopping list of official demands, including:

■ the option to do part-time work for a period of time on returning from maternity leave;

■ a statutory right to sick leave when a child is ill;

■ two hours' paid leave each day for breastfeeding the child;

■ restrictions on overtime, shiftworking and long business trips during the lactation period.

Another of the TUC demands is paid leave for visits to antenatal clinics; while legislation aimed at making this a statutory right was going through Parliament, the Secretary of State for Employment (James Prior) answered a TUC submission on the subject and is reported as saying that he was impressed by the contention that unskilled women workers were statistically most at risk and in greatest need of care 'and that *it is just these women who stand the greatest chance of finding their employer unhelpful in giving them time off*' (*The Times*, 25 March 1980) [Emphasis added].

This was soon to become a statutory right under the Employment Act 1980 (see 'Employment legislation', pages 150–54).

Very few British employers have improved on the statutory minimum requirements; for example, a GMWU survey in 1979/80 of 91 chemicals firms found that only *three* had agreed to better conditions and a survey by the same union of 326 engineering companies showed that only *two* offered better terms. This impression is further borne out by a study (in *Bargaining Report No 8*, LRD) of 20 *top* employers – 10 in the public sector, 10 in the private sector, employing altogether 4.8 million people:

■ only six out of the 20 (all in the public sector) have reduced the statutory service qualification period;

■ only seven out of the 20 (all but one – Grand Metropolitan – in the public sector) have improved on the statutory maternity pay.

On the whole, negotiated maternity rights in this country present a pretty dismal picture, but it would be a mistake to judge a pregnancy/maternity scheme by just *one* of its elements; if we take paid leave as an example, is three months on *full* pay (UK Atomic Energy Authority) 'better' than 29 weeks on *half* pay (Marshall Cavendish)? Or is 18 weeks on full pay with a *two*-year qualification (Mercury House) 'better' than 13 weeks on full pay with a *one*-year qualification (the Post Office)? All the elements of a scheme need to be looked at *together* and in the light of the needs of the people concerned.

This chapter is now divided into six sections, the first five dealing with maternity rights and the last one looking at time off for the father, as follows:

- Eligibility;
- Maternity leave;
- Maternity pay;
- Effect on other conditions of employment;
- Job back;
- Paternity leave.

As locally negotiated rights are always *related* to statutory minimum rights, it might be useful to check up on the legislation first (on pages 150–54).

The Labour Research Department publication already quoted (*Bargaining Report No 8*, 1980) also contains details of a number of the better deals negotiated in this country, and this chapter uses some of these figures; the rest of the information is drawn from several sources, notably a 1979 study by the NUJ and six surveys published in 1979/80 by the GMWU of industries where they have substantial membership.

Eligibility

The eligibility hurdle usually consists of two tests:

- Do you work enough hours a week? and
- Have you worked enough months/years for the firm?

These two questions reflect the legislation (see 'Employment legislation' (pages 150–54)). As 40 per cent of all working women are 'part-time', it is particularly difficult for a very large number of women to qualify for maternity rights – this despite the fact that employers have different cutoff points for 'full-timers':

- in the Civil Service, you are a part-timer if you work less than 18 hours a week;
- under the Universities Non-Teaching Staffs agreement the cutoff point is 15 hours a week.

So, if you don't work long enough hours, you may not qualify for anything – but there are a few exceptions:

■ *pro rata* maternity benefits for part-time workers at Arthur Guinness, the British Institute of Management, British Nuclear Fuels, Carlton, the Independent Broadcasting Authority and the Post Office.

The 'service qualification period' (i.e. have you worked enough months/years for the firm?) usually takes the form of a number of months or years of employment up to 11 weeks before the expected date of birth (see 'Employment legislation' (pages 150–54)). As the Employment Protection (Consolidation) Act 1978 sets two years as the minimum period of employment to qualify for *statutory* maternity rights, any company agreements which have a shorter period are encouraging. Here are a few:

■ *21 months:* Beechams (Walton Oaks), Longman Publishing;

■ *18 months:* Containerlink, Norfolk Capital Hotels, Roussel Laboratories, Thomson Books;

■ *12 months:* Albright & Wilson, Associated Dairies, British Airways, Butlins, Edinburgh University, Electricity Supply, Hotel Intercontinental, National Health Service, Rowntree Mackintosh (York), Sperry Univac;

■ *10 months:* Stratford Express Group;

■ *6 months:* Labour Party;

■ *nil:* National Coal Board.

A small number of agreements do not bother with the 11-week stipulation, and say that the service period leads straight up to the birth:

■ *one year prior to birth:* British Film Institute, Greater London Council, *Time Out*;

■ *nine months prior to birth: New Statesman.*

A useful feature of certain public-sector agreements is that employment with 'associated employers' counts towards this qualification period:

■ teachers moving from one Local Education Authority to another;

■ NHS workers moving from one Area Health Authority to another;

■ Water Service workers who have previously been employed in another public-sector industry with reciprocal pension arrangements.

Finally, there are a few organisations where women can

officially apply for *unpaid leave* if they have not been able to qualify for maternity leave/pay in the normal way:

■ at Oxford University Press, women with 10 months' service are eligible for 52 weeks' unpaid leave; this is changed to 20 weeks' paid and 32 weeks' unpaid leave after 15 months' service.

Here are some other firms that give unpaid leave:

■ British Steel Corporation (manual workers: 12 weeks; staff: 13 weeks);

■ National Health Service (18 weeks);

■ Civil Service (six months);

■ British Shipbuilders (40 weeks after one year's employment);

■ Containerlink (63 weeks after nine months' employment);

■ British Film Institute (at management discretion).

Maternity leave

It is unusual for there to be any leave *before* maternity leave begins, although time off for sickness during pregnancy is already protected by law (see page 150). There is much better provision abroad for antenatal care: in Sweden, for instance, a pregnant woman with a heavy job has the legal right to ask for a lighter job for up to 60 days before the estimated date of birth; if the employer cannot find a suitable alternative job, the woman is entitled to receive a pregnancy allowance (equivalent to sickness benefit) for a maximum of 50 days. In this country, antenatal provision was unusual before it became a statutory right under the Employment Act 1980 (see 'Employment legislation (page 153)); however, there were occasional local agreements, particularly where there were a lot of women employed:

■ at the Dumbarton bottling plant of Strathleven Bonded Warehouses, pregnant employees are actively encouraged by the firm to attend antenatal clinics during working time on full pay; they also get a free pint of milk each day and are allowed to leave work five minutes early at lunchtime and in the evening in order to miss the rush hour;

■ similarly, at Keys Mail Order, women in the last six weeks before maternity leave begins may leave work five minutes early at midday and at the end of the shift and are entitled to a free pint of milk;

■ there is also paid time off for visits to antenatal clinics at Containerlink, Arthur Guinness, London and Manchester Assurance Co, Deloitte Haskins & Sells, Gallaher and the Independent Broadcasting Authority.

As far as maternity leave proper is concerned, we have to bear in mind that the legal minimum period is 40 weeks (see page 152); there are some agreements which are spectacularly better:

- 90 weeks: Open University (academic and related staff);
- 63 weeks: Containerlink;
- 15 months: the police;
- 1 year: Longman Publishing;
- 52 weeks: Beecham (Walton Oaks);
- 50 weeks: British Institute of Management.

Two companies to have made less dramatic, but encouraging, progress recently are:

- Crane Fruehauf Trailers (East Dereham): statutory minimum leave + 5 days at basic rate;
- Dorman Diesels (Stafford): statutory minimum leave + 5 days at 85 per cent of average pay.

More often, the leave entitlement under the Employment Protection (Consolidation) Act 1978 is adhered to but with a shorter qualification period than laid down in the legislation (i.e. two years); the following firms give the normal 40 weeks' leave without discriminating against those women who have worked for them for less than two years:

- 40 weeks' maternity leave after *one* year's employment at Albright & Wilson, British Airways, British Film Institute, Butlins, the Electricity Council, Esso Petroleum, Arthur Guinness (Park Royal), London Borough of Camden, the Post Office, Rowntree Mackintosh and the UK Atomic Energy Authority.

Unfortunately, it would be wrong to think that all the above agreements are without strings:

- the paid leave at Esso Petroleum and the UK Atomic Energy Authority is conditional on the woman returning to work (there is no such obligation to return at Butlins and Arthur Guinness, for instance).

This condition is also to be found in less generous agreements elsewhere:

- in the Probation Service you must return for at least three months;
- teachers must return for at least 13 weeks;
- at TAP Portuguese Airlines you have to return for an unspecified period.

Another way of qualifying for maternity leave without having been employed for two years is to have a *reduced* leave entitlement after one year's employment; this is, of course, discriminatory against women who have been unable to have the job for long enough, but it is nonetheless better than the statutory minimum rights. Here are a few examples of reduced leave after only *one* year's employment:

- 13 weeks' leave (Water Service);
- 18 weeks' leave (BBC, Local Authorities and teachers);
- 6 months' leave (Civil Service and the IBA).

Some agreements have written into them a clause dealing with extensions to the 'basic' 40-week leave entitlement; in at least one case, this refers to the four-week extension laid down by the Employment Protection (Consolidation) Act 1978 (see page 152):

- according to the Universities Non-Teaching Staffs agreement (probably the best national agreement for public-sector manual workers), 'Where an employer postpones a return to work . . . the employee will be entitled to normal pay from the first agreed notified day of return and as if her return had not been postponed by the employer.'

After this four-week period has passed, there are a few arrangements that a mother can take advantage of:

- unpaid leave at management discretion (Local Authorities, the NHS and the Probation Service);
- unpaid leave on medical or other reasonable grounds (BBC);
- the management 'may, at its discretion, extend the period of paid or unpaid leave in cases of special hardship' (Universities Non-Teaching Staffs);
- paid or unpaid leave at management discretion, and it can be paid 'where the employer considers it desirable in the interests of the child' (Water Service);
- return to work may be delayed by up to 12 months (Time-Life International and Edward Arnold).

If the baby is stillborn or dies, a lot of agreements say that the mother has to return to work almost immediately and forego the maternity leave:

- teachers get six weeks' postnatal leave if the baby dies;
- four weeks' postnatal leave in the London Borough of Camden and at the Electricity Council.

A small number of employers take a more sympathetic line:

■ at Hodder & Stoughton, the entitlement of 13 weeks on full pay and 13 weeks on half is *extended* by a further four weeks;

■ the Universities Non-Teaching Staffs scheme says 'There shall be no distinction between live and still births in the granting of maternity leave.'

Postnatal leave is sometimes available to people other than the natural parents:

■ teachers in secondary and further education qualify for postnatal leave if they *adopt* children, too.

Maternity pay

Of the two elements of maternity pay, the period of time for which it is paid is given less attention by unions. As the ultimate objective must be for the woman to be paid *throughout* her leave, two of the best agreements in this respect are:

■ 29 weeks at sick-pay rate (i.e. the employer making National Insurance benefits up to £44.75 a week) at Miles Redfern (Hyde, Cheshire); the *basic* rate here was £44.86 in 1980;

■ 24 weeks at 90 per cent at London & Manchester Assurance Co.

The other element in maternity pay (the amount of money paid every week) has attracted somewhat more attention. The legal minimum entitlement is 90 per cent of *basic* pay (see page 151 for more details) and bonus payments and other plus-rates are usually excluded. However, two agreements that do *not* exclude plussages are:

■ the pay for local government manual workers includes the rates for shift work, night work, split duty, rostered weekend work, unsocial hours payments, responsibility money, regular standby duty money and many other elements of the weekly wage;

■ maternity pay at Imperial Tobacco includes regular set overtime, shift premium and 1/52nd of annual service payments. It is also common for employers to subtract National Insurance benefits, but not invariably:

■ at the Open University, National Insurance benefits are not touched.

Fortunately, an increasing proportion of maternity agreements give *full (or average) earnings*; here are a few examples, listed according to the number of weeks they are paid:

■ 26 weeks: *Time Out*;

■ 18 weeks: Beechams (Walton Oaks), Guardian Newspapers (clerical staff), Longman Publishing, Open University (academic and related staff), Times Newspapers (clerical staff);

■ 3 months: British Film Institute, the Civil Service, the Independent Broadcasting Authority, the UK Atomic Energy Authority;

■ 13 weeks: British Nuclear Fuels, Grand Metropolitan, National Magazine Co, the Post Office, Visnews, Water Service;

■ 11 weeks: British Shipbuilders;

■ 10 weeks: Camber Pencils, Arthur Guinness, Pontins;

■ 9 weeks: Butlins;

■ 2 months: Norfolk Capital Hotels, TAP Portuguese Airlines;

■ 8 weeks: Esso Petroleum.

In this context, it is worth drawing attention to the two months on full pay at the National Coal Board: there is no service qualification period at all – but the time off comes out of sick leave.

In some other firms, the unions have not been able to make such a dramatic impact on the legal minimum requirements, but have nonetheless begun to make important inroads:

■ six weeks' leave on *average* pay at Baird Tatlock Hopkins & Williams, Blundell Permoglaze (Hull), Dunlop (Washington, Tyne & Wear), Sorbo Industrial Polymers (Woking), William Warne (Barking).

There have been a number of devices aimed at improving maternity pay, and this has sometimes involved giving additional leave *at a lower rate*:

■ 16 weeks on full pay, 24 weeks on half pay (London Borough of Camden);

■ 8 weeks on full pay, 16 weeks on half pay (Universities Non-Teaching Staffs);

■ 6 weeks on full pay, 12 weeks on half pay (Edinburgh University, Electricity Supply);

■ 6 weeks on 90 per cent, 12 weeks on half pay (British Gas Corporation);

■ 4 weeks on full pay, 14 weeks on half pay (Greater London Council).

This method has also been adapted to act as an encouragement to return to work – in the following three examples, the extra weeks' pay is conditional upon the woman returning:

■ Penguin Books: 16 weeks' full pay + 8 weeks' half pay;

■ Thames & Hudson: 13 weeks' full pay + 13 weeks' half pay;
■ Labour Party: 6 weeks' full pay + 6 weeks' half pay.

Another kind of clause is found when the firm is keen for you to stay on for a minimum period *after* the maternity leave:

■ at the British Publishing Co, the eight weeks' paid leave is augmented by another four weeks' pay on returning to work and by yet another month's pay three months later: 'A woman shall be entitled to receive pay by way of a bonus of one month's salary three months after returning to her job provided she has not given notice of her voluntary intention to leave the Group's employment.'

■ at Roussel Laboratories, a *single* mother may receive an extra 18 weeks' full pay if she chooses to return.

It is important to point out that maternity leave in two parts need not be dependent on a return to work:

■ after taking paid leave at Containerlink (9 weeks on full pay, 6 weeks on half pay), you return to work *only if you wish to*.

Another device used to increase paid maternity leave is to have service-related leave – i.e. the longer you've been with the firm, the longer maternity leave you'll get:

■ one week's pay for every four months' employment (BBC);
■ after 1 year: 4 weeks on full pay, 14 weeks on half pay; after 2 years, 4 weeks on full pay, 2 weeks on 90 per cent and 12 weeks on half pay (NHS and teachers in further education);
■ 1–5 years' employment: 6 weeks on full pay; over 5 years' employment: 12 weeks on full pay (Cassell);
■ after 1 year: 2 weeks on full pay; after 2 years: 10 weeks on full pay; thereafter, 2 extra weeks on full pay for every extra year of service – maximum: 20 weeks on full pay (Roadchef);
■ on joining the firm: 13 weeks on full pay minus National Insurance benefits; after 10 years with the firm: 26 weeks on full pay – this scheme uses the sick-pay agreement (Albright & Wilson, Whitehaven).

Ideally, the sick-pay scheme should not be used for pregnancy leave because pregnancy is *not* an illness, and if you fall sick after returning to work you may have exhausted your paid sick-leave entitlement.

■ other firms to insist that sick leave is used include the Civil Service, the Design Council, the National Coal Board and the UK Atomic Energy Authority.

Finally, it is important for you to be paid if you do fall ill as a result of pregnancy, childbirth, miscarriage or maternity; this is the agreement at the Inn on the Park: 'The company will pay sickness pay for absence due to pregnancy provided the employee qualifies for sickness pay and provided a medical certificate for such absence(s) is submitted.'

The effect on other conditions of employment

Because of the break in employment brought about by taking maternity leave, it is unfortunately common for a woman's rights to certain contractual conditions to lapse, although this is less likely to happen in large firms: IRRR's survey of big employers in 1979 found that

■ 70 per cent allow women on maternity leave to use staff shops and sports and social facilities, and to take advantage of company discount schemes;

■ 55 per cent permitted repayments of cheap loans and/or company mortgages *during* maternity leave – and the loans had to be repaid completely only if the woman did not return (10 per cent said that payments could be *deferred* until she returned).

Two interesting examples of this are to be found in the insurance business, where it is the practice for the absent employee to pay the full commercial rate on loans (i.e. that charged to the public) and to revert to paying the concessionary rate on returning to work; however,

■ at the National Provident Institution, the additional interest paid during the maternity leave is refunded if the woman returns to work for at least one year;

■ at the Prudential Assurance Co, the interest rate is not increased for the first three months of maternity leave, and the difference between the commercial and the concessionary rates is refunded *as soon as* the woman returns to work.

Very occasionally, nearly all rights are preserved:

■ at Intercontinental Hotel and Cadbury Schweppes (Bournville), all contractual rights (except holidays) accrue during the absence;

but it is more normal for only certain non-wage benefits to continue to be available:

■ eligibility for concessionary travel facilities for the first 13 weeks (British Rail);

■ car allowance paid throughout the period of the leave (Industrial Estates Corporation).

Benefits that are calculated according to the length of employment are usually the most difficult to negotiate, and probably the best example of this is annual holidays; however, here is an example:

■ at Edward Arnold, two weeks of the annual holiday entitlement are held back and can be taken after the maternity leave is over.

There is another service-related benefit – one that involves the expenditure of relatively large sums of money – that can cause negotiating problems, and that is pensions; IRRR reports that

■ 83 of the 261 firms they interviewed count the period of maternity leave for pension purposes *and* continue to pay the employer's contributions;

■ 13 companies allow women to make up their own contributions when they return to work.

Examples of this type of procedure are:

■ Monsanto, Beckman Instruments and Hercules Powder Co (all of which have non-contributory schemes) make contributions throughout the maternity leave;

■ Cam Gears, which has a *contributory* scheme, pays both the employer's *and* the employee's contributions during the period of absence.

For a complete explanation of how pension rights can be protected during maternity leave, you should consult a companion volume to this (Sue Ward, *Pensions*, Pluto Press 1981).

Job back

One of the biggest problems faced by women after their maternity leave is over is getting their old job back (see pages 152–53):

■ United Biscuits take on their manual workers as 'process workers' and not on specific grades, and a woman who goes off on maternity leave is warned by the company that she cannot be promised exactly the same job when she returns;

■ at Arthur Guinness & Son, you have to take the first job offered – providing the terms and conditions are not substantially less favourable.

However, there are other agreements where the flexibility is to the *woman's* advantage rather than the company's:

■ at Containerlink, you need not take your old job back if you think it is affecting your health or domestic circumstances;

■ air stewardesses with British Airways can be transferred

to ground duties if they are unable to perform their normal job. Occasionally there is a positive attempt on the part of the employer to take into account the wide range of medical and social problems that can arise as a result of inadequate maternity leave:

■ at Longman Publishing and Beecham's (Walton Oaks), there is a scheme of staggered returns to work: a woman need work a three-day week only (on full pay) for the first four weeks after returning.

■ at the Sheraton Park Tower Hotel, women are allowed to build up their hours slowly for the first few weeks after returning from maternity leave, and they need do only light duties if the doctor believes normal work would be too arduous.

Unless *local* agreements can be negotiated to ease the problems of women wishing to return to work after pregnancy and maternity leave, it is certain that the provisions of the Employment Act 1980 (see 'Employment legislation' (pages 150–54)) are going to effectively *prevent* many women from doing so. The GMWU has produced the following letter to be sent by full-time organisers and branches to employers requesting that the conditions obtaining *before* the Employment Act came in should remain (i.e. the statutory provisions of the Employment Protection (Consolidation) Act 1978 or any local improvements):

'Dear . . .

'Maternity arrangements:

The GMWU wishes to ensure that our members retain their present rights on maternity as set out in (either quote the relevant maternity agreement and/or Sections 33–48 of the Employment Protection (Consolidation) Act 1978).

'I am sure you do not wish to see any deterioration in our members' terms and conditions of employment in this respect. Will you therefore confirm that the company will honour present arrangements and not seek to utilise the provisions of the Employment Act 1980 on notices to the employee or the right of return to alter the present terms and conditions of our members which will remain unaltered in all respects except for the provisions for paid antenatal leave.

'I would ask that a joint circular to this effect be sent to all (female) members/stewards.'

Paternity leave

It is still proving very difficult to make it a condition of employment that fathers have the *right* to paid time off on the birth of their children – although legal backing for maternity leave has undoubtedly aroused considerable interest among male trade unionists.

The social consequences of the father not being able to play his part in the child's early days are not difficult to find: a Department of Employment survey in 1975 estimated that over half of all male manual workers with children under 11 were doing $8\frac{1}{2}$–$10\frac{1}{2}$ hours' overtime a week. As the TUC commented, 'Many fathers were therefore working such long hours that they would be unable to play a full part in their own family life, including sharing responsibility for their own small children.' (*The Under-Fives*, TUC). And a lot of women agree: a survey carried out by APEX of over 2,000 women employed at Lucas factories found that the vast majority were in favour of paternity leave; in fact, 95 per cent of those supporting the idea thought it should last up to one month (*Workplace Attitudes to Maternity & Nursery Facilities: A Case Study*, APEX 1980).

Paternity leave is a *legally protected* right in certain other European countries: for example, in Denmark there is a statutory right to one week's paid leave for the father. An interesting extension of this is the *parental leave* provision to be found in Sweden: under Swedish legislation, the parents have the right to *share* nine months off work (at 90 per cent of earnings); it is estimated that in 1978 a quarter of all applications to take parental leave in Sweden came from men.

In this country, there is no statutory right to paternity leave, and very few men have a contractual right to it either. One survey put a surprisingly high estimate on it: according to the Institute of Administrative Management, as many as 13 per cent of firms give paternity leave of 3–5 days (*Office Holidays: Sickness Entitlements and Other Benefits*, 1980); however, most men have to make do with a number of extremely unsatisfactory devices:

■ *sick pay:* Berger (Dunstan);

■ *unpaid leave:* M A Craven & Son (York), Rediffusion (weekly-paid technical staff), Sperry Gyroscope;

■ *'at management discretion':* Albright & Wilson (Oldbury, Stratford (London)), Berger Paints (Middleton), British Oxygen Chemicals, BSC Chemicals (Southampton), Bush Boake Allen (Stratford (London)), Leyland Paint & Wallpaper Co, London and Manchester Assurance Co, Oxford University Press, Pointing (Low Prudhoe), Scottish Agricultural Industries (Edinburgh).

When there *is* an entitlement to a certain number of days off, the employer sometimes writes in a service qualification period (in a similar way to the eligibility hurdle for maternity leave); this is the agreement at Norfolk Capital Hotels:

> 'Leave shall be taken during the period commencing at the eleventh week prior to the estimated birth and [terminating at] the thirteenth week after the actual birth . . . The employee may take this leave either in single days or in any combination of days up to the total entitlement.' The entitlement at Norfolk Capital Hotels is 10 days after 104 weeks' continuous employment.

Here are some more examples of qualification periods, with the leave entitlements in brackets:

■ 6 months: National Council for Social Services (10 days);

■ 1 year: British Institute of Management (5 days), London Borough of Camden (5 days);

■ 2 years: William Cox (5 days), Roadchef (10 days).

There is an extraordinarily wide range of paid leave entitlements, with one of the biggest sticking points being whether the leave is on full (or average) pay or not. Here is a selection of arrangements:

■ 28 days on average pay: *Time Out*;

■ 2 weeks on average pay: Fisons (Widnes) – in special circumstances only;

■ 10 days on basic pay: Hutchinson, Penguin Books, Woodmet (Cheshire);

■ 7 days on full pay: Edinburgh University;

■ 5 days on average pay: GLC (staff only), Longman Publishing, Velva Tyne Tanks, Wilson & Whitworth Publishing Co;

■ 5 days on 85 per cent of average: Dorman Diesels (Stafford);

■ 5 days on basic pay: Butlins, Crane Fruehauf Trailers (East Dereham);

■ 3–5 days on average pay: Fisons (Plymouth);

■ 3 days on average pay: Bass North Ltd & Bass Brewing (Tadcaster) Ltd, Fisons (Stanford-le-Hope), Leyland Vehicles, London Rubber Co (Sandwich), Stowe Woodward;

■ 2 days on average pay: Acorn Shipyard, Albright & Wilson (Widnes), Bank of Tokyo and Detroit, Boulton & Paul (Norwich), Hotpoint (Middlesborough), Hull Bros (Radcliffe);

■ 2 days on basic pay; British Aerospace (Brough), Borg Warner;

■ 1 day on average pay: British Rail, May & Baker (Norwich), Sabena Belgian World Airlines, TAP Portuguese Airlines.

Preparing for negotiations

Employment legislation

In 1980, there were important changes in the laws covering women employees who become pregnant; these changes are dealt with in considerable detail in a companion volume (Jeremy McMullen, *Employment Law under the Tories*, Pluto Press 1981). The following is a brief summary of the current legislation.

The first protective legislation concerning maternity pay and leave in this country was implemented in 1976–77, and is part of the Employment Protection (Consolidation) Act 1978; however, this has now been amended by the Employment Act 1980. As one of the major struggles for trade unions at the moment is attempting to keep employers to the terms of the *original* legislation, *both* pieces of law are explained here (see 'Maternity leave and job back' and 'Notifying the employer' (pages 152–53)).

With one exception, all the legislation referred to in this section applies to all women employees who are full-timers *in the legal sense* (see Glossary); there is no need for a recognition agreement (see Glossary) between the employer and the union(s). The exception is the legal protection against unfair dismissal when pregnant (see 'Unfair dismissal' (pages 150–51)).

Unfair dismissal

Under Section 60 of the Employment Protection (Consolidation) Act 1978, if you are dismissed because you are pregnant *or for any reason connected with your pregnancy*, it is what is called an 'automatically unfair dismissal'. *All* women workers – irrespective of the number of hours they work – qualify for this legal protection. If you do get threatened with dismissal in these circumstances and if you are unable to solve the problem by means of your Grievance Procedure with the help of your union, you can claim unfair dismissal at an Industrial Tribunal. The only exception to this would be if you were doing a job which was illegal for you or your employer in view of your pregnancy – this can sometimes happen under health and safety legislation; but in this case, your employer has got to look for suitable alternative employment for you.

Even if you *are* dismissed, you do not lose your right to

maternity leave and pay – as long as you are entitled to it in the first place, and your employer cannot select you for dismissal *on the grounds that you are unmarried* – even when you're pregnant.

Who qualifies for maternity pay and leave?

Under the same 1978 Act, entitlement to maternity pay and leave is restricted to *employees legally defined as full-timers* (see page 286). It also makes no difference whether you are married or not.

Qualification period

Two years' continuous employment (see page 285) as a full-timer (see page 286) must have been completed by the beginning of the week 11 weeks before the baby is *due* to be born. For example, if your baby is due on Thursday 31 December, you must have completed two years' continuous employment at least 11 weeks before the beginning of that week – i.e. by Sunday 11 October.

Maternity pay

The term 'maternity pay' is a misnomer as, during the period when the law protects the right to this pay, you are not yet a mother – a better phrase would be 'pregnancy pay'; however, as nearly everybody says 'maternity pay', we'll say the same thing.

Under Sections 34–35 of the same 1978 Act, your *minimum* entitlement is six weeks' paid leave at 9/10ths of your basic wage; 'basic' wage usually means that you do not get bonuses, overtime pay or other plussages – pieceworkers usually receive earnings averaged over the previous 12 weeks (minus overtime).

The employer does not provide all of the 9/10ths of basic pay: he can subtract State benefits, and his own contribution comes out of the Maternity Pay Fund which *all* employers pay into. The legal minimum maternity pay is made up as follows:

■ maternity allowance (whether or not you are eligible for this State benefit *and* whether or not you apply for it) PLUS

■ the balance from your employer (i.e. he makes it up to 9/10ths of your basic pay).

(Maternity pay also includes earnings related allowance, but this allowance is to be abolished by the Tory Government in 1982.) You are entitled to this maternity pay *whether or not* you are returning to work with the firm.

If you have a miscarriage, or the baby is stillborn or born prematurely *after* the point 11 weeks before the expected confinement (see page 151), you qualify for maternity pay – *whether you have started maternity leave or not*. If the miscarriage, stillbirth or premature birth takes place before the 11th week before the expected date of birth, you are *not* entitled to maternity pay under the law – and, under DHSS rules, you are not entitled to maternity allowance either.

Continuity of employment

While you are off on maternity leave, your continuity of employment is *not* broken; for the purposes of benefits related to the length of employment (e.g. holidays, increments, sick pay), your period of employment *before* the maternity leave is *added* to whatever period of employment *after* the maternity leave.

Maternity leave and job back

Under the new legislation (i.e. the Employment Protection (Consolidation) Act 1978 as amended by Sections 11–12 of the Employment Act 1980), your legal position with regard to leave and job back is as follows:

■ Maternity leave consists of the 11 weeks leading up to the confinement and 29 weeks after the confinement; this can be extended by up to four weeks *either* by you *or* by the employer.

■ Your employer does not *have* to give you your *old* job back: he can offer you 'suitable' and 'appropriate' employment on terms and conditions '*not substantially less favourable*' than before; if you 'unreasonably refuse', you automatically lose the right to a job in that company. (Originally, the job back had to be 'on terms and conditions not less favourable' – the addition of the word 'substantially' is a strong weapon in the employer's hand; also, there *used* not to be an automatic loss of right to a job in the company.)

■ If you work for a firm that employs *fewer than six workers* (including any workers employed by associated employers (see page 284)), your employer is exempt from having to give you your original job back if it is not 'reasonably practicable' for him to do so. (This exemption in favour of very small firms is *new*.)

■ If you feel that you are being refused a job unfairly, you can claim unfair dismissal at an Industrial Tribunal – but the Tribunal will be able to take into consideration the size and administrative resources of the firm in deciding how reasonable your dismissal was. (This favourable treatment of small firms is also new.)

Notifying the employer

Under the new legislation (i.e. 1978 Act as amended by Sections 11–12 of the 1980 Act), your legal obligations are as follows:

■ At least three weeks before your maternity leave begins, you must inform the employer *in writing* that you are taking maternity leave *and* that you intend returning. (Previously, this notification was in writing only if the employer requested it.)

■ The employer can insist on a *written* confirmation from you not earlier than seven weeks after the expected week of confinement that you intend to return to work. If your employer makes this request, you *must* comply within 14 days or you lose your right to return. (This additional confirmation is new.)

■ At least 21 days before you intend returning to work, you must inform your employer *in writing* of the exact date on which you intend returning. (Previously this had to be done only seven days before returning.)

Time off for antenatal care

Under Section 31 of the Employment Act 1980, you are legally entitled to a maximum of six half-day visits to a clinic offering antenatal care – irrespective of how long you have worked for your present employer. The visits must be on the advice of a doctor, midwife or health visitor, and your employer can demand to see evidence of the appointment.

Time off for sickness during pregnancy

Under Section 60 of the 1978 Act, you cannot be dismissed for 'any . . . reason connected with [your] pregnancy': this includes any time you may need to take off for *sickness* resulting from your pregnancy.

Paternity leave

There is no legal right in this country for fathers to have time off work to look after the child and/or mother.

Income tax

Any money received *from the employer* (i.e. excluding State benefits) as part of your maternity pay is subject to income tax (PAYE) in the normal way.

Sitting down with management

One (small) advantage about negotiating maternity leave is that there has got to be some provision – the law says so. The main task – and not an easy one – is to *improve* on the statutory minimum conditions.

The greatest problem with the employer may well come if/when he wishes to *reduce* the contractual rights from those set in the Employment Protection (Consolidation) Act 1978 to the amended rights set by the Employment Act 1980. This will particularly apply if your contract says that the terms of the maternity agreement will be 'the same as the legislation currently in force'.

If you think there is any chance of the employer weakening your rights, take a very close look at the original 1978 legislation and see if you could prove that there have been no disruptions to production caused by compliance with its provisions. You could then say to the management that:

■ there is no need to make any changes – particularly as any change would make the employer's image look very bad in the eyes of the employees, *and* in the eyes of the public locally.

If you suspect that the management is unsure about the legislation – the old and the new – you might try and turn this to your advantage:

■ it would certainly be a tactical advantage if you could catch the employer out on a point of law;

■ you could also (politely) suggest that the *new* legal requirements (if adopted by the firm) would probably be more difficult to understand – from everybody's point of view.

An example of this might be the requirement to *write* three times to the employer: you could say that this could be a particular burden for:

■ women whose written English is poor;
■ women under strain with the new baby.

At all events, in view of the complexity of the legislation – and possibly in view of any further complications of any *local* improvements you may have been able to negotiate – you could certainly try and persuade the personnel department to

■ explain the statutory and contractual situation to each pregnant employee *individually – as soon as* the department becomes aware that the employee is pregnant.

If your employer is unlikely to be persuaded on *social* grounds that women should be given very much better conditions before and after having a baby, you may have to resort to more commercial reasoning. One of the best arguments may be recruitment and retention – you may be able to say:

■ it is cheaper to pay good maternity pay and keep the job open than to spend a lot of money employing *new* people *and* training them;

■ continuity (e.g. in certain clerical jobs) is worth paying for.

If your employer happens to have gone to the trouble of writing out an Equal Opportunities Policy (or Programme), you could point out that:

■ there isn't much point in having one if women are to continue to be discriminated against.

It shouldn't be too difficult to find the reasons for the company taking on women in the first place – women in the area are happy to do the evening shift, to work part-time etc. See if you can find ways of persuading the local management that they won't find anyone else to do that particular work, so they had better be more generous to make sure that the women stay with the firm.

Many of the arguments in favour of maternity pay and leave can also be adapted for *paternity* pay and leave, mainly on the grounds that there is nowadays an increasing willingness – and *enthusiasm* – amongst fathers to help in looking after their children. Depending on the work patterns at your workplace, you may be able to argue that:

■ men may be unable or unwilling to do certain jobs (e.g. certain shifts, overtime etc);

■ the stresses and worries experienced on behalf of the mother can have a bad psychological effect on the father – and that is scarcely the best frame of mind for doing his job.

While trade unions will certainly continue to negotiate for better maternity/paternity pay and leave, the only hope for radical improvement on a national scale is by a change in the law. The original statutory protection for women which came in between

1976 and 1977 was far from the revolution that it was made out to be in certain quarters – and Britain continued to languish at the foot of the European league table; and the amendments in the 1980 Employment Act have mostly weakened the position of women workers. There is also, of course, *no* statutory right to paternity leave at all. It is of the utmost importance for unions at local and national levels and for the TUC to join with other groups – particularly in the women's movement – to put the greatest possible pressure on government to introduce better legislation.

10.
Child care for working parents

Introduction

This chapter deals with the employer's provision of facilities for looking after the children of his employees; the place where these facilities are to be found is usually called a *nursery* or *crèche*.

When employers set up nursery facilities, they do so in their *own* interests: the best example of this was during the Second World War when as many as 65,000–70,000 children when cared for in nurseries so as to encourage women to contribute to the 'war effort'. This figure contrasts with the provision of a mere 25,000 full-time nursery places in 1981. Furthermore, it makes a nonsense of the legal right of women to return to work after maternity leave (see 'Pregnancy, maternity and paternity' (pages 132–56)) if an already meagre provision of nursery places is to be slashed by public expenditure cuts.

Workplace nurseries should be seen against the background of those facilities provided by the *State*, since it is to the State that most people look when they wish to work *and* have children of preschool age. After all, the TUC's official policy is for a 'public service of day care and nursery schooling provided free for all under-fives', and a TUC-affiliated union (NALGO) has the following policy:

> 'NALGO is, of course, committed to fighting for a comprehensive State-provided service of care and education for the under-fives. That we are also campaigning for workplace nurseries in no way undercuts that commitment. *We see negotiations for workplace provision as complementary to the campaign for a comprehensive State scheme.'* (*Workplace Nurseries – A Negotiating Kit*, NALGO 1978) [Emphasis added]

State provision is extraordinarily complicated and bureaucratic – and there is also very little of it; early in 1980 it was estimated that there were places for only 0.7 per cent of the under-fives in Britain. It is clear that there is a very considerable need: the DHSS estimated in 1972 that about 32 per cent of women were prevented from going to work because they had to look after preschool children; the situation had deteriorated four years later when the General Household Survey for 1976 reported that **almost half of all women at home looking after children would take up employment if there were good enough child-care facilities** – this was found to be particularly true of low-income homes. The public expenditure cuts made by the Tory Government elected in 1979 have, of course, begun to make this situation even worse.

There are two sections of the community that are particularly vulnerable if nursery provisions are poor; one is *single-parent families*: in 1980, there were **over 20,000 single-parent families in Britain** (i.e. 12–13 per cent of all families in the country); it is exceptionally difficult for the parent in these families to go out to work if their children are of preschool age. The other group is *women wishing to undergo training*:

■ a survey carried out jointly by the Equal Opportunities Commission and the National Union of Students in 1979 found that, **of the 760 universities and colleges studied, only 146 had regular nursery facilities**; these crêches had altogether 2,300 places but fewer than half of them took children under the age of two; all had long waiting lists and fees ranged up to £20 a week. There is a college nursery recently opened at Brixton College of Further Education in South London; in the original NATFHE proposals for the setting-up of this crêche, equal opportunities for women students were specified as one of the principal aims:

> 'Past and present female students who have had to give up their studies and/or had poor attendance, and have been distracted from learning because of unsuitable arrangements for the care of their children, would be able to continue more satisfactorily and successfully.'

The Brixton College nursery was opened in August 1980, and has five workers and 20 places.

For working parents, State provision has certain advantages over any scheme at the workplace:

■ it gives more flexibility of work and more freedom of movement (if you work where there *is* a workplace crêche and you're thinking of moving, you may *have* to go to *another* job that has one as well – or stay put);

■ it has no effect on wage and other negotiations.

Workplace nurseries

There are often strong suggestions in the media that women do not want to go out to work and would *prefer* to stay at home; furthermore, it is suggested that mothers would prefer to look after their children themselves rather than let them be looked after by others. Quite the *opposite* picture has been revealed both by academic research and by surveys of women trade unionists.

In 1979, the Department of Employment asked the Policy Studies Institute to carry out a study of the operation and effects of the maternity provisions of the Employment Protection Act 1975. The author of this study, W W Daniel, makes this point about workplace nurseries:

> 'When we asked women what changes they would like to see to make it easier for mothers to work they gave overwhelming priority to improved child-care facilities, especially nurseries or crêches at the place of work.' (*Department of Employment Gazette*, May 1980)

Other research carried out by the Thomas Coram Institute showed that mothers actually like the idea: if the nurseries have hours that fit in with their own working hours, mothers find that their children become more independent as a result of the increased contact with several other children and adults (Hughes et al, *Nurseries Now*, Pelican 1980).

Trade unions, too, have been questioning their members about their views on workplace crêches: according to a survey undertaken by the National Union of Tailors and Garment Workers (NUTGW), women members of that union would prefer to have their children with them at work and to be able to spend free time with them (i.e. during the working day); they also felt that a workplace nursery was a positive advantage if there was an emergency.

A much more elaborate survey was carried out in 1977 by APEX among 2,300 of their women members at Lucas factories in different parts of the country. Entitled *Workplace Attitudes to Maternity & Nursery Facilities – A Case Study*, this survey provides conclusive answers to a wide variety of questions. Here is a summary of them:

■ 72 per cent preferred a workplace to any other type (e.g. local authority).

■ Nearly everybody thought that the nursery should be run by an administrative committee and, of those who agreed, it was felt that it should consist of representatives of the employer, parents and the union.

■ 42 per cent said that the circumstances of the mother should decide how the places should be allocated (rather than seniority, a voting system or a waiting list).

■ 83 per cent considered that places should be free.

■ Of those who thought there should be a charge, one-third said it should be related to earnings and 67 per cent that it should be less than £5.10 a week (1977 prices).

■ 87 per cent thought the crêche should cater for children up to the age of five.

■ 55 per cent said that the children of male employees should be eligible.

■ 88 per cent felt there should be a ratio of at least one member of staff to every five children.

■ 93 per cent said they wanted the crêche open throughout working hours.

■ 37 per cent (but a much higher percentage of younger employees) said they wanted to be able to visit the nursery during lunch breaks etc.

■ Other advantages mentioned included properly trained staff giving good supervision, access to medical facilities and visits by doctors and dentists, adequate play facilities including education, toys and an outside playground, sleeping facilities, facilities for older children during school holidays and facilities for breastfeeding.

Interestingly, two management studies have reached conclusions that correspond surprisingly closely to the findings above:

■ A survey by the Institute of Personnel Management in 1975 found that employers were pleased with crêche arrangements for the following reasons:

- better recruitment;
- a contented atmosphere in the workplace;
- a drop in absenteeism;
- a drop in turnover, and retention of skills and experience;
- assistance in the more rapid development of children;
- a good company image.

■ A study one year later by Incomes Data Services concluded that the following were the main reasons for workers liking nurseries:

– the parents were confident that their children were being properly looked after;

– the costs were not too high;

– the opening hours were usually satisfactory;

– they could be near their children if there was sickness or some other emergency during the day.

It is hard work organising a campaign to get a workplace nursery, and hard work negotiating for one; it is also hard work sometimes keeping it open, perhaps because it is too expensive: prices range from £4 a week (Clwyd Area Health Authority) to £20 a week in parts of London. This is a brief summary of the campaign to get a crèche for employees of the London Borough of Camden:

■ The idea was first mooted in 1974, but the then Leader of the Council said that funds were not available and the scheme should be given low priority – despite an energetic campaign by NALGO members who had been lobbying councillors and had circulated a questionnaire in order to assess demand. Two years later, statistical evidence was still being produced (using records from the personnel department) and valuable ideas had been gained from helping out in the organisation of the Kingsway Nursery (see page 163). The Council ultimately agreed to participate in the Kingsway scheme as a pilot venture, partly because they wanted to be seen as an 'equal opportunities employer'. The principle of subsidised child care had now been established and, when a questionnaire in 1977 showed a substantial demand for places, it was much easier to push for better provision – and more difficult for the employers to refuse. Finally, £20,000 was put into the estimates for 1977/78 to pay for capital costs and other subsidies. The Camden crèche is now open from 7 a.m. to 7 p.m. and charges the same prices as ordinary Council nurseries.

Here are some other workplace nurseries (some of them mentioned in *Labour Research*, August 1980), with some of the details of how they are run. The date when they were set up is given in brackets.

■ *BBC* (1980): the employer paid the cost of converting an existing BBC hostel, and subsidises it so that it is available to less well-paid employees; the nursery is run by a committee consisting of parents, union representatives and management.

■ *Centre for Environmental Studies (London)* (1975): there are 25 places and the charge is £117 per month.

■ *Church & Co (Footwear)* (1963): 36 places.

■ *Enfield District Hospital (London)* (1972): members of staff pay £2.07 for a full day and £1.32 for a half day (75p without lunch); the crêche is open from 7.30 a.m. to 5 p.m.

■ *Goblin BVC (Leatherhead)* (1974): this cost £12,000 to set up and remains open during the holidays; the company reports a very much lower turnover of staff since the nursery was opened.

■ *Hotpoint (Llandudno Junction)* (1975): this 'holiday play centre' has 50 places, charges 20p per day and has the use of two minibuses; in 1979, the six-week holiday scheme cost £1,570. The company reports that there is now a much lower absenteeism rate among the 300 women during the summer holiday period, and is quoted as saying: 'We feel that the play centre has added to our reputation in the area as a "caring" employer.' (*Labour Research*, August 1980)

■ *London & Manchester Assurance Co* (1979): this 'family centre' is run by three professionally qualified staff, has 24 places and charges £7 a week (including meals). Parents are encouraged to spend some time in the nursery (perhaps 3–5 hours a week on a rota basis); any time spent during working hours is unpaid but counts towards other benefits.

■ *Mentmore Manufacturing (Stevenage)* (1959): this crêche has 36 places and is open to a limited number of children of non-employees.

■ *National Health Service* (1980): this is open to NHS workers in South London and was set up with the help of an Urban Aid grant to cover the capital costs of the Portakabins; it is sited in the grounds of the new St George's Hospital. An interesting feature is that it caters for shift workers, being open from 7.15 a.m. to 9.30 p.m.

■ *Pye Communications* (1965): this nursery has 50 places and organises a play school during the holidays.

■ *Reed International* (1974): 50 places.

■ *Reliance Nameplates* (1964): this nursery has 36 places and the company gives priority to the children of manual workers.

■ *Stylewear Manufacturing Co (Birkenhead)* (1966): this crêche has 30 places and also looks after older children before and after school *and* during the school holidays; some of the crêche's earliest children (including its very first) now work for the firm. The company claims a low absenteeism rate.

■ *Tudor Processing (Cricklewood (London))*: this nursery also looks after children during the holidays.

And lastly, three examples that operate on slightly different lines:

■ The nursery at John Bright & Bros (Rochdale) was set up in 1950 but had difficulty in finding enough children to fill the places after a while; the Local Authority stepped in and took 40 of the 100 places for its own children. In 1980, the local authority took over tne exclusive running of the crèche.

■ Teachers employed by the London Borough of Tower Hamlets who take maternity leave can, on returning to work for the borough, place their children in one of the Council's (i.e. their employer's) nurseries.

■ The Kingsway Children's Centre (London) was opened in 1977 with 40 places. One of its distinctive features is that parents employed by *several* Central London firms can send their children ('facilities for the children of parents working for a number of different employers in Central London who, as separate organisations, are not yet able or willing to set up their own nursery facilities'). There is a ratio of one member of staff to four children. Employers pay an initial non-recurring sum of money as a contribution to capital costs; thereafter, the employer pays two-thirds of the fees and the employee pays one-third.

The physical and bureaucratic problems faced when trying to set up a workplace nursery are enormous; fortunately, there are a few books which give useful advice on how to counter these problems:

● There are **DHSS recommendations** on day nurseries (size of rooms, toilets, kitchen, staffing levels etc); there is a good summary of these recommendations in *Workplace Attitudes to Maternity & Nursery Facilities – A Case Study* (APEX 1977).

● Two most helpful publications about how to campaign for a workplace crèche *and* how to approach the employer are *Nurseries and Playgroups* (NATFHE 1978) and *Workplace Nurseries – A Negotiating Kit* (NALGO 1978).

For further advice on such matters as fire regulations and toilet and washing facilities, it is always worth contacting certain local government officers – e.g. the Fire Officer, the Environmental Health Officer and a senior official in Social Services.

Another aspect of setting up a workplace nursery is the people who will come to work in it. While employers, parents and unions are usually very happy with the staff employed, the existing provisions for the training of this staff leave a lot to be desired. Training schemes for nursery nurses are organised under the umbrella of the National Nursery Examination Board (NNEB), and much concern has been expressed about the standard and content of the training and about the lack of coordination of courses. The NNEB is only an examining board and it has no statutory function, nor is it responsible to any Government department. The main criticisms aimed at it are that:

■ it cannot respond to the widely differing demands of the various bodies it is catering for (e.g. Local Authorities, the DHSS, community groups etc);

■ students are not eligible after training for any further training in a related field (e.g. education or social services);

■ there are huge differences between individual schemes in the standard and content of courses.

NUPE has called for a public enquiry into this most unsatisfactory state of affairs.

There is one other type of child care organised by the employer: *childminding*.

■ The DHSS in Newcastle employs a full-time child-care organiser who selects 'care parents' who will look after children in their own homes, and who is also available to give other types of assistance to parents who are in difficulties of any sort. Employees pay a fee to the 'care parent'.

■ A similar scheme is in operation at the Office of Population and Censuses in Fareham; there are fewer children involved here, but the scheme also runs summer holiday child care at a local play centre. In view of the frequent and widespread criticism of childminding, it is difficult to see how employers and employees can usually get a satisfactory arrangement. A recent study of childminding concluded that: children were often left most abruptly with child-minders, there was often little or no communication between the minder and the child's own mother and the attitude of the minder towards the child often left much to be desired. (Jerome Bruner, *Under Five in Britain*, Grant McIntyre 1980)

Preparing for negotiations

Employment legislation

There is no law obliging an employer to provide any sort of

workplace nursery for his employees. If he did do so, the local council would use the DHSS recommendations for setting standards (see the *DHSS Guidelines to Local Authorities 1976*). As far as *State* provision of nursery places is concerned, there is no longer a statutory obligation on Local Authorities to provide nursery education (Sections 24–25 of the Education Act 1980).

If the employer discriminated against any employees on racial grounds in refusing access to the crêche, this would be illegal under the Race Relations Act 1976.

Income tax

Use of a workplace nursery is not considered to be a taxable financial benefit; but any fees or subscriptions that you pay are *not* tax-deductible. For the employer, however, the operating costs of a nursery *are* tax-deductible, since they are classed as 'staff welfare'.

Sitting down with management

Your employer's major objection to a workplace crêche will almost certainly be cost, and it is undeniably true that it is very expensive:

■ you might just as well say to your employer at the outset that you recognise this.

You must be able to demonstrate to the management that:

■ there is a huge demand;

■ employees will be clamouring to use it.

And you can only do this by having a long and energetic campaign among the members involving:

■ at least one survey that shows there is a great need for a nursery.

The 'commercial' arguments will weigh very little if the employer thinks that only a few parents will make use of the facilities. .

If it is clear that a lot of the members would benefit from on-site nursery facilities *now and/or in the future*, you can then put it to the management that certain advantages will accrue to them:

■ better recruitment and retention of staff;

■ less training of new or temporary replacement staff;

■ the skills and experience of existing staff will be retained;

- absenteeism will drop, particularly during school holidays;
- employees with young children will not be worrying about how their children are, and so will work better;
- the company will acquire a good, or better, reputation in the locality.

If your employer has had difficulties in keeping staff, you could say that:

- a crêche will, in the long term, save the firm money in fees to agencies (for temporary staff) – or even in the employment of a recruitment officer.

Lastly, you will need to ensure as far as possible that the costs (both at the beginning and later on) are not too high. You may need to engage in a lengthy discussion with your employer about the overriding need of the vast majority of women to come to work – for instance, you could point to:

- the rapidly increasing need to supplement the other parent's income and/or State benefits;

but, above all, you want to point out that:

- if the prices are too high, the children will be withdrawn – and then the employer's vast outlay of capital will be lost.

11.

Tied accommodation

Introduction

Tied accommodation is living accommodation that 'goes with the job'. This chapter reviews the arrangements for such accommodation and includes payments for such things as rent, fuel, laundry and food. Arrangements for meals eaten at the workplace during working hours are discussed in 'Subsidised meals' (pages 196–209), and allowances for meals taken during working hours but away from the workplace and payments for overnight accommodation while at work are dealt with in 'Subsistence' (pages 182–95).

Tied accommodation is inhabited by people doing an astonishingly wide variety of jobs: care staff in Local Authority residential homes, managers of Local Authority parks, school caretakers, hospital workers and agricultural workers, the police, firemen and members of the armed forces, workers in hotels and catering and the security industry and in self-employed retail. It is estimated by Shelter that there are about a million households – most of them with children – living in tied accommodation (about *twice* the number of people living in *privately* rented furnished accommodation); it is also claimed by the British Institute of Management that in 1977 as many as 8 per cent of *executives* lived in housing that was either free or assisted.

The amount of tied accommodation has, in fact, remained steady for a number of years: the 1966 Census found that 5 per cent of households lived in tied accommodation and, 10 years later, the General Household Survey of 1976 estimated that it was 4 per cent – all this at a time when the privately rented furnished sector was declining by over a quarter. According to the Department of the Environment, as much as a third of the entire private rented sector will consist of tied accommodation by 1986.

With certain exceptions (see 'Housing legislation' (page 178)), employed people living in tied accommodation have no security of tenure; in fact, they are usually not tenants but 'licensees' and therefore have no protection from eviction. The 150,000 or so *self-employed* workers who lease premises where they both live and carry on their business are at least protected by the Landlord and Tenant Act 1954; nonetheless, you are twice as likely to become homeless if you are in some form of tied housing: in 1977, according to the Department of the Environment, one in ten homeless households came from tied accommodation. This can happen also to local government workers: employers of Local Authorities living in tied property can often expect to be rehoused in council accommodation *on retirement* but, if the Local Authority is not a *housing* authority (i.e. it does not *own* flats or houses), it can be very difficult getting the appropriate housing authority to find something.

Usually, tied housing is offered in order to assist in the (relatively) smooth running of the firm (or hospital, hotel etc). There is much more of a bargaining lever for trade unionists when management uses another argument – that for some jobs (e.g. security work or other jobs involving surveillance of property) the employee's presence on the premises is absolutely necessary. At all events, managements show every sign of continuing to place large numbers of their employees in tied accommodation. Recruitment and retention of staff – often both young and from overseas – would otherwise be even more difficult in industries with chronically low earnings (e.g. hotels and catering) and where there is no suitable accommodation in the vicinity (e.g. city-centre and rural hospitals).

Invasions of privacy, both direct and indirect, seem to be a characteristic of tied accommodations: nurses living in nurses' homes often have grounds for complaint against hospital officers searching their rooms without permission, and staff in the hotels business similarly find their private lives invaded. One hotel worker is quoted as saying:

> 'We're not allowed to have guests after midnight. Lately we've been finding the caretaker hiding behind curtains downstairs to catch us. Last week, minutes after 12 o'clock, somebody brought a girl in. They threw her out. They do room checks when we're not in our rooms. Altogether, it's like living in a mental home.' (*Hardship Hotel*, Counter Information Services Report No 27 1980)

Furthermore, workers 'living above the shop' often find themselves on call – willingly or unwillingly – to do extra work; in the hotels and catering industry, for example, it is estimated that **55 per cent of living-in staff do over 50 hours a week**, against only 10 per cent of staff generally in the industry.

This particular problem is vividly described in yet another survey on tied housing: in a series of interviews carried out by the Low Pay Unit, one agricultural worker is reported as describing the tied-cottage system as 'a relic from the Victorian era', another saying he felt like a 'feudal serf' and a third as remarking that 'you're called upon at every odd moment to do something. If you say a word back you're told you can get out.' Nearly a third of the workers interviewed in this survey said they did extra work without being paid, and their attitude was summed up by one of them who is quoted as saying: 'If the boss says something to you, in other jobs you would tell him where to go. Here you have to bite your tongue.' (Marie Brown & Steve Winyard, *Low Pay on the Farm*, Low Pay Unit 1975)

Jobs with tied accommodation are also difficult to break away from *successfully*; they are, as a Shelter booklet put it, a 'closed institutional world . . . part of a paternalistic and all-engulfing situation that can encompass job, housing and social life under one roof'. (Steve Schifferes, *The Forgotten Problem*, Shelter 1979) The Low Pay Unit book referred to above quotes the attitudes of two other agricultural workers:

> 'If you have a good employer and a good cottage such as mine it's OK. But one day I shall retire or perhaps my boss will sell his farm. What happens then?'
> 'One does not feel secure in any way as anything can happen and one could find oneself without a home practically overnight.'

This problem is by no means confined to the private sector:
- it is the *practice* for GLC/ILEA schoolkeepers to be rehoused on retirement; it is *not* obligatory, and will not happen if they leave their job for any other reason.

Furthermore, tied accommodation nearly always goes together with low pay and other unsatisfactory conditions of employment. The public sector (including the NHS), hotels and catering, agriculture and domestic service are consistently among the lowest-paying industries in the country: according to the General Household Survey of 1977, when average male earnings were £79 per week, the average income of a 'head of household' in tied accommodation was £62 per week (*27 per cent below*).

The pay is so bad that workers in these and other industries often cannot find their own accommodation and may *have* to accept tied housing – and later on they may not want to jeopardise their position by negotiating for higher wages. The myth that tied housing 'made up' for poor wages was smashed by the Low Pay Unit study which showed that agricultural workers had a particularly *low* standard of living. Even when the employer subsidises the cost of the accommodation (as distinct from giving it rent-free), the other drawbacks remain: it is only a question of degree.

In agriculture, there seem to be considerable financial advantages *on the surface*; the Low Pay Unit study found that, in a sample of 95 agricultural families living in tied housing, 59 were living rent-free and 34 were paying no more than £1 per week (1975 prices) (Marie Brown & Steve Winyard, *Low Pay on the Farm*, Low Pay Unit 1975). Some agricultural workers also receive a certain amount of free food, or are allowed to grow it, while others are given firewood; the Low Pay Unit discovered that this was not quite the benefit it was sometimes made out to be:

■ *just over half* of their sample received food or fuel free *or at a reduced price* – the average saving to families was 79p a week (1975 prices);

■ one worker was not given permission to collect wood 'for fear of disturbing the pheasants';

■ only half of the sample were able to save money by growing their own fruit and vegetables – with an approximate saving of 50p–£1 a week (1975 prices);

■ the food had to be grown and tended in the worker's spare time anyway.

Generally, however, tied housing might be very slightly less intolerable if the accommodation were of a good standard. In fact, conditions are quite the opposite:

■ Workers in hotels and catering normally have to live in extreme squalor and discomfort – and with the constant fear of fires.

■ Hospital accommodation is frequently very cramped and is subject to appalling social restrictions, particularly in the older hospitals.

■ Typically, tied cottages in agriculture are little different: 'A dank smell from years of dampness. The bathroom . . . covered with mould. The walls of the kitchen and bathroom were literally running with damp . . . Woodlice and strange insects, even snails, were frequently found in the kitchen and bathroom . . . "We have learnt to live in a cold atmosphere but it is embarrassing when friends and relations come and sit and shiver." ' (Marie Brown & Steve Winyard, *Low Pay on the Farm*, Low Pay Unit 1975).

The only method of dismantling tied accommodation *on a nationwide basis* will be through Parliament – by amending existing laws (and introducing new laws) with the effect of making it impossible or disadvantageous for employers to continue with the present system; such legislative changes will also need to ensure that workers will *continue* to have somewhere to live. An important inroad was made as long ago as 1975 when the Department of the Environment and the Ministry of Agriculture, Fisheries and Food published a Consultative Document entitled *Abolition of the Tied Cottage System in Agriculture*; two of the guidelines for consultations on abolition read as follows:

'The principle of abolition is not in question, and the consultations should essentially be concerned with the means of achieving it.
'The legislation should remove the social objections to the tied cottage system in a manner consistent with the [Labour] Government's wider policies and objectives for the national economy as a whole.'

The result of these consultations – and of much Parliamentary negotiation – was the Rent (Agriculture) Act 1977 which applies exclusively to agricultural and forestry workers (see pages 178–79).

After Labour's electoral defeat in 1979, the Party NEC's Housing Sub-Committee produced a Discussion Paper entitled *When Home Goes with the Job: a Discussion Paper on Tied Housing* (Labour Party September 1979); this document contains some interesting ideas. The overall policy is considered under three headings:

● to minimise the extent of tied housing;

● to strengthen access to secure housing for those leaving a job in the tied housing that remains;

● to strengthen housing rights for those who live in tied housing.

The Discussion Paper then goes on to spell out how this objective might be achieved:

■ All employers providing tied accommodation would make a weekly contribution (estimated at £3 at *1979* prices) on behalf of each tied tenant, which would be transferable if the employee moved from one tied job to another. When the employee left tied housing (*voluntarily or otherwise*), one of two things would happen:

– the employer's contributions would be handed over to the employee if s/he chose to *buy* somewhere to live, or

– the employer's contributions would be given to the Local Authority if the employee went to live in council housing, but a proportion (say 25 per cent) would be paid direct to the tenant towards the purchase of furniture and other expenses.

On the other hand, if the employee gained security of tenure (e.g. as a result of an industrial tribunal hearing), the contributions would revert *to the employer*.

In those industries where workers do not yet have any protective legislation covering their housing rights, it occasionally happens that board and lodging is subsidised by direct payment.

■ There is a Special London Residential Allowance of £228 per annum for residential supervisory staff in certain posts in Children's Homes (in the Royal Borough of Kensington and Chelsea) and in Children's Homes, Mental Health Hostels and Old People's Homes (in the London Borough of Haringey).

It is much more common for the board and lodging payment to be *deducted from wages*.

■ Under the Wages Council Order 1980 for Licensed Residential Establishments and Licensed Restaurants, service workers (e.g. porters, waitresses, waiters etc) outside the London area must be paid a minimum of £48.40 for a 40-hour week. Under the Order, the employer may *deduct* from wages the following payments for board and lodging:

– *Full board & lodging, including sleeping accommodation (maximum of two to a room):* 40p per hour worked (i.e. £16.00 for a 40-hour week);

– *Full board & lodging, including sleeping accommodation (three or more to a room):* 34p per hour worked (i.e. £13.60 for a 40-hour week).

If the employer pays *more* than the minimum wage, he may deduct *more* for board and lodging on a pro rata basis.

■ Food and accommodation charges for members of the armed forces went up by £7.8 million in 1979 (the cost of the *pay* increase was £292.1 million).

The public sector employs a very large proportion of the tied workers in this country. The board and lodging of residential staff in

Community Homes, Probation Homes and Probation Hostels is paid for according to a lengthy formula negotiated every year; these 'emolument charges', as they are called, vary according to a number of criteria – for example:

■ if two employees share the accommodation and they are married; the husband pays £513 + £33 VAT, the wife pays £306 + £21 VAT;

■ if they are not married, they each pay £411 + £29 VAT;

■ if only one of them is employed, s/he pays £306 + £21 VAT.

(These charges are intended to include a reasonable amount of personal laundry.) There are also official weekly charges laid down for other members of the family and guests – this is calculated according to the ages of the people concerned:

under 1 year	No charge, but parents must pay for patent foods
1–4 years inclusive	£1.68 + 25p VAT
5–10 years inclusive	£2.91 + 44p VAT
11–18 years inclusive	£4.28 + 64p VAT
19 years and over & employees' guests	at discretion, due account being taken of the circumstances in individual cases, subject to the charge being not less than £5.97 + 90p VAT

The emolument charges are handed back ('remitted') if the officer is away from the accommodation *for at least 48 hours* on annual holiday, off-duty days, rest periods, Bank or public holidays and 'other authorised leave'. Absence on sick leave counts only if the period away is at least *three* days. One other reason for having charges 'remitted' is when a meal is taken in the course of work; the APT&C agreement states:

■ 'Where officers are required by their employing authorities to take meals with clients in the performance of their duties these should be provided free of charge. Suitable deductions from their charges should be made in the case of officers subject to full board and lodging charges.'

In the National Health Service, an employing authority with

even more tied workers than local government, the 'lodging charge' is closely linked to earnings; however, the employers' side of the Nurses and Midwives' Whitley Council has been endeavouring for some time to introduce *'fully economic lodging charges'*, a move that has been strongly resisted by the trade unions. For ancillary staff, the 1979 agreement on weekly lodging and laundry charges was:

	London zone	Outer London zone	National
lodging	£7.931	£4.690	£3.381
laundry	£0.784	£0.784	£0.784
total	£8.715	£5.474	£4.165

The NHS has the distinction of being one of the few employers in the country to produce its own standards for living-in employees; according to *Hospital Building Note No 24 – Residential Accommodation Staff,*

■ each student nurse needs a separate bed/sitting room for sleeping, studying, reading, writing etc; the Note also states that there should be one bath (or shower), one WC and one kitchen/utility room for every four to six people, and even deals with the appropriate size of common rooms, heating levels etc.
The existence of this Building Note does *not* mean that hospital residential staff benefit from precisely those standards, but it is – at least – a basis for negotiation.

Many factors can lead to the deterioration of the standard of the accommodation, and trade unions have consistently brought this to the attention of the employers. One of the biggest complaints among local government employees, for instance, is lack of privacy, and in 1974 it was accepted by the employers' side in London of the National Joint Council for APT&C Staffs (local government white-collar workers) that certain minimum standards had to be set for *all* housing. These were the criteria laid down at the time:

'(i) A resident officer (and his/her family) should be afforded a measure of privacy and relaxation as close as possible to that enjoyed by non-resident staff. In general, this requires the provision of quarters to which those in care and other staff do not have unrestricted access. Where staff facilities (e.g. toilet and bathroom accommodation) have to be shared these should only be shared with other staff, not with those in care.

'(ii) Staff should have reasonable facilities for privately entertaining guests, including private cooking facilities, other than those in the main kitchen, except in exceptional circumstances.

'(iii) Basic laundry facilities should be provided.

'(iv) Adequate heating should be available to all staff rooms.

'(v) The general standard of furnishing and decorations should be well maintained, with senior staff being allowed a reasonable voice in their selection. *The establishment is 'home' to resident staff* and dingy quarters which would not be tolerated in a private home should be renovated and made more acceptable.' [Emphasis added]

It should be pointed out that the above criteria were to be looked upon as 'an aid to staffing efficiency, morale, recruitment and continuity', but unions have had enormous difficulty in ensuring that these standards are adhered to.

It was also recognised in 1974 by the trade unions in London that Local Authority tied housing could not be upgraded quickly enough to satisfy the members, so the employers agreed to reduce the proportion of the charge that related to *lodging alone* (i.e. *not* to board). This 'abatement of emolument charges' applied to resident staff in children's homes, to residential accommodation provided under the National Assistance Act 1948 and the Mental Health Act 1959 and to residential nurseries. The standard charge is £513 a year; here is an extract of the *reduced* charges:

	Lodging	Board	Total
sharing any facilities with residents and lacking exclusive use of quarters	NIL	£306	£306
sharing any facilities with other staff	£36	£306	£342
having exclusive use of staff kitchen and/or bathroom/WC, but no separate staff entrance:			
1 room	£123	£306	£429
2 rooms	£150	£306	£456

A serious threat to the continued *existence* of living accommodation can arise when employers sell their stock – and their employees – to one another. An example of this occurred in 1979–80 when the Greater London Council passed over most of its housing to some London boroughs and certain other Local Authorities in the South-East of England. One result of this was that hundreds of GLC employees (e.g. estate managers and caretakers) in tied housing found their accommodation under threat, but the Greater London Council Housing (Staff Transfer and Protection) Order 1979 was passed by Parliament and stated that tied employees would *not* have to move out of their homes whether

– they were transferred and the dwellings were not, or
– they were transferred and the dwellings were transferred to yet another Local Authority, or
– they were not transferred but the dwellings went to another authority.

Another problem that arose with regard to this particular transfer concerned heating charges: while employed by the GLC, Resident Assistant Caretakers had been paying 75p a week for heating, but the 'receiving authorities' (i.e. the Local Authorities to which the staff were transferred) tried to impose a more 'commercial' rate; only prompt action by the unions ensured that the existing conditions were protected.

Until such time as appropriate legislation comes through to give decent housing *and* security of tenure to tied tenants, one of the few strands of hope is a decision of the employer to pass over the accommodation to the employees concerned. There have been two interesting examples of this in recent years:

■ In the early 1970s, the National Coal Board (NCB) adopted an energetic policy of selling its properties to serving miners, sometimes via an arrangement with the Halifax Building Society. The exercise has had its problems, though: the new owners have sometimes not been serving miners but ex-miners, their surviving relatives or even people with no connection with coalmining at all – and the property that has been less easy to dispose of (because of widespread pit closures) has often been in poor condition. In January 1980, the NCB put 5,000 of its houses in Scotland up for sale and the sitting tenants were offered prices at *half the market value*. A Coal Board spokesperson was quoted as saying: 'We will be happy to get out of housing management altogether and concentrate on the primary function of producing coal.' (*The Times*, 1

February 1980) In July of the same year, the NCB sold 136 houses at Newstead Colliery, near Nottingham, to Gedling Borough Council for £1 each; the buyers agreed to spend £98,000 on improvements;

■ A similarly encouraging move was made in 1979 by Unilever when they decided to sell 800 homes at Port Sunlight on Merseyside. The problem faced here is that most of the tenants are over 45 and cannot afford the deposit because they have been paying rent throughout their working lives; however, the scheme preserved about 100 homes for the elderly and also allowed the workers the option to carry on paying rent.

Preparing for negotiations

Employment legislation

There is no law obliging an employer to provide an employee with accommodation, but there are important tactical steps to remember if you have been *dismissed* (i.e. you are not employed any longer and the employer says he is no longer bound under the employment contract to provide you with accommodation):

■ if you are summarily dismissed (i.e. without notice) *and* your union is unable to establish a status quo (i.e. both sides agree to take no further action until the problem has been resolved) *and* you decide to go to an Industrial Tribunal, you can say: 'I'm not moving – get a Court Order if you want to evict me.' You can say this whether you are living on site (e.g. *in* the hotel where you work) or some distance away (e.g. in a hostel). The negotiation can now go something like this:

– the *employer* claims that, as he has dismissed you, he can remove you from the accommodation;

you claim that the employer has broken *his* side of the contract by unfairly dismissing you (e.g. you don't accept that you have refused to obey a reasonable order, or you think that your work *is* up to standard) – therefore, you are staying.

The employer *cannot* evict you without a court order – and may well fear the bad publicity that may surround the issuing of one. For as long as you stay in your tied accommodation, you will not be entitled to any *food* that may have been a condition of your employment.

■ If you take your dismissal to an Industrial Tribunal, you

cannot be evicted unless the Tribunal hearing ultimately goes against you. If this happens, your tenure is unlikely to last for more than a week, as the court is almost certain to uphold the employer's claim that he has been 'reasonable' up to now and that he needs the room for another employee.

The only other legal obligation that your employer has under employment legislation is to provide any tied housing without sex or race discrimination – i.e. within the terms of the Sex Discrimination Act 1975 and the Race Relations Act 1976 (see page 13).

Housing legislation

There is a lot of sometimes very complex legislation surrounding the legal rights (or lack of them) of workers living in tied accommodation. The legal protection may, for instance, depend on whether you are in exclusive occupation (i.e. you don't share the accommodation with another employee): in these circumstances you have a right to remain, even if you are dismissed, until evicted with a court order; on the other hand, if you *are* sharing, you have virtually no legal rights at all.

For a thorough explanation of the Rent Act 1974 and of the rights of tenants and licensees, there is an excellent reference book entitled *Housing: Security & Rent Control* by Andrew Arden (Sweet & Maxwell); but here is a brief rundown of some of the main pieces of legislation that have an effect on tied tenants:

Protection from Eviction Act 1977

Tied tenants are covered by this law to the extent that any harassment against them is a criminal offence; furthermore, if you are in exclusive possession of the accommodation (i.e. in a single room), the employer needs to have a court order to evict you and the court must give you a period which is 'reasonable in all the circumstances' before you have to leave.

Rent (Agriculture) Act 1977

This law applies only to:
1. full-time *agricultural workers* in England and Wales who have worked for at least 91 out of the last 104 weeks (including sick leave); it does not apply to other agricultural jobs (e.g. gardeners and gamekeepers), even if the employees concerned live in;
2. forestry workers.

The law protects tenants *and* licensees (i.e. those not covered by the Rent Act 1974) equally.

The principal protection of the Rent (Agriculture) Act 1977 is that, on terminating employment with a farmer, an employee becomes a normal statutory tenant – i.e. like any other tenant covered by the Rent Act 1974; s/he can only be evicted for the sort of reasons that a Rent Act tenant could be evicted for (e.g. destructive behaviour or not paying the rent). On application from the farmer, however, the Agricultural Dwelling House Advisory Committee (ADHAC) can decide that the worker must leave the accommodation 'in the best interests of efficient agriculture'; the onus is then legally *either* on the ex-employer to find other accommodation that he may own *or* on the Local Authority to 'use its best endeavours' to rehouse the worker and his/her family in 'suitable alternative accommodation'. This will, of course, depend on the availability of council housing and, anyway, it may well not be in the same area; the worker may, therefore, not be able to continue in his/her present type of work; this is an acute problem as ADHACs nearly always recommend rehousing. In spite of certain shortcomings, both employers and trade unions say that they are generally pleased with the operation of the Act.

Agriculture Act (Scotland) 1970

As agricultural workers in Scotland are not covered by the Rent (Agriculture) Act 1977, they do not have the right to become statutory tenants on leaving their employer. They are only protected by the very much weaker Agriculture (Scotland) Act, which says that an agricultural worker cannot be evicted for six months after ceasing to work for a farmer – although even this can be reduced if the court considers that there are exceptional circumstances. After eviction, the worker must rely on the Local Authority.

Housing (Homeless Persons) Act 1977

Under this law, anyone who does not have a home has theoretically got the right to be rehoused by the Local Authority. However, the law does not apply to several categories of people, including the 'intentionally homeless': this clause is a major obstacle for tied tenants as many Local Authorities will class as 'intentionally homeless' anybody who *voluntarily* leaves tied accommodation (i.e. not just because you have resigned, but also because you have retired – perhaps through ill-health); other councils will provide assistance only to workers who have been evicted with a court order.

Housing Act 1980

This Act specifically excludes workers in tied accommodation from the rights given to public sector tenants.

Income tax

According to Section 33 of the Finance Act 1977 (assuming you are not 'higher-paid' (see pages 9–10)), you do not have to pay income tax on the financial benefit brought by rent-free or low-rent accommodation that comes with the job, as long as it can be successfully argued that:

■ you need to live there in order to do the job properly (e.g. you are a caretaker), or

■ you can do the job more effectively (what the Finance Act calls 'the better performance of the employee's duties of employment') by living in (e.g. you are a warden in sheltered housing), or

■ you live in as part of security arrangements *and* are in some danger (e.g. you are a security guard or look after a sports ground). (If you *are* 'higher-paid', the financial benefit of subsidised accommodation is never tax-free unless you have to live there as part of the security arrangements.)

If you are exempt from paying income tax on your tied accommodation, you will have to pay tax on the financial benefit of certain services (such as fuel, lighting and furniture, but on not more than 10 per cent of your net emoluments.

Sitting down with management

If the members that you represent do not already live in tied accommodation:

■ the constant invasions of privacy, the insecurity of tenure (job *and* home) and the social problems that arise on leaving the job must rank as powerful arguments against the introduction of such a scheme.

If your employer claims he is having difficulties in recruiting/retaining workers because of the shortage of suitable housing,

■ you might suggest he offers *normal* tenancies to new starters who have nowhere to live.

If, on the other hand, your employer does provide tied housing you are not going to eliminate it at a stroke; but in the meantime, you can raise a few points:

■ does your employer have a conscience about what employees will do when they retire (or just leave early)? Some employers *do* and, in local government, for instance, workers can often benefit from a transfer to *other* council housing;

■ the standard of the accommodation can nearly always be *substantially* improved;

■ the system can be *abolished* – by selling the accommodation to the tenants.

12.
Subsistence

Introduction

This chapter is concerned with the money your employer may give you to cover meals, overnight and other expenses you run up in the course of your work – but while you are away from your normal place of employment. Allowances for meals taken at work *during* working hours are dealt with in 'Subsidised meals' (pages 196–209), and subsidies on food that might be available *out of* working hours are discussed in 'Sports and social facilities' (pages 210–15).

White-collar schemes

Executives' subsistence often takes the form of 'all "reasonable" expenses being paid on production of receipts'; a lot of firms operate a scheme like this, including:

■ Hymatic Engineering, Knowles Electronics, Porvair, Smith Kline & French, Sun Alliance and Williams & Glyn's Bank.

For the most part, it is executives alone who qualify for these allowances, but considerable differentials exist between them in the majority of firms:

■ at Knowles Electronics, all allowances depend on one's status within the company;

■ at Fisons, senior management have all reasonable expenses reimbursed while sales staff have an allowance for lunch;

■ the National Health Service scheme excludes all ancillary staff.

As it is recognised by many employers that local circumstances can make predictions of costs impossible, some agreements give guidance on what can 'reasonably' be claimed; here are some examples:

Hambro	evening meal: £8.00
	lunch: £4.00
Pedigree Petfoods	evening meal (management): £4.95
	evening meal (sales staff): £4.30
Gillette Industries	lunch (junior management): £3.00
	(higher management qualify for more)

Some managements lay down set amounts of money for all meals:

■ journalists on *Public Service* (NALGO's newspaper) get £2.40 for lunch, 85p for tea and £3.10 for dinner;

■ at Thomson Newspapers the journalists' rates are £1.75 for breakfast, £3.50 for lunch and £4.65 for dinner.

The choice of hotel for white-collar staff in the private sector tends to go according to grade:

■ at Gillette Industries, the choice is between 4-star, 3-star and 2-star according to status within the firm;

■ at the Automobile Association, managers and above can stay at 3-star hotels and everyone else who is eligible stays at 2-star hotels.

Overnight expenses, too, can be very variable:

■ Pedigree Petfoods pay their sales force £17.00 a night;

■ Black & Decker pay theirs £12.50;

■ editorial staff employed by commercial radio stations get £20.00 a night for accommodation.

Other organisations *also* operate a sort of *away-from-home allowance*:

■ at United Biscuits there is an allowance of 50p for being away from the office for up to 12 hours, £1.50 for being away for more than 12 hours and £1.50 for every additional day spent away;

■ NUJ members employed by the Labour Party get £4.86 for Saturday and Sunday work, £10 a day when abroad and £2.70 when involved in running Party schools.

White-collar workers also sometimes enjoy subsistence allowances when working late – i.e. on top of whatever pay they may be receiving for working after hours; this is particularly common in publishing, but it is to be found elsewhere:

■ Cassell pay £2.75 after 7.30 p.m.;

■ BPC, the Labour Party, FT Business Publications and

Hutchinson's pay £2.00, £3.24, £4.50 and £5 respectively after 7 p.m.;

■ Time-Life International pay £4 for working more than 2½ hours late;

■ the NHS pay £1.30 for 'late-night duties'.

In those organisations where employees make a lot of journeys, the subsistence schemes tend to be very elaborate – and nowhere more so than in the public sector. Public-sector agreements may be long, and sometimes a little complicated, but at least all the information is on paper with no possibilities of management

---

Travelling or outside officers
Where the total absence from the administrative centre is less than 24 hours:

bed and breakfast	£10.12 (£12.92 in London)
breakfast	£ 1.45
lunch	£ 1.37
tea	£ 0.59
dinner	£ 1.67

Where the total absence is 24 hours or more:

per day (or part thereof	£ 6.72
per night	£10.12 (£12.92 in London)

Other officers
Where the total absence from the administrative centre is less than 24 hours:

bed and breakfast	£10.12 (£12.92 in London)
breakfast	£ 1.45
lunch	£ 1.99
tea	£ 0.79
dinner	£ 2.49

Where the total absence is 24 hours or more:

per day (or part thereof)	£ 6.72
per night	£10.12 (£12.92 in London)

---

discretion or favouritism of any sort. Here are two such schemes – in local government and the Health Service:

■ *Local government (APT&C)* (see table above, page 184).

Here, a distinction is made between:

– the 'travelling or outside officer' who is 'normally engaged for the major portion of his time on duties away from his administrative centre' and

– other officers (i.e. those who occasionally travel away from their administrative centres).

In 1980 the unions representing APT&C grades attempted to negotiate that *no* distinction should be drawn, on the grounds that prices are the same for everyone; the claim has not yet succeeded, but the unions will continue to place the matter on the agenda with the employers. The subsistence allowances at present are as shown on page 184:

■ *National Health Service*

The NHS has an equally elaborate system of 'night allowances' that

Class I	London	elsewhere
first 30 nights	£33.49	£29.63
after first 30 nights:		
married officers	£13.50	£13.00
other cases —		
non-householders	£8.55	£7.45
householders	£10.00	£9.00
Class II		
first 30 nights	£27.00	£21.20
after first 30 nights:		
married officers	£11.30	£10.30
other cases —		
non-householders	£8.55	£7.45
householders	£10.00	£9.00

The NHS also pay 'day allowances':

	absence of 5–8 hours	absence of over 8 hours
Class I	£1.87	£3.98
Class II	£1.50	£3.59

depend on how long is spent away and on the officer's domestic situation. An important distinction is also made between:

– Class I (officers with a national salary maximum above that of the Senior Administrative grade – in 1980: approximately £7,700) and

– Class II (other officers).

Ancillary workers are specifically excluded from this scheme.

Manual schemes

Manual workers, too, have negotiated a good number of subsistence allowances but these are, almost without exception, less generous than white-collar schemes. It may be this very lack of generosity that has caused so much bad feeling amongst manual workers: an ill-thought-out scheme, or one whose unfairness causes resentment, can easily lead to trouble: an example of a badly organised scheme came to light in 1976 when several thousand lorry drivers in London and Bristol went on strike over an attempt to introduce a method of *certifying* that overnight expenses had in fact been incurred. Many of them complained that **they were being obliged to justify some of their expenses in a way that their executives were not**, and several weeks passed before a mutually satisfactory agreement was eventually reached between the employers' federations, the unions and the Inland Revenue. The drivers accepted certification in return for a higher subsistence allowance.

Sometimes the origin of subsistence allowances is the lack of access to canteen facilities, and today part or all of some schemes are paid to compensate for the unavailability of subsidised meals (see pages 196–209) – either because the canteen is closed or because it is too far away, as in these examples:

■ 57p for a meal for craft, engineering and technical grades at Findus;

■ 85p for lunch when the canteen is closed (e.g. on Bank Holidays) at Nabisco;

■ £2 a week for shift workers at Cambridge Scientific Instruments Ltd (this includes compensation for not being able to use the firm's subsidised transport service).

However, a lot of workers (particularly drivers) receive their subsistence allowances *regularly* as part of their normal terms and conditions of employment. We will now look at the various components of manual workers' subsistence schemes under the following headings:

- Breakfast;
- Lunch;
- Tea;
- Evening meal;
- General subsistence;
- Overnights including meals;
- Staying with friends;
- Updating the scheme;
- Normal place of employment;
- Allowances while abroad;
- Subsistence on training courses.

The examples below, many of which are quoted by Incomes Data Services, refer to drivers unless otherwise stated.

Breakfast

Allowances for breakfast are usually included in payments for overnight stays (see 'Overnights including meals' (pages 188–89)), but there are a few exceptions:

- £1.45 for anyone working away from base (Visnews);
- 75p for the early-start meal allowance (GKN);
- 70p if starting work before 7 a.m. (Borden (UK) (Thermoplastics Division);
- 55p for maintenance and warehouse staff (NAAFI).

Lunch

Drivers are not the only hourly-paid employees who spend time away from work in the middle of the day; sometimes this allowance is to make up for the lack – or unavailability – of a works canteen. This is the agreement for manual workers employed by the London Borough of Merton:

- '£1.12 per day payable when men are working more than 10 minutes, either by van, bicycle or on foot, as appropriate, from messroom facilities.'

Other similar arrangements include:

- £2.45: Visnews (anyone working away from base);
- £1.82: Weetabix (manual workers);
- £1.25: Bovril, GKN;
- £1.20: Borden (UK) Thermoplastics Division;

■ £1.00: Chard Meat Co (manual workers), Tucker Fasteners (manual workers);

■ 80p: Boots (joiners).

Tea

There is sometimes a little confusion about whether this allowance is for a meal in the afternoon or later in the evening; the low sums of money offered would suggest a light refreshment in mid-afternoon:

■ £2.00 (weekly): Boots;

■ 33p: NAAFI (clerical, maintenance and warehouse staff).

Evening meal

As with breakfast, this allowance is often merged with the payment for overnight stays, but sometimes the two are separated in order to cover workers who do not return to the depot until late in the evening:

■ £3.65: Visnews (anyone working away from base);

■ £1.50: Borden (UK) Thermoplastics Division (drivers returning home after 10 p.m.);

■ £1.20: Weetabix.

General subsistence

This payment is intended to cover a wide variety of *general* expenses, not specified elsewhere in the subsistence agreement:

■ £8.50: London Carriers (for any 24-hour period away; over and above the overnight allowance of £8);

■ £7: Electrical Contracting NJIC (when starting and finishing work over 25 miles from base);

■ £4.10: Batchelors Foods (to cater for any meals costing more the ordinary meals allowance);

■ £1.25 Christian Salvesen (for journeys of over five hours and not qualifying for overnight allowance);

■ £1.20: Furniture Manufacturing JIC – GB (while away from the normal workplace);

■ 80p: SPD/Unicold (for each meal taken away from base during recognised meal breaks);

■ 65p: Victoria Wine (branch managers).

Overnights including meals

The range of payments for overnight accommodation is

surprisingly wide given that hotels and boarding houses are seldom cheap:

■ the GMWU's survey of conditions of employment in the engineering industry found that allowances ranged from £2.71 to £15 a night (including breakfast); the average was £8.

Under most agreements, there is a flat allowance irrespective of distance covered or time spent. However, other agreements go into some detail; for example:

Fine Fare:

first night	£10.00
second and consecutive nights	£12.00
some Scottish journeys:	
first night	£10.50
second and consecutive nights	£12.50

Here are some examples of flat-rate allowances for bed and board:
■ £18.00: Reynold Ltd (Bradford);
■ £15.00: M T Chemicals (Tividale), Swish Products (Tamworth);
■ £11.75: Mobil Oil;
■ £11.50: Boots (drivers);
■ £10.80: Boots (joiners employed on shopfitting);
■ £10.60: Esso, Petrofina;
■ £9.50: Container Base, London Carriers, SPD/Unicold, United Biscuits;
■ £9.25: Tate & Lyle;
■ £9.00: Christian Salvesen.

Staying with a friend

If, when you are sent away from home on company business, you are able to sleep at a friend's house or even have a meal there, you *might* be able to pocket your subsistence allowances; on the other hand, it has been known for employers to demand it *all* back. We usually like to thank our hosts for their hospitality, and some firms have recognised this in their agreements. Here is an example:

■ *Batchelors Foods*: if you stay at a friend's home, you can claim $1\frac{1}{2}$ times the incidental expenses of £4.10 (i.e. you can claim £6.15); if your friend gives you a meal, you can claim up to half the cost of the meal if you make some contribution (e.g. a bottle of wine).

Updating the scheme

Some union negotiators have found the annual (or more frequent) discussions around an adjustment to subsistence allowances an unacceptable burden; others have felt aggrieved that annual (or more frequent) negotiations have left their members with an inadequate increase. The result in some firms has been to opt for a mechanism independent of both the employer and the trade union. Here are some examples of this:

■ move in line with the Retail Price Index (RPI) (meal allowances at Singer Machines and Esso Petroleum, other subsistence allowances for drivers – e.g. under the York & District Road Haulage Employers' Federation, and in the building industry);

■ move in line with prices in a chain of hotels (Merchant Navy seamen's expenses are calculated according to price rises in Merchant Navy Hotels);

■ in the light of increases in the Government's food price index (under the Thermal Insulation Contracting Industry (NJIC);

■ annually every 31 July according to the yearly increases set out in the Department of Employment's *Meals Bought and Consumed Outside the Home* (editorial staff employed in commercial radio stations).

The advantage of such schemes is that there is an automatic 'trigger' and concessions do not have to be any part of the horsetrading that characterises most negotiations. The disadvantages are that:

■ there is no trade union pressure brought to bear at any stage on any of the details – the union is abdicating its own power to wrest the initiative from the employer;

■ there is no certainty that the 'independent' agencies, such as the RPI, accurately reflect the increases in food and accommodation that the members experience.

Normal place of employment

Most agreements state that subsistence allowances are payable as long as the employee is away from the 'normal place of employment' or 'away from base'. While it is very clear to most workers that the machine shop or the kitchen or the office is the 'normal place of employment', it is less clear for workers who travel around. An unusual arrangement had to be worked out for Merchant Navy ratings who, while on leave, do not eat or sleep on their ships.

■ Merchant seamen now receive a daily subsistence allowance of £2.35 while on leave. The employers argued that it was a contribution to the family budget, but the men's union, the National Union of Seamen (NUS), rightly claimed that it was the cash conversion of the food and accommodation provided on board. The NUS won the day, and the allowance is now *consolidated*.

Another problem of the precise definition of the 'normal place of employment' arose in 1979 in the Water Service:

■ In the Water Service, the national agreement states that subsistence allowances are payable for work done by employees 'other than at their normal place of work or in the area where they are usually employed'. The disputes machinery had to be invoked in cases where the local management was refusing to pay allowances because they were interpreting the 'area' to be a whole 'Division', perhaps 100 miles across.

Allowances while abroad

As with overnight allowances (pages 188–89), many firms go in for flat-rate allowances for international trips, for example:

■ £16.00 a night.; international routes under the Road Haulage (Western Area) agreement;

■ £9.50 a night: continental journeys at Chard Meat Co.

Other firms set out the expenses in elaborate detail:

Air Products:

Continental deliveries	
per night	£17.42
meal allowance	£7.46
extra meal allowance	£6.22
rest period (Continental)	£20.57
rest period (Dover)	£16.78
Irish deliveries	
subsistence on boat	£21.28
subsistence in Ireland	£12.95
meal allowance	£2.86

Subsistence on training courses

Arrangements for paid release to go on training courses are dealt with in 'Time off for study' (pages 118–31); some firms pay special expenses on these occasions to cover:

- the extra expenditure unavoidable in hotels;
- the higher prices of meals in a locality that you don't know;
- incidental expenses, such as drinks.

The easiest way of doing it is to say that the company will pay for all reasonable meals and that any other reasonable expenses will be reimbursed; the companies that do this include:

- Cambridge Scientific Instruments, Cheeseborough-Pond's, H J Heinz (who also give £2.00 for unreceipted expenses), Reckitt & Colman (Hull), Weetabix.

As far as transport costs are concerned, the rule is that second-class rail fares are paid or reimbursed; there are a few exceptions:

- at Cheeseborough-Pond's, for instance, both manual workers *and* staff travel first-class to all courses.

Some organisations spell out their arrangements in detail:

- at Batchelor Foods, manual workers receive £9.25 for meals and £4.10 for incidental expenses – this is the same arrangement as for assistant managers;
- employees of Pedigree Petfoods who go on courses organised by the company qualify for up to £7.00 a day for bed and breakfast, hotel car park charges, tea, a newspaper and one phone call home a day; they also receive a daily allowance of £5.00 to cover lunch;
- under the agreement for Environmental Engineers, student apprentices get £21.69 a week;
- under the Furniture Manufacturing JIC – GB, apprentices on courses receive 60p a day for lunch.

Preparing for negotiations

Employment legislation

There is no legislation in this country obliging your employer to give you an allowance of any sort towards any expenditure you incur while away from your normal place of employment; any discrimination in providing such allowances on the grounds of sex or race, though, is illegal under the Sex Discrimination Act 1975 and the Race Relations Act 1976 respectively (see page 13).

Income tax

Under Section 189(1) of the 1970 Income and Corporation Taxes Act, subsistence allowances to cover meals and overnight expenses incurred in the course of employment are tax-free. To quote the *Employer's Guide to PAYE* (Inland Revenue 1979):

> 'The following items should not be treated as 'pay' for tax deduction purposes: . . . Lodging or out-working allowances which are no more than reasonable payments for the extra living expenses incurred by employees employed temporarily away from home and normal place of employment.'

Strictly speaking, it is only the *extra* cost that is tax-free, but the Inland Revenue normally takes the view that there will be continuing expenditure at home while you are away – so the whole lot is allowed. If, however, you have no permanent home, you could be liable for tax on the subsistence allowance.

Subscriptions both to clubs that supply 'cheap' accommodation for business travel and to luncheon clubs used for business entertaining are also tax-deductible, as is the use of a company flat which you occupy while away from home on company business. All your expenses have to be 'reasonable' and take into account your status within the company and if, at the end of your trip, you go and see friends or 'tag on' a holiday, the business expenses are still tax-deductible.

Lastly, it is the employer's job (not the Inland Revenue's) to establish that the expenses are 'reasonable', and that you actually spent the night in the hotel.

Sitting down with management

The trouble with subsistence is that it consists of so many different bits (meals, refreshments, tips, hotels, high-cost areas, localities where you don't know the cheap places), that it is surprisingly difficult to quantify. An employer might easily say to a worker who is only occasionally employed outside that an allowance for one meal is enough: but the employer needs to have it brought to his attention that:

■ loss of access to the works canteen represents considerable extra expenditure and must be compensated for.

The boss can also easily forget, it seems, that the absence of a regular timetable should also be recognised in allowances: you could say that:

■ while a worker is in his/her normal place of employment, there is a clear meal break which everybody knows about; but if you're working outside, it can be very difficult to find that hour *and* something decent to eat – a sandwich eaten in the park should be compensated for by a generous allowance.

The biggest argument you are likely to have with the employer will be over the amount of money he is prepared to give you. He might say that he will only give you the *extra* money needed to buy a meal out – after all, he may say, you would have bought food for home out of your wages:

■ you may need to remind your employer of café prices, and that the total cost of decent meals taken outside is *very much greater* than the cost of meals taken at home (or in the works canteen);

■ also, virtually all of your domestic costs are continuing during your absence.

If practicable, you could try and do a survey of suitable cafés (restaurants, hotels etc) to show your employer, and you could point out that:

■ it can be very difficult – sometimes impossible – to find reasonably-priced eating-places in localities you rarely visit (but be careful you are not weakening the claim of members who travel more frequently).

You should also resist any attempt by the employer to establish that the subsistence allowance is intended to 'top up the housekeeping when you get back home':

■ it is extremely important to keep wages and expenses quite separate, or else it could prove difficult to increase wages at a later stage – it might also be difficult to do something about expenses.

If you cannot find a system that will automatically trigger increases in the subsistence allowance scheme, it means that you will have to negotiate – and renegotiate – the allowances whenever necessary; if your management tries to steamroll a system through, just keep saying 'No' – and they will eventually *have* to agree to periodic negotiations.

Some firms like to reimburse all the expenses that their employees (particularly their executives) claim – but this idea is not always the best:

■ elaborate and detailed schemes of payments for this or that item of expenditure (perhaps in the way the public sector goes about it) are at least fair.

If the employer argues that he would prefer a system that is 'unbureaucratic and uncluttered', you might be able to say that

■ the union(s) would prefer a system that is *open and above board* and does not permit any favouritism or discrimination – at least, if there is any, it is there for all to see.

This will mean regular and frequent reviews of the scheme, but this is *very much in the interests of the members*:

■ it forces management – and the unions – to take a regular look at prices.

13.

Subsidised meals

Introduction

This chapter deals mainly with the provision by the employer of subsidised eating facilities at work: for the most part, these consist of the eating place itself, food costs, the wages of the catering staff and other overheads. This chapter also looks at the supply of meal vouchers.

Workers who are given accommodation as part of their jobs may well also receive subsidised meals or an allowance that goes towards the cost of the food: the meal subsidies of *residential* workers are dealt with in 'Tied accommodation' (pages 167–81). Some company agreements incorporate meal subsidies and subsistence allowances under one heading, but it is the intention of this chapter to deal exclusively with subsidised meals *at work*; food allowances for people working *away* from their normal place of employment are explained in 'Subsistence' (pages 182–93). There is also an element of employer subsidy in the provision of such 'in-house' facilities as a bar or social club: these are discussed in 'Sports and social facilities' (pages 210–15).

The supply of subsidised food and drink is a huge business, with an estimated seven million people taking lunch every day in works canteens up and down the country: in the Civil Service alone, the body responsible for organising subsidised meals – the Civil Service Catering Organisation (Cisco) – serves no fewer than 19 million main meals a year, and sells 20,000 cups of tea every day just in its own restaurants. Probably the most important reason, both in the public sector and the private sector, for the flourishing of subsidised meals in the last ten years was the Government's pay policies in the late 1970s:

■ in the 1977 wage negotiations at the Lucas Group in Birmingham, pay increases were already limited by the pay policies to £2.50–£4.00 a week, so some of the lost ground was made up by a six-month freeze on canteen prices;

■ during Phase 2 of the pay policies, the BBC introduced huge reductions in canteen prices – this policy was not reversed until 1979 when the pricing system was switched to a cost-of-materials + VAT basis.

When the effects of the pay policies of the 1970s had worn off, subsidised food continued to be high on the agendas of unions and managements alike: in 1980, it was reported that **about two-thirds of medium-sized and large establishments had meal facilities on the premises**, although the proportion was lower in inner-city areas; about half were charging 41–60p for a three-course meal (*Office Holidays, Sickness Entitlements and Other Benefits*, Institute of Administrative Management 1980).

The standard of subsidised food varies enormously from firm to firm; it also depends on your grade in the firm. Most canteens limit themselves to the basic 'meat and two veg' type of meal – and not all of them come anywhere near the standard of the canteens at Southampton General Hospital (which came top in an Egon Ronay survey of hospital canteens) or Marks & Spencer. Boardroom catering would appear to be on a different level: the woman in charge of cooking for the boardroom of an unnamed City merchant bank is quoted as saying that the menu for a typical week included:

> 'blinis with caviar, smoked salmon and sour cream to start, followed by steak, kidney, mushroom and oyster pie, then meringue piled high with strawberries and cream. During the week they also had Lamb Cutlets Reform (rolled in egg, breadcrumbs, chopped ham, and fried), with gherkins in port, cheese soufflé, boeuf en croûte, Armenian lamb, whitebait, fillet steak, home-made ice cream, loin of veal in cream and brandy.' (*Guardian*, 11 February 1980)

This firm is, later on in the same article, described as 'relatively modest'. Top executives certainly do well for food: according to *Executive Remuneration and Benefits Survey* (John Courtis and Partners 1980), **20 per cent of directors and heads of department receive free lunch**.

According to another survey carried out in 1977 (*Fringe Benefits for Office Staff*, Alfred Marks Bureau), subsidised meals then constituted a benefit to all employees of anything between £200 and £500 a year on average, free of tax. If these figures are adjusted broadly in line with rises in the cost of living since then, there would now seem to be a tax-free benefit of £300–750 a year; that is a lot of money, particularly if you work out how much your *gross* annual earnings would have to go up by if the scheme were to be withdrawn:

■ when a direct subsidiary of a large City firm moved out of the head office into new premises, the employees lost access to the dining-room facilities: they succeeded in obtaining an extra payment of £600 a year (before tax) to compensate.

The financial loss is the amount you will have to spend on food that is *not* subsidised. This applies also to workers who are transferred (perhaps only temporarily) to a place that does not have a canteen. You may well find that the members you represent have little or no awareness of the value of a subsidised canteen: this can leave you in a very weak bargaining position if the employer ever threatens to withdraw it. Equally, if your employer wants to share existing facilities, the price can be quite high:

■ a company *taken over* by the City firm referred to above were told that they would have to pay £750 per employee per year to use the dining-room facilities; as 35 employees were involved in the move, this came to £26,250 p.a.

Poor canteen standards are frequently the result of inadequate or non-existent monitoring. The most common complaint is that the food is no good; this may be because the caterers are using reconstituted meat (rather than fresh meat), 'catering' sausages (i.e. with a very low meat content) and 'catering' butter (half butter, half margarine):

■ if you think that the caterers might be breaking the food regulations, get in touch with the Trading Standards officers through your local Town Hall.

Another source of discontent is low standards of hygiene – this may be because of where the canteen is sited (near certain departments, or downwind from others):

■ insist that any health and safety inspections and measurements that are carried out elsewhere in the workplace are also carried out in the canteen;

■ if all else fails, contact the Environmental Health Office of the Local Authority in which you work.

Pressing for higher standards is important not only because it will result in better meals, but also because the management will find it a lot easier to close the canteen down if nobody is using it any more.

Subsidised meals are sometimes reckoned to be 'part of the job', particularly among workers who prepare food for others to eat

– catering workers, for instance: cooks and helpers employed in civic restaurants and staff canteens run by Local Authorities get free meals: 'No deduction shall be made from wages and no charge shall be made in respect of meals available during the period of duty.' However, this is not necessarily as attractive as is sometimes made out – to quote from a leaflet produced by NUPE school meals assistants: 'We do get a lunch as part of our wages – if we get time to eat it.' Teachers, too, have had the option of free meals in return for doing 'dinner duty'; when the teachers' unions began to take a firm stand on who should have the *unpaid* responsibility for supervising the students, very few teachers regretted the passing of what outsiders had often felt to be a pleasant 'perk'.

For the majority of workers, subsidised eating facilities are usually provided in what may be called the 'works canteen' or the 'staff restaurant', and the catering is done either by company kitchen staff or by an outside catering firm. A few examples of companies that have canteens are:

■ Borden (UK) Thermoplastics Division, Bovril, Chard Meat Co, Colgate-Palmolive, Knowles Electronics, Nabisco, Pfizer, Tucker Fasteners.

The cost to employees of canteen meals varies a lot from company to company; in the City, for instance, prices are generally round the 50p mark, but there are examples of better arrangements – for example:

■ meals are free at the Chief Office of the Sun Life Assurance Society and at the Head Office and certain other offices of the Eagle Star Group;

■ at Brooke Bond Liebig, 25p is the cost of a nutrionally well-balanced meal with good helpings of meat; the meal consists of soup and main course.

Incomes Data Services quote the following examples of prices – and what you get for them:

30p for a three-course meal	Grindlay's Bank
50p for a three-course meal	{ Abbott Laboratories Black & Decker
50p for main course and sweet	Gillette Industries
60p for main course and sweet	Firestone Tyre and Rubber Co

The following charges are made in Local Government (to employees who do not live in) and in the National Health Service (non-residential staff):

breakfast	33p
dinner or main meal	57½p
tea	16p
snack supper	26½p
(All prices include VAT)	

In the NHS, juveniles (workers who have not yet reached their 18th birthday) pay half price unless they are already taking advantage of the meal voucher scheme.

One of the greatest troubles that trade unionists experience in negotiating subsidised meals schemes is being able to challenge the employer when he claims it would cost x thousand pounds a year to run. It can in fact be very difficult to get sound advice on this, but the following sources have proved useful:

■ School Meals Supervisors (who are responsible for most of the ordering of food for school dinners and also know about prices); if you're not already friendly with one, you might be able to get to know one through local trade union contact points;

■ the Treasurer's Department of your local Council (they know about civic restaurants – as well as school meals); if you don't know anyone personally in this department, try the contact points on page 12;

■ other trade unionists in your area who might have been able to extract from *their* employers over the years how much their canteen costs – or at least how much their employer *says* it costs; they will certainly be able to tell you how much it costs them as customers, and also the going rate for LVs in the area.

Canteen prices have a habit of breeding much resentment among the 'customers', and workers will often dig their heels in over wages or shift allowances but not over the alleged inadequacies of the canteen; however, this is not always the case:

■ at the engineering firm of James Dickie in Ayr, 150 workers came out on strike in early 1980 because the price of the bread rolls had gone up from 12p to 15p.

It is clear from those employers who do reveal how much they contribute to the running of the canteen that the subsidies are given in a whole variety of ways:

■ by underwriting a percentage of total costs (e.g. 50 per cent at the Automobile Association);

■ by paying for specified items only (e.g. heating, lighting and fixed equipment in the Civil Service Department);

■ by paying for everything except the cost of the food (e.g. William Blythe, Shell Chemicals, Johnson Matthey and Ratby Engineering);

■ by charging for food + VAT and paying for everything else (e.g. Independent Broadcasting Authority);

	Subsidy	*Subsidy pays for*
Abbott Laboratories	£350 per employee per year	heating, lighting, equipment, canteen staff's wages
Fisons	50 per cent of total	labour and heating
Gillette Industries	75p per employee per day	heating, lighting, equipment, canteen staff's wages
Grindlay's Bank	£1.50 per meal:	cost of part of the food
	£2.50 per meal: (total: £4.00 per meal)	heating, lighting, cost of the premises, wages
Pedigree Petfoods	£300 per employee per year	everything but the food
Smith Kline & French	80p per employee per day	everything but the food

■ by charging for food + 25 per cent and paying for everything else (e.g. British Airways);

■ by charging 120 per cent of food prices and paying for everything else (e.g. Batchelor Foods).

Even if they know *what* they spend the money on, it is common for employers not to know *how much* they spend. However, some managements actually do their sums:

■ in mid-1978, Brooke Bond Liebig were paying a contractor (Gardner Merchant) £9,000 a month to provide 250 people with one meal a day – this included lunch in a separate dining room for directors, higher executives and visiting executives living in three flats in the same building.

In 1980, IDS were able to report the costs to certain employers (see page 201). IDS estimate that, when *all* costs are taken into consideration – including long-term costs such as the cost of the pennies – the employer's subsidy on average is approximately £4 per employee per day.

It is almost a tradition in much of industry and commerce for there to be separate eating areas for different grades, for example:

■ at the Head Office of Molins in Deptford;

■ at the Head Office of the P&O Steam Navigation Co where senior grades qualify for membership of the company's executive luncheon clubs.

Increasing union pressure since the late 1960s for 'single status' within companies (i.e. the abolition of any formal distinction between monthly-paid, weekly-paid and hourly-paid) has, however, encouraged a number of employers to have *one* canteen/restaurant for *all* employees:

■ Associated Octel and Cossor Electronics (Essex) do this;

■ at IBM the same facilities are even used by the Managing Director when entertaining guests;

■ the visitors' dining room at Alcan (Lynemouth) is open to *all* employees.

Certain difficulties automatically arise when there are people still at work but the canteen is closed for the day. Works canteens are often closed, for instance, when shiftworkers are on duty; in these circumstances,

■ at Johnson Matthey meals are available from a machine at subsidised canteen prices;

■ at the Carrington site of Shell Chemicals a mobile canteen service is brought to amenity rooms.

To compensate for meals that cannot be taken because of overtime worked without notice,

■ Associated Octel give a free meal;

■ a free prepacked meal at H P Bulmer (Hereford) is available when overtime is expected to last more than $1\frac{1}{2}$ hours;

■ ancillary workers and craftsworkers in the NHS can claim back the cost of a meal if they are told they are required to do overtime *after reporting for work*.

Vouchers, usually with a specified value (e.g. 15p), are tokens that can be exchanged for food. They may be non-transferable and cannot therefore be used outside the works canteen – in such cases, they are often called 'meal vouchers'. Alternatively, they are so-called Luncheon Vouchers (LVs) produced by Luncheon Vouchers Ltd, and can be exchanged in the works canteen *and* in ordinary restaurants, cafés, sandwich bars and pubs.

It is thought that LVs are much more likely to be found amongst inner-city office staff, who work in areas where office space can be extremely costly and where catering is also likely to be prohibitively expensive (*Fringe Benefits for Office Staff*, Alfred Marks Bureau 1977). There is now a well established trend to introduce LVs in major cities outside London, but there is little evidence to suggest that many manual workers are benefiting from this. LVs have long been a feature of the private sector, rather than of the public sector – although the BBC is a notable exception. White-collar workers (e.g. in head offices) also do substantially better than manual workers, and this pattern is beginning to creep into the public sector:

■ since 1977, at least two nationalised industries (the UK Atomic Energy Authority and the British Transport Docks Board) have introduced LVs for their head office staffs;

■ in the GLC, only APT&C grades (i.e. white-collar staff) qualify.

Other employers have taken a decision in principle to offer LVs *only when no canteen facilities are available*:

■ vouchers are given to workers in outlying offices and depots of the Independent Broadcasting Authority, Abbey Life and Pilkington Bros;

■ staff at P&O who are not eligible for membership of the company's executive luncheon clubs qualify for LVs instead.

Others have opted for helping out low-paid young employees:

■ British Nuclear Fuels and the Civil Service Department give

LVs to workers who are under the age of 18 and not yet earning the full *adult* rate of pay.

The value of LVs varies considerably:

- 15p: Fisons, Hambro;
- 25p: Brooke Bond Liebig, Sun Alliance;
- 30p: Black & Decker, General Accident;
- 40p: Air Products, United Biscuits (London and Maidenhead only);
- 45p: Thomson Magazines;
- 50p: Co-op Insurance Society, International Publishing Co;
- 55p: Bass North & Bass Brewing (Tadcaster);
- 60p: National Magazine Co;
- 75p: Penguin Books (London office only), Phoenix Insurance Co;
- 95p: Mobil Oil (drivers and depot workers).

A less common way for the employer to provide financial assistance is to give a lunch allowance:

- Grindlay's Bank has a package consisting of a £1.50 daily allowance plus concessionary prices at specified local restaurants;
- the Automobile Association gives 45p daily to those employees who have no access to canteens.

The reason for the relative rarity of this method is probably that it *can* incur a sizeable income tax liability (see pages 205–206).

Lastly, some workers are fortunate enough to be able to use their LVs *in a subsidised canteen*:

- at the National Coal Board, LVs can be exchanged in the canteen when you are doing overtime without notice;
- at Hambro and the London & Manchester, you can spend them in the canteen all the time.

Preparing for negotiations

Employment legislation

There is no law in this country that forces your employer to open a works canteen or give you meal vouchers, nor is there any legislation obliging him to keep prices below a certain level. However, the Sex Discrimination Act 1975 and the Race Relations Act 1976 make it illegal for your employer to offer better or worse conditions on grounds of sex or race (see page 13).

There is some protective legislation covering women and

'young persons' (i.e. up to the age of 16): this is Section 86(c) of the Factories Act 1961, which mentions breaks 'for a meal or a rest'. Unfortunately, it is hedged around with a large number of exemptions (Sections 102–113) which make Section 86(c) even less enforceable that it already is, but it is a bargaining lever that is worth knowing about when discussing the matter with management. The Equal Opportunities Commission has recommended in one of its reports *(Health and safety legislation: Should we distinguish men and women?*, Equal Opportunities Commission 1979) that this legislation should be repealed; all adult male workers – and *all* other workers not covered by the Factories Act 1961 – have *no* legal entitlement to meal breaks, and the effect of the EOC's proposals would be to reduce the overall rights of everyone. The TUC has rejected the EOC's recommendations.

Income tax

There is plenty of scope for reducing tax liability in the field of subsidised food – and this extends to those occasions when the boss entertains his own employees: therefore, the company can get a tax deduction on the cost of the office Xmas party.

As for the more everyday forms of subsidised food, the Inland Revenue has different rules for meals taken in works canteens and for meal vouchers:

Subsidised meals

Meals taken in canteens subsidised by the employer are *tax-free* to those taking the meals – *provided that the facilities are available to ALL employees* – and you must be an employee to qualify. The tax position is *not* altered if different grades are eligible for different facilities (e.g. if hourly-paid manual workers use 'the canteen' and supervisory grades and above can use 'the restaurant'). Cheap or free coffee, tea, biscuits etc are also a tax-free benefit.

For the employer, the costs of running a subsidised canteen are *tax-deductible* – as are the costs of providing cheap or free coffee etc.

Meal vouchers

Whether they are of the non-transferable type (useable only in the canteen) or of the transferable type (exchangeable outside in cafés etc), vouchers are a tax-free benefit *provided that*:

■ they are for meals only AND

■ (if restricted to certain grades) they are available to lower-paid workers AND

■ they are not worth more than 15p per day actually worked for each employee (if they are worth more, the amount *over* 15p is taxable).

If you get vouchers to spend in a subsidised canteen, they are also tax-free providing they are *for employees generally*.

The fact that subsidised food in a canteen is *not* taxable and that the Inland Revenue is resolutely opposed to raising the tax threshold on luncheon vouchers above 15p make canteens very much more preferable for workers. Luncheon vouchers were introduced – with the 15p limit – to act as a *subsidy* on meals consumed during working hours; they no longer subsidise a cup of coffee. Only a change in legislation *raising* the tax threshold on vouchers to a more realistic level will make them more attractive; meanwhile, subsidised canteens remain far and away the best bet for workers.

As far as your employer is concerned, the running of a meal voucher scheme is tax-deductible, as is the amount of money *over* 15p that the vouchers are worth – there is even a formula whereby the tax on the excess can be borne by the employer. Schemes whereby employees can charge up to a certain amount in specified restaurants are also tax-deductible to the firm – and tax-free to the employees. They need to be negotiated with the Inland Revenue.

Sitting down with management

If you are trying to negotiate a completely new subsidised meals scheme, the first thing you may choose to do – and the only thing you may succeed in doing initially – is to get the management's agreement *in principle* to the idea. The financial and organisational commitment is enormous, and the entire negotiations could take many months.

Your employer is going to object all along the line – whether it is a question of a new scheme or an improved one – on grounds of cost; he is also going to bring up the trouble and upheaval involved in setting up a subsidised canteen. There is no point in rejecting this as it is certainly true, but:

■ ask him what his figures are;

■ ask for a complete breakdown of what he thinks the cost will be;

■ remind him of tax allowances – the real cost is never as bad as it looks.

You can also argue that the employer would soon see a *net gain* in terms of:

■ better timekeeping;

■ improved efficiency and conditions of work.

It shouldn't be too difficult to persuade the management that people will not be late back for work because *they will already be on site*, and that this will make for better efficiency overall. There are also some managers who think that one advantage of a works canteen is:

■ a measure of control over the nutritional content of the main meal during the day;

you could try that argument if you think there is a member of your management who might be convinced by it.

Probably your best selling point for a subsidised canteen is that it will have a positive effect on:

■ recruitment and retention of staff.

The best supporting arguments are (and they apply equally to a canteen and to LVs):

■ they make an immediate impact on job adverts;

■ they slow down the turnover of temp and agency staff (by encouraging them to become permanent);

■ they can make a good impression when employers are competing among themselves for workers.

The management will also be worried about insufficient takeup – i.e. that not enough workers will make use of the canteen for it to be financially viable. This is fair comment, and it might be worth getting in first and saying that you appreciate management's anxieties; but the anxieties are also on your side:

■ the union would lose a lot of credibility if it managed to negotiate a canteen – which then nobody used. Question members from all departments (men and women, young and old) very closely about what sort of facilities they want, what standards they are prepared to pay for – *and how much* they are prepared to pay.

As a result of your survey, you might be able to put forward some of the following arguments:

■ there aren't *any* eating places in the vicinity;

■ there aren't *enough* eating places in the vicinity;

■ there *are* eating places in the vicinity, but they are difficult to get to (e.g. in bad weather);

■ subsidised meals are cheaper than meals in cafés – and a meal subsidy of some sort will lead to improved industrial relations;

■ a canteen is a tax-free benefit for employees, and therefore is 'good for morale'.

If your employer can *prove* to you that there is no land available or that it is ridiculously expensive, you will regrettably have to accept it as a fact of life – but you can still move forward on a new tack: if the management, at the very beginning of the negotiations, said that they agreed to a subsidised canteen *in principle*, see if you can hold them to it and:

■ say that you would like luncheon vouchers instead. You can support this claim by saying that:

■ there are generous tax deductions for the company;

■ vouchers are extremely cheap to administer.

If you already have a canteen, the management might one day say that they want to close it down; try and find out if they intend keeping the facilities open for themselves – if so, you can point out that:

■ a 'restaurant' open only to executives would no longer be tax-free to them.

You can make a similar point if they say that they want to have special facilities for themselves:

■ it is usually much more difficult to persuade the Inland Revenue that meals should be tax-free if the executives' meals are cooked in a separate kitchen.

The executives with whom you are negotiating may well not know this side of income tax law. The management may also say that they want to close the works canteen down for a different reason: cost; if they offer you LVs instead (and you want to keep the canteen),

■ say that you do not believe there will be a saving *on balance*, because the canteen acts as a valuable *social centre* for the workforce.

However, the offer of LVs instead of access to a works canteen can be most acceptable in other circumstances: if you happen to work for a firm that has more than one location, your employer may try to avoid setting up a canteen on the grounds that it could not cater for all the employees:

■ say that you believe that there are still more than enough people who remain on site *and* that those who are off site *should be given LVs* to compensate them for not being able to use the canteen.

Finally, always keep the subsidised meals scheme on the agenda for negotiations with management – particularly if you have not yet got everything you want (e.g. you have vouchers but no proper canteen). Also, don't forget that the catering staff are workers, too – and they can be key people if you ever have industrial action; it is the *management* that is supposed to be subsidising your meals, not the catering staff doing it through low pay and other bad conditions of employment. Therefore:

■ recruit them into the appropriate union;

■ try and get them onto the common wage structure (otherwise, they can be left behind when *your* wages go up).

14.
Sports and social facilities

Introduction

Sports and social facilities, as provided by the employer, consist of some or all of the following:

- a sports 'club' with pitches and courts for such activities as football, cricket, tennis and squash, and (probably) including changing facilities and/or
- facilities for social gatherings, which might include a bar and a restaurant (probably at subsidised prices), a television room etc.

The provision by the employer of meals at reduced prices during working hours (e.g. in the works canteen) is dealt with in 'Subsidised meals' (pages 196–209).

Sports and social facilities are often known as the 'sports club' or the 'social club' – and sometimes, more familiarly, as the 'club'; furthermore, a feature of these clubs is that membership is often open to spouses and children (perhaps up to the age of 21); it is also common for ex-employees who have become pensioners to be eligible. Some clubs, particularly those with a well developed sports side, offer a 'social' (or non-playing) membership.

There is growing evidence to suggest that the provision of such facilities greatly improves the standing of the employer in the locality: two surveys carried out in 1978 (*Employee Benefits Management Survey Report 37*, British Institute of Management, and *Fringe Benefits for Office Staff*, Alfred Marks Bureau) both found that sports and social facilities were one of the most effective ways of developing what they called the '"good employer" syndrome'. Their existence is also thought by employment agencies to be a successful method of encouraging 'temp' and agency staff into permanent employment.

Furthermore, there is evidence to support the view that there are many other spinoffs for employers: Gillette Industries are quoted by IDS as saying that a cheap, well run club has **particular appeal for younger employees**; and there is certainly no need for full-time involvement on the part of the management:

■ the BBC club is run by a committee consisting mainly of members (i.e. employees), with the employer taking a back seat and just making sure that the accounts balance.

Some sports and social facilities seem to be common to virtually all companies, while others are much more unusual or imaginative; this is borne out by the following list of firms together with only a selection of their activities:

■ Abbott Laboratories: a bar with subsidised prices; sailing and angling;

■ Batchelors Foods: annual outings;

■ Gillette Industries: dances, football, squash, tennis, cricket and sailing;

■ Grindlay's Bank: saunas; squash and badminton;

■ Porvair: dances and outings; golf;

■ Sun Alliance: dances; squash, tennis, football, rugby, badminton and archery.

The sports and social club is sometimes concerned with the firm's discount scheme:

■ the sports and social club at Abbott Laboratories has its own club discount card which is used by employees at local shops to obtain lower prices under the company's discount scheme (see 'Company Discount' (pages 216–21).

Also, certain facilities are sometimes to be found in staff lodgings:

■ Grand Metropolitan Hotels own three hostels near Central London for living-in staff – sports and social facilities are provided (see 'Tied Accommodation' (pages 167–81).

The cost of membership of sports and social clubs is nearly always nominal; typical subscriptions quoted by IDS are:

■ £1.00 a year: Automobile Association, Fisons, Grindlay's Bank (Blackheath club);

■ £2.00 a year: Grindlay's Bank (sports complex in London);

■ 20p a month (i.e. £2.40 a year): Thomas Cook Group, Porvair;

■ 5p a week (i.e. £2.60 a year): Gillette Industries;

■ 22p a month (i.e. £2.64 a year): Abbott Laboratories;

■ 25p a month (i.e. £3.00 a year): Sun Alliance.

Companies are traditionally reticent about exactly how much they themselves pay – it frequently happens that they do not know:

■ for instance at Molins, where there are sports and social facilities at all their major locations, the company simply says that the subsidy varies according to the type of facilities provided;

■ the club at Gillette is 'self-financing' with large sums of money being raised from fruit machines, bar football, bingo and dances.

Sometimes, membership of the firm's sports and social club brings with it additional 'perks' over and above the advantages of a bar, low-cost sports facilities etc:

■ Pedigree Petfoods finances part of the leisure centre at Melton Mowbray, and employees can take part in its activities including darts, squash and skittles;

■ employees at the Swindon office of Hambro Life Assurance Ltd have free membership of the W D & H O Wills club;

■ members of the British Gypsum club can take part in group-sponsored competitions (e.g. golf) free of charge;

■ at J C Bamford Excavators, discounts are negotiated with local retailers.

In conclusion, it is fairly common for the club to be used for activities other than the strictly sports and social activities of the members:

■ the cricket pitch belonging to Colman's Foods in Norwich is good enough for Norfolk to play Minor Counties cricket on it;

■ some of the rooms in the same club are used for a variety of internal meetings, and have also been used for shop stewards' training courses organised by the trade unions.

Preparing for negotiations

Employment legislation

There is no legislation protecting the right of workers to any sports and social facilities. The only laws affecting employees under this heading are those relating to discrimination: the Sex Discrimination Act 1975 and the Race Relations Act 1976 outlaw any discrimination on the part of the employer in the way he affords access to these facilities (see page 13).

Club and licensing legislation

There is a strict legislation surrounding the setting-up of

private clubs, particularly if it is the intention to sell alcohol. It will be a good negotiating gambit to have a working knowledge of these laws when you go in to talk with management. For a clear and helpful explanation, read *The Law of Clubs* by J F Josling and Lionel Alexander (Oyez Publishing 1973, 3rd edition).

Income tax

Sports and social facilities are a tax-free benefit to *you*, and they are *tax-deductible* to your employer (they come under 'staff welfare').

Sitting down with management

If you are talking to management for the first time about sports and social facilities, you can be quite certain that they will not agree to the idea at once; in fact, at the initial stages of the negotiations you might be well advised to establish with the company that they are prepared to consider the idea *in principle*. If you can get over this hurdle, you could ask for a joint working party to be set up to look into the various problems.

Certainly one of the first objections that your employer will put up is 'Will enough people use the club to make it cost-effective?' – i.e. will enough employees patronise the club to make it worth all the expense and administrative trouble? The management might point out that not everybody plays sports or drinks *and* likes the idea of spending free time with workmates, even if the subscription is small. It is important to be able to establish that the members *really* want a club, and it would be a good idea to arrange for a *wide* selection of members to be canvassed as to their views. For example, it would be useful to be able to say to the employer that, on the basis of your survey:

■ a certain percentage of the members who play sports would find it attractive since the facilities will be *very much* cheaper than anything outside;

■ those who like a drink also like the idea of subsidised prices;

■ other members would like to entertain their friends and or family at the club.

Your employer might then say that, even if the club were well patronised, it would still cost too much money. You want to be able to rebut this on two grounds:

- Has the employer done his sums correctly?
- Won't there be an overall gain to the employer?

When the employer tells you that sports and social facilities cost a lot of money, you might just as well concede the point – because it is absolutely true; but don't let him get away with any bland statement to this effect:

- challenge him to justify his figures. If your employer does so – and you can reasonably claim that he is exaggerating – he might ask *you* to substantiate your claim; it would be an impressive negotiating counter if you could:

- quote approximate costs of rent and ground maintenance, and running costs of items such as sports equipment and general wear and tear (this information you can get hold of via a union member who is also a member of a local sports club);

- give your views on negotiations with brewers, bar prices, 'profits' and how to get custom (you can find this out from your local CIU (working men's) club – or perhaps a local tenants' association – but you'd better be discreet because they might not always be too keen on you taking away some of their custom).

If you can show that you, too, know about the costing of a sports and social club, your employer will know that he cannot get away with bluff. You may also need to remind the employer that he does not bear the *full* cost of a social club:

- it is *tax-deductible* to the employer.

The management may be worried about having such a large investment tied up for very limited use (i.e. it is only being used at weekends or in the evenings – unless the bar is on-site); this is a reasonable point of view, so you could suggest that:

- the facilities could be put to other uses – e.g. conferences, courses etc.

Your employer might then ask 'But what's in it for us?', and it will be important to have a number of arguments that will convince him that he is going to get a return on his outlay. You might be able to argue that:

- the opportunity to socialise will encourage 'company spirit and loyalty';

- a club is an ideal place to break down internal barriers within the firm (e.g. if the employer has been unhappy about a great divide between monthly-paid and hourly-paid);

- it will help to recruit and retain many of the employees;

■ if the firm has *more than one location*, a club is the obvious place to meet.

You may also be able to take the argument out of the workplace and into the locality – you may be able to play on the company's need to have a good 'image' locally:

■ the regular appearance of the company's name in the sports pages of the local paper puts over the idea of a firm 'doing things' for its employees;

■ a popular bar/clubhouse/pavilion makes a very favourable impression on visiting teams and their supporters, and on visiting business representatives of other companies.

It is also becoming very common for companies to sponsor *local* sports – in addition to national and international competitions:

■ if there were good sports and social facilities, it would be possible for the firm to *host* certain sporting events and thereby *advertise* the firm (this, too, is tax-deductible).

If the management balks at the prospect of increased administrative work, you can say that:

■ the majority of clubs are run by committees of club members (i.e. employees) with management themselves not being closely involved except to ensure that the books balance at the end of the year.

At the end of your negotiations, the employer may turn you down flat on ground of cost, but he may also accept your arguments in favour of the *idea* of a sports and social club; you could then suggest:

■ *sharing* facilities with another firm or using the facilities of a local private club.

Later on, the *existence* of such an arrangement can be a useful bargaining lever if you want to move on to having your *own* club.

If you *are* going to have your own club, or there is one already in existence, it needs *non-stop monitoring* by the trade unions – with regard to both the quality of the facilities and the prices. However the club is run on a day-to-day basis, try to keep the subject permanently on the agenda of your meetings with management – the sports and social club is not simply a benefit supplied by management, it is a condition of employment *to be negotiated on a regular basis*. And whatever happens, make sure that the club staff are unionised.

15.

Company discount

Introduction

This chapter deals with opportunities to buy, or otherwise obtain, goods and/or services – generally those which *you* are involved in producing in your job. The goods or services may be obtained at a discount from the employer or by discount arrangements made with *other* firms. This chapter does not deal with mortgages that can be obtained in the finance sector (see 'Relocation' (pages 261–76)); nor does it deal with free or subsidised accommodation and food that is sometimes available in the hotels and catering industry (see 'Tied accommodation' (pages 167–81)).

A survey conducted in 1980 by Incomes Data Services discovered that a lot of companies saw in a discount scheme the sort of non-wage benefit that had 'immediate impact' when it came to attracting (and keeping) staff; a number of firms also said that it had the virtue of being substantially less expensive than other benefits (e.g. pensions), which tend to commend themselves to members *in the long term.* Company discounts are also fairly widespread: a 1980 survey of benefits found that **48 per cent of employees were eligible for discounts on company products.** (*Executive Remuneration and Benefits Survey Report*, John Courtis and Partners 1980)

The income tax position is key to an understanding of company discount schemes. It was one of the original intentions of the 1976 Finance Act Bill that this type of concession should be taxed, but the mere suggestion brought forth a howl of protest from a number of employers – notably British Rail and British Airways. The latter canvassed opposition to the proposal on the grounds that employees do not have the same rights as ordinary passengers: 'the employee passenger will only be carried on the flight if the seat would otherwise have been empty'. The British Airways argument was that, far from offering a cheap perk to their staff, they were actually obtaining a small amount of money for a seat when they would otherwise not have filled it at all. The clause that British Airways – and other employers – found so unacceptable was withdrawn from the Bill. In some other service industries (e.g. travel agents, catering etc), the opportunities for such concessionary prices are much greater, because the employer can much more easily claim that the service would have brought in no money at all – but for the employee.

It is unusual to find 100 per cent discounts on company products and services (i.e. they are free), although there are some examples in the transport industry:

■ British Rail give a number of free second-class rail tickets to employees – the number depending on the amount of service. Examples in the private sector include:

■ the Automobile Association, where you can get free AA membership and Relay vehicle recovery service;

■ Pedigree Petfoods, where each employee can have one free case (i.e. 48 cans) of cat or dog food per week;

■ W D & H O Wills, where each employee is entitled to 40 cigarettes (or tobacco equivalent) every week.

The majority of 'internal sales' are not free, however. The employer usually knocks off a percentage of the retail price; for example:

■ at the Automobile Association you can get $7\frac{1}{2}$ per cent off AA travel services and 20 per cent off the company's publications and other merchandise;

■ Porvair offer their own products at approximately $33\frac{1}{3}$ per cent off;

■ Firestone sell their tyres at 40 per cent off;

■ Sun Alliance make their own insurance policies available at discounts that vary according to the type of policy.

The discount does not always take the form of a percentage:

■ Fisons usually sell their own goods at trade prices;

■ the prices in the company shop at Gillette are cost + VAT;

■ clerical staff at Thomson Holidays qualify for a reduction in the price of holidays that is related to how long they have been employed on the day they leave for the holiday:

Service qualification	Reduction allowed
3 years	£24
6 years	£48
10 years	£71

IDS also quote a most unusual system in operation at Marks & Spencer:

■ instead of paying less over the counter, full-time staff use tokens worth £28.80 per annum; these tokens represent a discount of 20 per cent of goods worth £144 at shop prices (part-time employees receive tokens worth £14.40).

This kind of arrangement (the one at Marks & Spencer was specially agreed with the Inland Revenue) is of particular interest to people working in such industries as the retail trade. For a manufacturing company, it is relatively easy (from an administrative point of view) to sell some of its goods to its employees: it can deliberately withdraw goods from the end of its production line and, for example, sell them in its own 'staff shop'. By contrast, a *shop* might have considerable administrative problems with employees buying a lot of goods – many of them costing relatively small sums of money – *and* claiming their staff discount. That is why the Marks & Spencer scheme is so important.

Company discounts are well established in the food manufacturing industry, where managements find them a useful way of making at least some money out of goods that are not up to the standard required in the High Street:

■ the company shop at United Biscuits sells, among other things, cakes, biscuits and other packaged goods: if they are damaged, the discount is 50 per cent; if they are undamaged, the discount is 25 per cent;

■ 'Staff Sales' at Pedigree Petfoods offers damaged goods at $66^2/_3$–75 per cent off, and undamaged goods at $33^1/_3$ per cent off.

Sometimes the discount scheme will extend beyond the confines of the firm; for example:

■ the National Coal Board's deal on concessionary coal applies also to miners' widows;

■ Thomas Cook holidays are open to family and friends

accompanying the employee: the normal discount of 25–30 per cent applies to the immediate family or to one friend, but other friends can also benefit to the extent of a $7\frac{1}{2}$ per cent reduction.

The discount scheme can also extend to other *firms*:

■ Pedigree Petfoods, being a member of the Mars Group, offers its normal discounts on other Mars products (e.g. Uncle Ben's and Yeoman products, sweets etc);

■ Thomas Cook take 10 per cent off holidays booked with other holiday operators, and travel staff get a 75 per cent reduction from airlines;

■ Penguin Books give a 33 per cent discount on other publishers' books, in addition to charging only half price for their own.

Some companies do not offer discounts on their own products, and instead make arrangements with retail shops:

■ Gillette Industries *supplement* their internal discount scheme: special company cards entitle employees to buy a limited range of goods at specified local shops at a discount of 5–15 per cent.

■ 'Company visiting cards' are also used at Brooke Bond Liebig when purchasing goods at 'selected warehouses': this company sometimes makes arrangements with certain firms whereby trade cards issued to the employees attract the same discounts there.

■ Staff at Abbott Laboratories can make purchases (minimum order: £25) at specified local shops on production of the firm's sports and social club discount card (see 'Sports and social facilities' (page 211)). The goods have to be ordered through the company and staff pay only cost price, with Abbott making up the difference.

■ Knowles Electronics, being in the business of manufacturing electrical components of little practical use to their employees, have come up with a scheme of inviting representatives from local shops to visit the firm. Any goods bought in this way are charged for at wholesale prices, with the company paying the difference between wholesale and retail prices.

Preparing for negotiations

Employment legislation

There is no law in this country covering the employer's

provision of goods or services at a discount, except for the anti-discrimination legislation (the Sex Discrimination Act 1975 and the Race Relations Act 1976 (see page 13)) which outlaws any favouritism on the part of the employer on the grounds of sex and race respectively.

Income tax

If your employer offers you his own goods or services at a discount, you are not liable for income tax on the saving as long as you do not pay any less than they cost the employer in the first place. If the employer arranges for other companies to sell their goods or services at a discount, this too is tax-free to you.

Sitting down with management

Since it is *you* who are directly concerned in producing the goods and services for your employer, you might feel that:

■ you are *entitled* to a share of the product;

but if your employer is going to be opposed to this stance, you had better concentrate on more 'commercial' arguments. The first of these is that a company discount scheme is remarkably cheap to run:

■ there are no transport costs;

■ there is no 'middleman';

■ there is likely to be a spinoff in the shape of cheap advertisement of the goods/services with family and friends;

■ not much space is needed.

There are also the advantages to the employer that:

■ it is a way of getting rid of goods that have been damaged;

■ it is a way of getting round overproduction or a temporary lull in sales.

If the employer can demonstrate that there isn't enough room on site, you can always suggest:

■ an arrangement with other firms (either in the same group or simply in the locality) to sell their goods/services at a discounted price.

It certainly costs the employer very little to run a discount scheme, but you can also point out that there can be useful operational advantages as well:

■ if it is an attractive scheme, people will think the firm is a good (or better) one to work for – i.e. recruitment and retention of staff will be easier;

■ workers may feel some identification with the company and the goods/services it sells;

■ if the discounted goods are available in a company shop, workers are more likely to stay on site during meal breaks to do their shopping.

Above all, you need to impress on management that prices should be 'competitive', or else:

■ not enough employees will take advantage of the scheme, and it may have to close.

16.

Using your own transport

Introduction

This chapter is concerned with financial assistance given to you by your employer for *using your own car in connection with your job*, and there will also be some discussion about the basis of how some of these expenses are often made up. These expenses are sometimes called 'mileage allowances'. There are other types of assisted travel which are dealt with in two other chapters: 'Company car' (pages 250–60) – which also looks briefly at mileage allowances for driving the *firm's* car – and 'Travelling by public transport' (pages 236–40).

Allowances to cover expenses incurred in driving your own car are worked out in a variety of ways but, theoretically, the overall aim is that the employer pays for the business use of the car with regard to:

- petrol,
- oil,
- servicing,
- general maintenance,
- repairs (including accidents),
- tyres,
- depreciation (wear and tear),
- motor insurance,
- personal insurance,
- car licence,
- garaging,
- parking,
- breakdown service.

It is certainly not always the case that the employer pays for everything; for example, at Brooke Bond Liebig, 'An employee using his own car on company business must ensure that his insurance policy covers such use.' Furthermore, as we shall see later (on page 225), a very large number of company schemes exclude depreciation.

If unions have had trouble in persuading employers to agree to decent schemes, they have also had problems persuading some of their members to *claim* the allowances! Even if the sums of money concerned are quite small, shop stewards often enough have to argue with members that:

■ the money is theirs;

■ not claiming gives the employer a completely false idea of how much the business or service really costs to run;

■ not claiming causes problems for colleagues who really *need* the money;

■ not claiming causes problems for their successors.

It is unusual for driving expenses to be itemised clearly, except where there is a separate heading for petrol. The most common schemes are the following:

■ mileage allowance;

■ mileage allowance according to engine size;

■ mileage allowance + lump sum.

The first and simplest method consists of giving a set sum of money per mile *irrespective of engine size*. The spring 1980 issue of the salary survey magazine *Reward* reported that these so-called 'flat rate' allowances ranged from 6.5p to 21.0p, and that 55 per cent of companies gave financial assistance in this way. The details of *Reward*'s survey are on page 224 together with some examples (an explanation of the terms on the top line is to be found in the Glossary):

■ There is also a 15p a mile allowance at Abbott Laboratories, but that is only for journeys of up to 100 miles; for longer trips, you have to take public transport.

■ A feature of some of the more generous schemes is that the management will make efforts to discourage the use of private cars: at Fisons, for example (see the above table), the use of a pool car (see page 259) is strongly encouraged.

■ A few mileage allowance schemes also give small payments for carrying company property in the car (e.g. the BBC, the British Railways Board and the Civil Service); the British Waterways Board and the Independent Broadcasting Authority also pay a mileage allowance for taking another employee as an 'official' passenger.

Lowest	Lowest decile	Lowest quartile	Median	Upper quartile	Upper decile	Highest
6.5p	10.0p	10.0p	12.0p	13.0p	15.0p	21.0p

Here are some examples of this type of allowance:

Chard Meat Co ⎫ Rolls Royce Aero Engines ⎬	14.5p/mile
Gill & Macmillan ⎫ Hambro Life ⎪ Marks & Spencer ⎬ Nabisco ⎭	15.0p/mile
Black & Decker	16.0p/mile
Baxters (Butchers) ⎫ Incomes Data Services ⎬	17.0p/mile
Gillette Industries	18.0p/mile
Colgate-Palmolive	20.0p/mile
Pedigree Petfoods	20.5p/mile
Fisons	21.0p/mile

The *second* most common method of calculating allowances to cover business use of a private car consists of a set sum of money per mile varying *according to the engine capacity*. This method has its origin in an elaborate formula of 'estimated standing and running costs' produced by the Automobile Association twice a year; although the AA brought in a *new* formula in 1980, the old system is still used by employers.

Dividing cars into five categories of engine capacity, the AA estimated annual 'standing charges' and 'running costs per mile': the 'standing costs' were car licence, insurance, depreciation, interest on capital, garage/parking and the AA subscription; the 'running costs per mile' were petrol, oil, tyres, servicing, and repairs and replacements. The formula then produced a 'total cost per mile' based on 10,000 miles' driving a year. The AA figures were criticised on a number of fronts:

■ they assumed that the driver had taken out the most expensive insurance cover, did not carry out any maintenance privately and would sell the car after 80,000 miles or eight years;

■ 'interest on capital' denoted the loss of capital you would have earned if you had invested your money instead of buying the car (!);

■ a survey by the New Towns Study Unit in 1977 estimated that the AA's figures were 150 per cent higher than estimates of private motoring costs produced in the Family Expenditure Survey. (Stephen Potter, *The Cost of Motoring to the Consumer*, New Towns Study Unit, Open University 1977)

The AA's revised formula is as follows:

■ petrol;

■ servicing and repairs (including engine oil);

■ insurance;

■ all other costs (including road tax, AA subscription, accessories, parking fees and 'miscellaneous items').

This new system is still open to at least one very important criticism from the point of view of the private motorist using his/her car for work, which is that depreciation is excluded from the formula.

The spring 1980 issue of *Reward* claims that the AA's method of calculating mileage allowances according to engine size is used by 45 per cent of companies; their more detailed conclusions are as follows (the terms in the left-hand column are explained in the Glossary):

	up to 1,000cc	1,001– 1,250cc	1,251– 1,500cc	1,501– 1,750cc	1,751– 2,000cc	2,001– 2,500cc
Lower quartile	9.0p	10.0p	10.5p	12.0p	12.0p	12.0p
Median	10.0p	11.0p	11.0p	13.0p	14.0p	14.0p
Upper quartile	11.5p	12.0p	13.0p	15.5p	16.0p	18.0p

A lot of individual firms adhere more or less to the AA's format. Some keep very closely to the AA's calculations, for example:

■ Knowles Electronics, Macmillan Books, Thomson Magazines, Penguin Books.

Other employers take the *idea* of the AA format, but reduce it to only two, three or four engine capacities:

two engine capacities	Engine capacity	Allowance per mile
Sun Alliance & London	up to 1,300cc	14.0p
Assurance Group	over 1,300cc	15.0p
IPC Magazines	up to 1,360cc	14.5p
	over 1,360cc	17.0p
IPC Business Press	up to 1,490cc	12.0p
	over 1,490cc	13.5p
Smith Kline & French	up to 1,500cc	13.0p
Laboratories	over 1,500cc	15.0p
United Biscuits	up to 1,500cc	18.2p
	over 1,500cc	22.8p

three engine capacities

	up to 1,500cc	1,501– 2,000cc	over 2,000cc
Thomas Cook Group	11.5p/mile	13.8p/mile	20.1p/mile
Grindlay's Bank	12.0p/mile	14.5p/mile	21.0p/mile

	up to 1,300cc	1,301– 1,800cc	over 1,800cc
Shell (UK)	15.5p/mile	18.0p/mile	22.5p/mile

	up to 1,000cc	1,001– 1,350cc	over 1,350cc
The Boots Co	17.51p/mile	19.54p/mile	23.10p/mile

	up to 1,199cc	1,200– 1,999cc	2,000cc and over
Mobil Oil	15.5p/mile	19.0p/mile	28.8p/mile

four engine capacities

	up to 1,000cc	1,001– 1,500cc	1,501– 2,000cc	over 2,000cc
Reckitt & Colman Products (Hull)	11.8p/mile	13.0p/mile	16.2p/mile	24.0p/mile
Pfizer	14.5p/mile	16.0p/mile	19.5p/mile	29.0p/mile

Sometimes, this format is further complicated by being linked to the number of miles driven:

	up to 1,300cc	over 1,300cc
Porvair Ltd	first 300 miles in a month 15p/mile thereafter 13p/mile	first 300 miles in a month 17p/mile 301–600 miles 15p/mile thereafter 13p/mile

(This company uses calculations prepared by the RAC, rather than by the AA.)

This formula is also used in the banking sector, with somewhat more generous allowances:

Bank of Scotland

	first 5,000 miles	over 5,000 miles
up to 1,500cc	20p/mile	10p/mile
1,501–2,000cc	23p/mile	12p/mile
over 2,000cc	29p/mile	15p/mile

Lloyds Bank

	first 2,000 miles	2,001–10,000 miles	over 10,000 miles
up to 1,000cc	24p/mile	15p/mile	6p/mile
1,001–1,500cc	27p/mile	17p/mile	7p/mile
1,501–2,000cc	33p/mile	21p/mile	8p/mile
over 2,000cc	50p/mile	32p/mile	11p/mile

Barclays Bank

	first 2,000 miles	2,001–5,000 miles	over 5,000 miles
up to 1,000cc	28.34p	17.60p	14.05p
1,001–1,500cc	32.37p	19.97p	15.84p
1,501–2,000cc	40.50p	24.71p	19.44p
over 2,000cc	59.96p	36.31p	28.42p

An interesting variation on this system is to be found at Gillette Industries when an employee is transferred by the firm (see 'Relocation' (pages 261–76)); this special entitlement lasts for only six months:

up to 1,000cc	15p/mile
1,001–1,500cc	16p/mile
1,501–2,000cc	17p/mile
over 2,000cc	18p/mile

The *third* most common method of calculating driving expenses consists of two components: the mileage allowance + a lump sum. Whereas the single sum of money in the first two methods has to cover *all* motoring expenses, the idea of a lump sum in this third system is that it should pay for 'fixed' costs like car licence and insurance.

This type of scheme is particularly common in the public sector where the nature of many of the jobs calls for big differences in the amounts that private cars are used for work. This is the mileage allowance scheme operating in the Fire Brigades:

	Lump sum	First 9,000 miles	Over 9,000 miles
up to 999cc	£249	13.5p	7.1p
1,000–1,199cc	£282	15.1p	7.9p
1,200–1,450cc	£300	16.1p	8.5p
1,450–1,750cc	£363	18.4p	9.1p

Because some public employees use their private cars very much more than others, some national agreements distinguish between what are often called 'essential users' and 'casual users':

■ an *'essential user'* is someone who regularly uses, or is *obliged* to use, his/her own car for work purposes;

■ a *'casual user'* is someone who occasionally uses his/her private car for work purposes at the request of management.

Public sector agreements are sometimes criticised for being too long and detailed; in their favour it should be said that it is quite clear to *all* concerned exactly what their entitlements are. Here is some information on two such schemes – in the National Health Service and in the Water Service:

■ The National Health Service places a lot of reliance on the ability of certain employees to use their own cars *in order to provide appropriate health care* – nurses and midwives, for example, have long complained that their car and motorcycle allowances are too low. In the NHS, 'essential users' are called 'regular users' and 'casual users' are entitled to what are called 'standard user allowances'. The following allowances are in force from 1 April 1981:

Regular users	501–1,000cc	1,001–1,500cc	1,501–2,000cc	Over 2,000cc
lump sum per annum	£266	£310	£395	£395
up to 9,000 miles	12.9p	14.5p	17.7p	19.5p
thereafter	6.9p	7.6p	8.9p	10.8p

Standard user allowances	501–1,000cc	1,001–1,500cc	1,501–2,000cc	Over 2,000cc
up to 3,500 miles	17.6p	20.0p	24.7p	26.6p
3,501–9,000 miles	14.7p	16.6p	20.4p	22.3p
thereafter	6.9p	7.6p	8.9p	10.8p

If an NHS employee goes in his/her own car 'where travel by public service (e.g. rail, bus) would be appropriate', the allowance is reduced. At all events, the employer will refund in all circumstances 'reasonable garage and parking expenses and charges for tolls and ferries necessarily incurred'.

■ The Water Service scheme, like the local government scheme, is *not* open to manual workers; however, *unlike* the local government scheme, the Water Service formula offers relatively high lump sums and lowish mileage allowances: this fractionally favours employees doing a relatively low number of miles. An interesting feature is the 'Excess depreciation rate' which is intended to cover any decrease in the car's value. Class 1 employees are lower-ranking white-collar staff, Class 5 employees are very senior executives:

Motor cars

Regular users

Class	Annual lump-sum allowance	Mileage allowance	Excess depreciation allowance
1	£636	7.07p/mile	4.31p/mile
2	£720	7.52p/mile	5.21p/mile
3	£924	8.94p/mile	6.99p/mile
4	£1,020	9.75p/mile	7.71p/mile
5	£1,416	12.87p/mile	11.54p/mile

Casual users

Class	up to 3,000 miles p.a.	over 3,000 miles p.a.
1	19.84p/mile	7.07p/mile
2	22.03p/mile	7.52p/mile
3	27.49p/mile	8.94p/mile
4	30.13p/mile	9.75p/mile
5	41.26p/mile	12.87p/mile

Three-wheel vehicles and motorcycles

Regular users

Class	Annual lump-sum allowance	Mileage allowance	Excess depreciation allowance
1	£204	2.33p	1.42p/mile
2	£288	3.18p	1.94p/mile
3	£384	4.24p	2.59p/mile
4	£480	5.30p	3.23p/mile

Casual users

Class	up to 3,000 miles p.a.	over 3,000 miles p.a.
1	6.55p	2.33p
2	8.93p	3.18p
3	11.90p	4.24p
4	14.88p	5.30p

Given the rapidly increasing costs of private – and public – transport, it is not surprising that more and more company agreements are setting out allowances for motorcycles and mopeds. We have already seen allowances for them in the Water Service schemes; here are three private sector agreements:

■ *Pfizer:*
Motorcycles and mopeds

up to 125cc	5p/mile
126–250cc	6.5p/mile
251–500cc	9p/mile
over 500cc	11.5p/mile

■ *Cambridge Scientific Instruments:* a flat rate of 12p per mile for motorcycles and mopeds;

■ *Baxters (Butchers) Ltd:* a flat rate of 6p per mile for motorcycles.

Yet another kind of allowance is to be found in the Civil Service – one that takes account of the future world shortage of fuel as well as

Monthly mileage	Allowance
up to 100 miles	2.9p per mile
100–150 miles	£3.03 per month
151–200 miles	£3.67 per month
201–250 miles	£4.06 per month
251–300 miles	£4.43 per month
over 300 miles	£4.62 per month

the ecological hazards of lead poisoning from petrol fumes: bicycle allowances. On page 231 are the allowances given to civil servants who use their bicycles for work:

Despite the large increase in the price of petrol (not to mention other items) in the last few years, unions have experienced difficulty in persuading employers to adjust allowances more often than once a year. There are, however, a few exceptions to this:

■ in the first half of 1980, local government white-collar staff had a review on no fewer than three occasions (1 January, 1 March and 1 May);

■ in the Water Service, future adjustments arising out of increases in petrol prices will be based on an initial premium of 5p over the AA's base price as published in April each year, and further adjustments will be subject to increases or decreases of 5p in petrol prices within the Retail Price Index (RPI);

■ at Pedigree Petfoods, there is an automatic review as soon as the price of petrol has gone up 10p since the last agreement;

■ in the Electricity Supply agreement, as soon as 4-star petrol goes up or down 1p, so the allowance goes up or down by between 0.028p and 0.043p a mile (according to engine size).

It can sometimes happen that an employee is liable to income tax on mileage allowances (see 'Income tax' (page 231)); when this happens, some of the allowance is lost. At least one company has written into the agreement a method of avoiding any financial loss of this kind:

■ at Pfizer, the car and motorcycle & moped allowances (on page 226 and page 231 respectively) are increased by 1½p to compensate those employees who have to pay tax on driving allowances.

Preparing for negotiations

Employment legislation

There is no legislation in this country obliging an employer to give financial assistance to employees who use their own cars (or motorcycles or mopeds) on company business. However, any sex or race discrimination in the provision of such assistance is illegal under the Sex Discrimination Act 1975 and the Race Relations Act 1976 (see page 13).

Income tax

Under Section 60(2) of the 1976 Finance Act, expenses given to you by your employer to cover motoring costs are tax-free, providing you are necessarily obliged to incur these expenses in the performance of your job. Insofar as the mileage allowances (and/or the lump sum) are expected to take care of such expenses as depreciation, this too is covered – but by earlier legislation (Section 47 of the Finance Act 1971).

The cost of travelling between your home and your normal place of employment – *and* payments for the time spent travelling – are *not* tax-deductible (Income and Corporation Taxes Act 1970, Section 189). (See also 'Travelling to and from work' (pages 241–49)).

It is argued by some authorities that it is financially more advantageous to drive one's own car than to have a company car:

■ 'If the amount of private motoring [a 'higher-paid employee'] does is small in relation to his business mileage the tax he pays for having a company car may well outweigh the advantage of having it available for private use. He *may* therefore be better off using his own car and charging his company when he uses it on business.' (*Economist Intelligence Unit Special Report No 71*, 1979) [Emphasis added]

Sitting down with management

It is unlikely that your employer will admit that he wants to pay you *less* than it really costs you to drive your car for work purposes; if he offers you less than you have asked for, you can initially reply by:

■ giving him a detailed run-down of how much the *members* think it costs to run their cars for work;

■ challenging the employer to tell you how *he* reached *his* figure(s).

It is not unknown for small, paternalistic employers to 'expect' their workforce to do things for love, but you *probably* won't have to argue the *principle* of mileage allowances as the big national agreements include them almost without exception. What you could more frequently find yourself doing is trying to incorporate a new group of the workforce into the mileage allowance scheme. The employer may not like the idea of paying out more money, but you could try and persuade him that *flexibility* would be an advantage to him; you might be able to argue that:

■ members would welcome some variety in their work (by being able to leave the workplace from time to time);

■ this variety could lead to increased 'job satisfaction'.

If your employer were to propose a two-tier scheme (along the lines of 'essential/casual users'), you would need to examine the proposal *in every detail*; after discussing the matter with the members, you might still find that it was essentially exploitative:

■ the 'essential' category pays better, but involves more driving;

■ the 'casual' category *should* involve only occasional driving – but it can happen that the employer puts pressure on them to do a lot more (for little reward).

Throughout the life of a mileage allowance scheme, the employer will probably continue to resist claims for increases; so as not to have to be negotiating for an improvement long after prices have risen, you could try and:

■ introduce an automatic calculator or 'trigger' mechanism (see page 232).

But there are many *other* hidden, or 'forgotten', expenses involved in running a car, and the management may tell you that the allowance (particularly if there is a lump sum) is *intended* to cover 'fixed' costs – 'fixed' costs are the non-recurring items such as car licence and insurance. You may need to remind them that:

■ the car will *depreciate in value* even more quickly than it would otherwise have done precisely because it is being used in connection with the job; that part of the allowance needs to be maintained – or even increased.

Finally, you could find yourself trapped by ownership of a car being 'a condition of employment': you want to investigate this carefully if the employer brings it up, because it may have been no more than a sentence like 'Own car an advantage' in the original advertisement. If the company tries to keep the allowance artificially low on the grounds that you are (allegedly) obliged by your contract to have a car anyway – and therefore the firm does not need to reimburse you for all expenses – you might consider:

■ calling a temporary halt to the negotiations on driving allowances at once and

■ setting up other discussions to clarify the contract *immediately*.

If the management eventually accept that a private car is no more than 'an advantage' – and not compulsory – you could point out that:

■ the workforce would feel cheated if there was any financial loss from driving their own cars.

You could also say:

■ retention – and even recruitment in the long run – will be favourably affected;

■ nobody should have to *pay* to work for the firm;

■ does the employer want a resentful workforce?

17.

Travelling by public transport

Introduction

This chapter deals with financial assistance given to you by your employer for *using public transport while at work*. Assistance in getting you to work and back home again is in 'Travelling to and from work' (pages 241–49), and any free or low-cost travel you may be entitled to by being employed in the travel industry (railways, travel agencies etc) is looked at in 'Company discount' (pages 216–21).

Travelling on public transport on company business is not *exclusively* an activity of middle and top management – but it very nearly is, and so arrangements are generally made for this group only. However, managers are often bound by quite a strict scheme of differentials themselves. As far as *rail* travel is concerned, arrangements can be very varied:

- some firms send *all* their employees first-class (e.g. Abbott Laboratories, Black & Decker, Colgate-Palmolive and Grindlay's Bank);

- sometimes first-class travel is restricted to top management (e.g. Firestone Rubber, Hambro, Hymatic Engineering, Knowles Electronics, Porvair, United Biscuits, Local Authorities and the NHS);

- sometimes the formula *can* be expressed very simply: monthly-paid go first-class, weekly-paid go second-class (Gillette Industries).

Life is not *always* so luxurious for management, though:

- at least one firm sends *all* its staff second-class (Smith Kline & French Laboratories).

Sometimes the arrangements aim to take into account the circumstances of the journey:

■ at the International Publishing Corporation there is first-class travel for all journeys of more than 50 miles;

■ at Nabisco, first-class travel is reserved for senior managers travelling over 150 miles;

■ at Pedigree Petfoods, *anyone* travelling over four hours or out of normal working hours can go first-class.

Air travel is subject to similar differentials:

■ first-class air travel is a perquisite of main board directors at Thomas Cook;

■ however, most business representatives go tourist class (e.g. Abbott Laboratories, the AA, Black & Decker, Firestone, Fisons and Grindlay's Bank).

Sometimes, first-class travel is available – but subject to certain conditions of the journey:

■ at Porvair, staff travel first-class on long-distance journeys (e.g. to the United States or the Soviet Union) but, to make up for it, they have to start work on their first working day;

■ Pedigree Petfoods employees going on all transatlantic and other intercontinental journeys may travel first-class;

■ sometimes the first-class fare will be paid if the journey takes more than a certain time (over 10 hours at Thomas Cook, over 8 hours at Gillette, over $7\frac{1}{2}$ hours at Smith Kline & French and over $5\frac{1}{2}$ hours at Grindlay's).

Company agreements on travel by public transport do not solely cover the cost of the bus/train/plane tickets:

■ the NHS Whitley Council (which, in this case, does not cover ancillary workers) pays for 'extra expenditure necessarily incurred on Pullman Car or similar supplements, reservation of seats, and deposit or porterage of luggage.'

The same agreement also covers taxi fares and tips.

Most agreements and contracts state that travel on public transport will be paid for by the employer as long as the journey is connected with work – in most cases, this is because the benefit would otherwise be taxable (see 'Income tax' (page 239)). A problem can arise when there is a dispute about whether the trip is or is not connected with the job; the employer may be persuaded to pay the travelling expenses, but the Inland Revenue may want to tax them:

■ a Birmingham teacher got travelling expenses from her employer to travel to a parents' meeting after school hours, but the Inland Revenue said they were taxable. The teacher then appealed, with the assistance of her trade union, the National Union of Teachers (NUT), to the Inland Revenue Commissioners and won her case.

The opportunity to travel by public transport is rare among manual workers – i.e. workers who do not have managerial/supervisory responsibilities. In both the public and private sectors of the construction industry and civil engineering there are, of course, many manual workers who travel around in the course of their work, but their transport is usually organised by the employer.

Manual workers are usually excluded from the first-class travel referred to elsewhere in this chapter, except for a few firms such as those mentioned earlier.

And it is not only the private sector that provides attractive travelling arrangements for its employees:

■ from 1 July 1982, half a million members of the armed forces (together with their spouses and dependent children aged between 14 and 18) will be given 'rail cards' by their employer (the Ministry of Defence); these 'rail cards' will entitle holders to a 50 per cent discount on rail travel.

By far the most common arrangement for manual workers in either the public or the private sector is second-class travel:

■ NHS maintenance staff on 'detached duty' (i.e. away from home for at least one night) have fares paid by the employer: 'The fares payable shall be the cost of travel by public conveyance, not by taxi. Rail fares shall be those for second-class travel.'

Other firms to pay for second-class rail fares for manual workers, as quoted by IDS, include:

■ Avon Cosmetics, Batchelors Foods, Baxters (Butchers), The Boots Company, Borden (UK) Thermoplastics Division, Cambridge Scientific Instruments, Chard Meat Co, Cheeseborough-Pond's, H J Heinz, Knowles Electronics, Reckitt & Colman Products (Hull), Pfizer, Tucker Fasteners, United Biscuits, Weetabix.

Preparing for negotiations

Employment legislation

There is no law in this country obliging your employer to give you any money to cover any costs that you may run up while using public transport in the performance of your duties as an employee.

However, it would be illegal for him to provide this assistance in a discriminatory way on grounds of sex or race under the Sex Discrimination Act 1975 and the Race Relations Act 1976 (see page 13).

Income tax

Under Section 60(2) of the 1976 Finance Act, you do not pay tax on any travelling expenses you necessarily incur while doing your job. If you were to receive travelling expenses for travelling *to and from work*, that *would* be taxable (see 'Travelling to and from work' (pages 241–49)).

As with most tax claims, a lot turns on what the Inland Revenue calls 'reasonable', and they tend to judge the 'reasonableness' of the expenses on why the journey is being made, the suitability of the transport chosen and *the employee's status within the company*; also, if you use the trip to go and see some friends or have a few days' holiday, the expenses are still tax-deductible.

Sitting down with management

Unless you happen to work for a company that expects you to pay for your own business travel, you *ought* not to have any particular difficulty in, at least, getting the bare minimum: as with expenses to cover driving your own car for work (see pages 222–35), the sole criterion while negotiating with your employer must be that:

■ you do not pay a penny out of your own pocket.

However, unlike driving costs, public transport costs are laid down in black and white and there can hardly be any argument about how much you can claim – remember, *other* expenses you might run up while travelling are dealt with in 'Subsistence' (pages 182–95). If you do find yourself eligible to put in for public transport fares, make sure you include *all* fares – for example:

■ don't forget to see to it that any travelling to and from, say, the railway station is also paid for.

Assuming that the various trips on behalf of the company are necessary to the company's general well-being and survival, it is difficult to claim that the trips should not take place. However, it *is* difficult to justify the facility to travel first-class: while you may not find it possible to dissuade your employer from sending his executives first-class, it is an item you can bear in mind *in totally different negotiations* when your employer is claiming that he just can't afford something:

■ if what you're asking for is relatively cheap, it could be useful to be able to say it could be paid for by *x* executives travelling second-class in the previous year.

And beware of *elevating* first-class (or second-class, for that matter) travel into something it isn't:

■ flying around the world – first- *or* second-class – is *not* considered a wonderful perk by the vast majority of executives.

The only way of making yourself eligible for rail and air travel on the firm is to:

■ change the nature of your job;

you *might* be able to make a start by suggesting that:

■ certain work is shared amongst a *larger* number of employees. After all, even if most executives don't find the travelling so very appealing, they have two important advantages over nearly all other workers:

■ they do some of their work *in different surroundings*;

■ travelling to those different surroundings is another break from any monotony they may experience.

It can be worth reminding your employer of these points from time to time: even if you don't manage to negotiate the occasional trip by air, you might be able to begin to persuade your employer that *you* should be given *something else to compensate*.

18.
Travelling to and from work

Introduction

In this chapter, we look at assisted travel from home to work and back home again – probably by means of a 'company bus', perhaps by public transport or taxi. This chapter does not deal with allowances given to cover travel *at* work; these are dealt with in 'Company car' (pages 250–60), 'Using your own transport' (pages 222–35) and 'Travelling by public transport' (pages 236–40). The most common form of assistance is the 'company bus', but there are also several types of arrangement for workers doing overtime and for workers whose place of work changes. There are also a few schemes for young workers.

It is becoming increasingly difficult to get to work; there are four main reasons for this:

- the length of many journeys;
- the complexity of many journeys (particularly in inner-city areas);
- the unavailability or unsuitability of public transport;
- the rapidly increasing cost.

It is true that a good many people come to work by car – according to the Automobile Association, 60 per cent of car owners use their vehicles to drive to and from work – but that still leaves millions of workers who must rely on other means of transport, and both employers and Government are convinced that lack of suitable transport is a significant obstacle to getting to work. In 1977, IDS reported that both public and private sector organisations which moved to new industrial developments – such as the new towns surrounding London – often felt '*obliged* to provide some form of assisted travel for their employees to and from their place of work'. [Emphasis added] Two years later, in 1979, the Manpower Services Commission (MSC) carried out a survey of six of their Employment

Services Division districts: the MSC concluded that 'some hard-to-fill vacancies offer low wages, [and are] *even less attractive when coupled with travelling costs*'. [Emphasis added]

A few employers pay for their employees' travelling costs: according to an Alfred Marks Bureau survey in 1978, 8 per cent of employees in the London area had their tickets bought for them; but this advantage is sometimes felt to be nullified when the worker is thinking of moving on to another job: if you want to move to another job in the same locality or to a job with the same travel problems, and that job has no assisted travel scheme, **either you lose out financially or you stay in your present job**. Furthermore, there is no income tax allowance on travelling to and from work, although: travelling to and from work is **totally or partly tax-deductible** in Belgium, Denmark, France, Luxembourg, the Netherlands, Sweden and West Germany.

It is being claimed that at least part of the problem will be alleviated by a new scheme launched in the summer of 1980; the scheme works briefly as follows:

■ the firm of LV Travel Ltd has gone in with London Transport to sell to employers annual bus/tube season tickets at a bulk discount (anything up to 50 per cent); the employers then give them to all, or some, of their employees as a free perk. The holder of a 'London Traveller Ticket' will then be able to travel on London buses and underground free of charge at any time during the day or night. LV Travel say that an employer will be able to save half of the increase in gross annual earnings needed to compensate an employee already paying £8 a week on getting to work; they also claim that the benefit will be tax-free because it is not part of earnings, not convertible into cash and not bought by the employee with money or a voucher provided by the employer.

The scheme is open to criticism on a number of counts, not least:

■ it is by no means certain that this sort of travel will turn out to be tax-free, particularly in view of the 1979 Conservative Government's hostility towards many types of fringe benefit;

■ the scheme militates against people who work for small firms (the bulk discount strongly favours large companies) or for firms that employ a small number of commuters.

This London Transport scheme – and other elaborate schemes – also present trade unionists with another danger: an employer operating in one area with a relatively *low* level of unemployment might organise the bussing (at fairly low cost) of workers from another area with a *high* level of unemployment – **and then pay them low wages**.

Employers are now saying that the 1980 Transport Act will improve public transport: one of the provisions of the 1980 Act breaks up the State's near monopoly of public transport – it is claimed that this will enable (and encourage) small, local operators to run services responding to *local* needs. The reality of the situation is that private operators will **only run those services that are profitable** – and that will exclude the majority of local runs (for example, to the factory gate).

The form of assisted travel to and from work that receives most publicity is that offered by employers already in the public transport business:

■ British Rail and London Transport both give their employees free passes to travel to and from work by rail and bus/tube respectively.

However, probably the *most used* type of assistance is the 'company bus'; this is run – and possibly owned – by the firm, and picks up its passengers along an established route; invariably, the service is timed to fit in with the starting and finishing times of shifts. On the whole, employers seem pleased with the idea: an IDS survey in 1980 quotes several employers who are more than satisfied: bad time-keeping has been reduced at one firm (Knowles Electronics), and at another (unnamed) firm 'the bus service gives our company the edge over others in recruiting staff.' A third firm is quoted as saying: 'The buses were brought in when we were desperate for people. We don't need the service now but long-serving members still need it so we cannot phase it out despite the immense cost.'

Company buses are to be found in many industrial sectors; for example, some of those quoted in *IDS Study 221* are:

■ Baxters (Butchers), Lesney Products, Molins, Nabisco, Pfizer and United Biscuits.

One of the most common reasons for introducing the service is the difficulty in reaching the site:

■ Knowles Electronics in Burgess Hill, Sussex, is in a relatively remote area and public transport facilities are not adequate, so the company decided to have a free coach service to bring the hourly-paid workers in.

Where the service is free to employees, the company picks up the entire bill; where the employees pay a nominal fare, the scheme is operated like this:

■ at Boots in Nottingham, the buses go round the different sites, arriving and leaving at times which fit in with manual and white-collar shifts; the company which runs the buses collects the reduced fares from the passengers, and Boots pay the balance later on.

Fares are almost invariably subsidised by the employer; sometimes the journeys are *free*:

■ Adams Foods (Leek), Bovril (to and from Burton Town Hall), Knowles Electronics, Porvair (to and from the bus station), Weetabix.

Some other companies make a charge:

■ Batchelors Foods: 7p per trip on local routes in Sheffield, 32p for longer trips of up to 25 miles outside Sheffield;

■ Cambridge Scientific Instruments: 30p from Royston into Cambridge, 15p if you pick the bus up between Melbourne and Cambridge;

■ Adams Foods (Uttoxeter): 75p per week;

■ Avon Cosmetics: 35p each journey.

The employers' subsidies also vary, but usually because of the considerable differences in the size of the operations:

■ United Biscuits: 50 per cent;

■ Adams Foods: 75 per cent;

■ Avon Cosmetics: 75 per cent (approximately £26,000 a year for a service consisting of five coaches a day);

■ Batchelors Foods: 70–80 per cent (approximately £70,000 a year for 30 trips a day, including some many miles outside Sheffield).

Most of these services are regular, having the same timetable every day; sometimes there are variations:

■ at Weetabix, workers required to do overtime are guaranteed transport home afterwards.

At other firms, the bus does not only bring people to and from work:

■ at both Bovril and Borden (UK) Thermoplastics Division, there is free transport during meal breaks for workers who wish to go shopping.

Some other companies have found that running a company bus service might be too expensive, and have decided to share the service with other local firms:

■ Shulton (UK) Ltd has gone in with several other firms in the area to have a bus go round all the factories.

In most cases, small numbers of employees are likely to make a company bus scheme uneconomic; other kinds of arrangement are then made:

■ journalists at Marshall Cavendish get the taxi fare home if they work more than $1\frac{1}{2}$ hours late;

■ you have the right to a taxi home or to the railway station at Hutchinson and IPC (if you work after 7 p.m.), at Cassell (after 7.30 p.m.) and at Time-Life International (after 10 p.m.).

There are not all that many manual workers who work off-site, and they are often transported to their temporary workplace in vans, buses or cars – at the employer's expense. However, this is not always the case; *travelling allowances* to and from work are sometimes given to manual workers in the public sector, and they are invariably less generous than those offered to white-collar workers.

■ In the National Health Service, workers employed under the Ambulancemen's and Ancillary Services Councils are entitled to certain expenses when sent away on 'temporary detached duty' (i.e. not at the normal workplace); the travelling allowance is worked out strictly according to the following formula: 'When an employee travels from or returns to his/her home, the fares admissible will be those for the journeys from or to home *less the fares normally spent on the journeys between home and the usual place of duty.*' [Emphasis added] The agreement goes on to say that '[The] fares payable . . . shall be the cost of travel by public conveyance, not by taxi. Rail fares shall be those for second-class travel.'

■ Local government craftsworkers often find themselves starting and/or finishing their working day at sites or deopts where they do not normally report for work: under their *national* agreement, they only receive travelling expenses (i.e. fares both ways) when they travel both to and from the job on public transport during time for which wages are *not* paid.

Other employers prefer to give an allowance for travel rather than reimburse fares; here are some examples from both the private and public sectors:

■ Electricity Supply (clerical, administrative & sales staff and manual workers): the assisted travel scheme for employees working at 'remote' sites is:

3–6 miles	80–90 p per week
6–10 miles	£1.30–£1.40 per week
over 10 miles	£2–£2.15 per week

■ construction industry: the daily fare allowance ranges from 10p (sites seven kilometres from home) to £2.76 (sites 50 kilometres from home);

■ County Council roadworkers (Local Authorities manual workers): the allowances for distance travelled each way to and from work or the pick-up point are:

under 3 miles	nil
3–5 miles	25p
5–7 miles	30p
7–9 miles	40p
9–11 miles	50p
over 11 miles	to be negotiated locally

■ thermal insulation engineers: the daily allowances paid for travelling from home directly to a job are:

up to 5 miles	£2.02
5–10 miles	£2.72
10–15 miles	£3.43
15–20 miles	£4.13
20–25 miles	£5.07
25–30 miles	£6.63
30–35 miles	£7.79

Another travelling problem that can arise is when the whole firm or department is transferred to a new locality; during the periodic reorganisations of Local Government, this is what council workers are entitled to:

'An employee incurring additional travelling expenses shall be paid . . . an allowance equal to the difference between the costs of travelling (a) from his home to his new place of work, and (b) from his home to his old place of work. Such an allowance shall be paid *for a period of four years* and shall be based on public transport rates (second-class, if rail).' [Emphasis added]

There are also a few arrangements for young workers who are perhaps living away from home for the first time:
■ at Barclays Bank, workers under the age of 21 who are receiving a lodging allowance qualify for four free return journeys home a year;
■ in the Civil Service, workers under 21 in lodgings get three journeys home a year, and low-paid staff living in hostels or in receipt of a lodging allowance are entitled to assistance in travelling to and from work.
Finally, people who work in remote spots can have considerable difficulty in having any life outside the workplace:
■ the Ancillary Staffs Council of the NHS 'expresses the hope that' resident staff in hospitals and institutions situated in isolated areas will be afforded travelling facilities for recreational purposes. Unions in the Health Service have had the greatest difficulty in having this clause translated into action.

Preparing for negotiations

Employment legislation

There is no law obliging an employer to provide any transport for his employees to get to work and back home again, nor is there any obligation to give any financial assistance. If there is a subsidy of some sort, it is illegal for the employer to discriminate on grounds of sex or race under the Sex Discrimination Act 1975 and the Race Relations Act 1976 (see page 13).

Income tax

Financial assistance from the employer to help you get to and from your *normal* place of work is taxable; *however*, as long as the assistance *cannot* be transferred or converted into cash (e.g. a company bus or a free season ticket), it is tax-free. If you do *not* have a 'normal' place of work (for example, you are a sales representative, a civil engineering worker – or a full-time trade union official) and go to *different* places to do your work, all reasonable travelling expenses are tax-free.

Sitting down with management

The main trump card you will be able to play when negotiating this type of transport with management is the threat of problems in the area of recruitment/retention of staff:

■ if your employer can be persuaded that he might not be able to get hold of the workers he wants – and hang on to them – you should be able to make him see the value of free (or low-cost) travel to and from work.

If your employer accepts – or if you just happen to know – that there is a problem in hiring and keeping workers, there are several points you can make to support your case, according to the circumstances:

■ public transport is inadequate from certain surrounding districts or at certain times of the day;

■ only a limited number of employees can afford to run a private car *and* drive it to and from work.

Perhaps the reason for your employer having trouble with recruitment/retention is that he is in a competitive market for labour; in order to press your point, try and find out if:

■ the management is particularly on the lookout for workers of a special type or with a special skill;

■ rival companies in the neighbourhood are paying better wages.

If the firm is having to pay out large sums of money on temporary or agency workers, you could say that:

■ they might well be tempted to stay if they did not have the inconvenience and expense of travelling to and from the workplace.

If your company produces goods or services that need to be advertised, you could say that:

■ a company bus could have the name of the firm and/or its best known product painted on the side of the coach.

You might also try and find out if other grades are eligible for assistance with transport (e.g. season-ticket loans).

Similarly, when it comes to late working, you will be able to put maximum pressure on the employer:

■ if he finds that he cannot recruit/retain certain grades of worker because they can't get home late in the evening or at night.

If the pool of labour is large and the amount of work is relatively small, the employer will probably sit back and rely on *a few* doing all the evening/night work. It is when the situation is *reversed* that you are suddenly in a stronger bargaining position: you might be able to say that:

■ if facilities are not available immediately to assist people to travel to and from work, the firm will probably be unable to take advantage of the commercial upsurge.

In other circumstances, you may prefer to argue about the *composition* of the evening/night shift: you could say:

■ only those with no domestic duties will be happy to stay on;

■ only younger workers will feel it's worth it;

■ those who do have to get home may have to leave the firm.

If *pay* for shiftworkers or other lateworkers is not high enough, you can point out to the employer that:

■ he may have to face a chronically high turnover in this department.

It is always worth doing a few sums to work out really how much it costs members from different parts of the area to get to work by car or public transport; if the results are clearly favourable, you could say that:

■ the small sums of money involved (hiring a bus, taxi fares etc) are tiny compared with the goodwill and high workrate that they generate.

Lastly, if you find yourself negotiating on behalf of workers who do not work in a single office or factory but who are directed to work anywhere in a given 'area' (e.g. construction and civil engineering), do not give the employer a chance to say that they must simply go to work where the work is; make sure you have *already* had negotiations to clarify and define their 'workplaces'.

19.

Company car

Introduction

The company car is a benefit given to middle and senior management, including sales personnel; it is *never* given to manual or clerical workers. The purpose of this chapter is to give trade unionists an idea of how well *some* other employees do.

This chapter is about the provision by your employer of a car which you are to use in the course of your job and (probably) which you can use for private driving as well. This chapter will also deal with any payments that have to be made *to the employer* for the right to drive a 'company car', and any expenses that can be claimed *from the employer* for distances covered. Expenses for driving your *own* car are discussed in 'Using your own transport' (pages 222–35).

According to the British Institute of Management (BIM), a company car (sometimes called a 'fleet car') is worth anything between £1,000 and £2,000 a year, taking into consideration depreciation, income tax, maintenance and insurance. (*Management Survey Report: Business Cars*, BIM 1979) The magazine *Reward* goes into greater detail, into the extra gross pay that would need to be added to present earnings in order to compensate for the loss of a company car, and permit the employee to run his/her own car: see page 251.

It is, of course, much more difficult to put a figure on the value of a company car to an employee who would not normally have had a car at all.

The British Institute of Management also estimate that about 80 per cent of *new* cars on the road technically belong to firms, and it is also thought that approximately half of *all* cars in Britain are company cars. These figures suggest that about one million new cars will be bought by companies in 1981 – at an overall cost to the companies of £3,500–4,000 million. In addition, the BIM survey

Present company car	Gross annual pay increase to compensate for loss
Chevette (1,250cc)	£1.196
Cortina 1600L	£1,270
Princess 2200 HLS	£1,987

(*Reward Salary and Living Cost Report*, Reward 1979)

found that about half of the companies they questioned had a 'buy British' policy (*Management Survey Report: Business Cars*, British Institute of Management 1979). British employers have the distinction of being the most generous in the world when it comes to giving company cars to their employees – Britain being a country where cars are particularly expensive by comparison with earnings.

Why do employers provide so many of their employees with company cars? Given the uniquely favourable tax position in this country, it is certainly a cheap way of improving an employee's standard of living – i.e. in view of the tax advantages to both employer *and* employee, it costs a lot less to buy a car for the employee than to pay the extra *gross* salary necessary for him/her to afford to run it. Companies were given a special impetus, however, during the various pay policies of the mid- to late-1970s: big increases in wages/salaries were more or less out of the question and employers quickly saw that a method of reducing the anxieties of their management personnel was to give them a car. People who did not need a car for their job now got one, and those who already had a car got a 'better' one. The social distinction for many had become, not to be able to afford a car, but to have *a company car*. And there were financial advantages yet to be properly appreciated: when the company paid for periodic servicing and repairs due to wear and tear, this covered private, as well as business, motoring.

What with income tax legislation failing to keep pace with devices for getting round successive pay policies in the mid-1970s, the number of people with strong *expectations* to have a company car began to overtake those who had a more or less objective *need* for one. Although employers would prefer to pay their managers in cash rather than in kind, an IDS survey in 1978 found that recruitment and retention of suitable staff could be extremely difficult if there were no perks: the 'total remuneration package' (see pages 3–4) was not complete without a company car. And the BIM are quoted as saying it is 'unlikely anyone would move from a position with a car to one without'.

The very highest levels of management have long enjoyed the benefit of a company car: as long ago as 1971, the management survey firm of AIC/Inbucon reported that **92.5 per cent of managing directors had a company car; by 1977, this figure had risen to 95.2 per cent.** But it is at the slightly lower levels of management that most of the biggest strides have been made in recent years. The following statistics supplied by AIC/Inbucon show how other managerial grades have been acquiring cars on the firm:

	1969 *percentage*	1977 *percentage*
general managers	81	94.8
company secretaries	62	75.4
managers	49.7	63.8

This overall picture is borne out by a BIM survey in 1977 which estimated that company cars were being given to 91.4 per cent of directors and 51 per cent of 'supporting managers'. Estimates of how far the provision of fleet cars has extended to *employees in general* are less certain:

■ 18 per cent according to *Executive Remuneration and Benefits Survey Report* (John Courtis and Partners 1980);

■ 37 per cent (*Reward Salary and Living Cost Report*, Reward 1979).

When it comes to allotting company cars to different grades, it is clear that there is a form of pecking order:

■ *top management* certainly cream off the most luxurious models – directors and senior management at United Biscuits, Porvair, Gillette Industries and Black & Decker get Jaguars, Mercedes, Volvos or Rovers;

■ *middle and executive management* at Firestone Rubber, Knowles Electronics and Pedigree Petfoods get Granadas, Princesses, Cortina Ghia 2000s or Lancias;

■ employees who spend much of their working time 'on the road' usually get a Cortina 1600 or an Escort 1300 – for example, the sales forces at Abbott Laboratories, Black & Decker, Nabisco and Firestone Rubber.

Occasionally, special care is taken in the selection of company cars so that the appropriate one is bought:

■ at Pedigree Petfoods and Porvair, the sales force receive estate cars if they have to take large amounts of samples around with them.

But the granting of a company car is sometimes openly used to spur employees on:

■ at Selkirk Metalbestos, the sales team get Cortina Ghias and move up to Rover 2600s on fulfilling certain quotas – but revert to Ghias if they later fall below the target.

The above information, largely derived from an IDS survey, gives a clear picture of a pecking order; a very similar conclusion is reached by the BIM who, in the summer of 1979, reported that slightly under a third of chairmen and managing directors got a Jaguar or Rolls-Royce, and a quarter of directors got a Rover or Granada (the Granada having taken over from the Jaguar since the previous BIM survey in 1976). The various models of Cortina, according to the BIM, are very popular among junior and middle management and sales personnel, and it is also surprising to find that as many as 12 per cent of firms in the BIM sample give 'status cars' to *junior* managers. This *overall* picture of a pecking order is also confirmed by the independent survey, Ford Analysis of Car Transport Statistics (FACTS), published by the computer firm Hoskyns Systems.

Although the system described above (a given grade qualifies for a given car) is the most common, some companies operate certain variations:

■ Abbott Laboratories, for example, also give three grades a maximum purchase price:

junior management	up to £4,600
senior management	up to £5,100
directors	up to £7,500

■ Pedigree Petfoods have a similar system:

senior managers	up to £7,750
directors	up to £15,000

■ Grindlay's Bank offer a particular car *or* another that the employee can choose him/herself *as long as it is no more expensive*:

Grade A: Cortina 2000 GL
Grade B: Rover 2600 automatic
Grade C: Rover 3500 automatic
(or another car of equivalent value)

At Grindlay's, those on Grade A were earning at least £11,760 in 1979.

■ Nabisco, on the other hand, give fleet cars not on the basis of earnings or the name of your job but on how high (or low) you rank on the company's job evaluation scheme: those at the top of their Hay/MSL scheme get a Granada 2.8 and those lower down get a Granada 2.3 or 2.0.

It is the general rule for companies to supply a fleet car free of charge, and for such items as road tax, insurance, servicing and repairs to be paid for by the employer; it is also likely that the driver will have the right to take the car abroad on holiday. As far as business use is concerned, this is usually free. Arrangements can vary quite considerably:

■ the car is usually supplied free (Penguin Books, Fisons);

■ there is no charge for business use (Firestone and Hambro);

■ unlimited private driving (Gillette);

■ up to 5 per cent of the cost of any extras – e.g. cassette players or car radios (Grindlay's Bank).

Sometimes, though, employees have to *pay* to have the company car:

■ at Sun Alliance, branch managers pay £48 a year and others pay £25 a year;

■ at the AA, employees who qualify for a perk car and earn less than £8,500 a year pay £10 a month (those earning over £8,500 p.a. pay nothing);

■ at Grindlay's Bank, Grade A employees pay £190–380 a

year according to the car's engine size, although better-paid staff pay nothing.

It is normal for petrol and oil for business use to be 'free' – i.e. fuel is bought either with a credit card or in cash (in which case the money is reimbursed on production of receipts). Some companies, however, operate a mileage allowance scheme similar to that applied to workers using their own cars (see pages 222–35), and *pay* a set sum of money for every mile driven on company business:

Automobile Association	4.5p
Hymatic Engineering Co Ltd	5.7p (first-level salesmen – Cortina 1600) 6.3p (second-level salesmen – Cortina 2000)
Pedigree Petfoods	4.5–4.88p (according to engine size)
Thomas Cook Group	4.4–8.6p (according to engine size)

Private motoring is usually a matter for the employee concerned, but some employers – while not putting any limitation on the number of miles that can be driven outside work – put a charge on it:

Porvair	4.0p/mile
Automobile Association	6.0p/mile

When it comes to deciding on the frequency of replacing company cars, employers have to juggle several important factors: how many (or few) miles a particular car has done, the seniority of the employee, the car's likely resale price and (not least) the employee's expectations of a new car; there is also the question of the company's image – an insurance company may wish to keep a lowish profile whereas the sales force of a manufacturing company may opt for a more flamboyant image. According to the BIM, company cars are usually replaced after three years or 40,000–50,000 miles – whichever happens first – although there is a tendency for perk cars to be replaced more frequently. Cars are disposed of either by resale to the motor trade, or by sale in part exchange for new company cars or by sale to employees (either at or below the market rate).

Sometimes very high-ranking employees have not only a company car but also a company chauffeur to drive it for them: a BIM survey in 1977 found that over 14 per cent of directors had prime use of a chauffeur-driven car – and that 90 per cent of them *also* had sole use of a company car. In answer to a Parliamentary question in May 1980 suggesting that top civil servants need not be picked up at main-line railway stations every morning, a government spokesperson justified the expense on the grounds that they could use their time in chauffeur-driven cars to 'go through their papers in privacy and concentrate on complicated matters'. BIM statistics strongly suggest, however, that chauffeurs are very much more common in the private sector than in Government.

Preparing for negotiations

Employment legislation

There is no law in this country obliging an employer to provide a car for any of his employees – or to give any financial assistance towards running costs; discrimination in the provision on the grounds of sex or race, however, is outlawed by the Sex Discrimination Act 1975 and the Race Relations Act 1976 (see page 13).

Income tax

As the British income tax system uniquely favours those employees fortunate enough to be given a company car, it is worth knowing exactly *how* the system operates in favour of the few – at the expense of the many.

Until 1976, taxation on the use of a company car had depended on one's accuracy – and honesty – in estimating the annual ratio of business mileage to total mileage. The 1976 Finance Act, however, drew a clear line between the 'higher-paid' (see pages 9–10) who paid tax and the rest who didn't. The Act introduced a system whereby a sum of money is added to annual gross earnings for tax purposes, this sum being calculated according to the car's original market value and present engine capacity.

The rapidly rising cost of living soon made a nonsense of the 1976 figures, and the proliferation of 'legal' perk cars fuelled widespread criticism of the system. The first shot of any importance was fired by the Inland Revenue who argued for 'a realistic scale of car benefits' (*The taxation of cars and petrol as benefits in kind*, The Board of Inland Revenue 1979). At the time the Inland Revenue were collecting about £65m a year from company cars, and they thought that £350m was more 'realistic'. The response from management organisations was fierce: the BIM was unhappy that cars should be singled out and wanted 'some of the lesser and more frivolous benefits' included in any reappraisal of tax liability – by this term the BIM said they meant such things as holidays on the firm, flats, yachts, suits, furniture, servants, entertainment and concessionary travel. The Confederation of British Industry (CBI) called for even more income tax cuts for middle management before company cars were subjected to a less favourable tax liability, particularly in view of the harmful effects such a move would have on the British car manufacturing industry – BL had already complained that sales of Rovers and Jaguars would be critically reduced if company cars were more heavily taxed. The employers failed to meet the Inland Revenue's point that 'a taxpayer who is provided with a company car which is available for his private use is treated much more favourably for income tax purposes than *one who provides for his own private motoring.' (The taxation of cars and petrol as benefits in kind*, The Board of Inland Revenue 1979) [Emphasis added]

It is now being increasingly recognised that 'personal taxation has become an important tool of economic management' (*PAYE – Possible Future Developments*, The Board of Inland Revenue 1979), and the tax ratings for company cars effective from the beginning of the 1981–82 financial year (i.e. from 6 April 1981) – set by the March 1980 Conservative Budget – are a lot less punitive than had been expected.

Under the 1976 Finance Act (as amended), *if you are earning less than £8,500 a year you are NOT liable for income tax on the value of a company car*; you *would* be liable, though, if you took a drop in pay – or refused a rise – in exchange for a company car, if that rise would have taken you to £8,500 p.a. or more.

'Higher-paid' employees (see pages 9–10) *are* liable for income tax but it is, in the main, higher-paid employees who get fleet cars in the first place, and even so their tax advantages are impressive. For example, an executive with a car under four years old in the 1,301–1,800cc range and with an original market price of less than £9,600 would add only £300 to his/her annual gross earnings; in other words, if the executive pays income tax at the standard rate (currently 30 per cent), s/he would only pay £90 (i.e. 30 per cent of £300) a year in tax for the benefit of having a car s/he has not had to buy. Furthermore, payment for such items as insurance, petrol and repairs is tax-free as long as the employer settles up *direct* with the insurance company, garage etc.

Sitting down with management

Company cars are a fiddle. And cars that are needed for work – let alone perk cars – are not just a tax fiddle for that particular employee: the fact that so little tax is being paid on company cars means that *all* taxpayers are subsidising them. What this means is that the cars of middle-class/executive/better-off employees are being subsidised by *lower-paid* workers.

There can be no trade union justification for negotiating a company car – particularly when manual workers and clerical workers are never offered one:

■ research for this book has failed to unearth a single example.

There is a trade union school of thought that says you have a right to go and ask for anything that anybody else has; it tends to be an unsuccessful theory:

■ when the unions at Chrysler (Coventry) asked for company cars for manual workers, they were turned down flat – on the grounds that they are part of the total remuneration of *senior management only*.

That is not to say, however, that 'business' use of motor cars cannot be justified. There are innumerable types of job which would be done less efficiently without a car:

■ sales/marketing;
■ supervision;
■ 'caring' jobs (e.g. local government social services);
■ out-of-doors jobs (e.g. construction, civil engineering and public utilities).

Some people would add full-time trade union officials to that list.

■ There are many arguments that can be adduced in favour of

'assistance' on the employer's part in providing you with transport:
- speed (e.g. in an emergency);
- convenience (i.e. choosing the best time to travel);
- comfort (not arriving tired)

are only three such arguments. You can also point out that
- a car is infinitely more suitable for carrying equipment, papers etc.

With the best will in the world, it is difficult to imagine public transport improving sufficiently in the foreseeable future to cater for the needs of manufacturing and service industries in both the public and the private sectors. There is therefore a need to find other satisfactory means of performing certain jobs: one of these, driving your own car, is dealt with elsewhere in this book ('Using your own transport' (pages 222–35)). Another method, which is particularly common in the public sector, is the pooled car system: the employer has a stock (or 'pool') of cars which are used by employees only when they need them. If you think you need cars in your job, but don't fancy the idea of 'fleet cars', you may like to put the pooled car system to the employer; there are, however, disadvantages as well as advantages. Here are some of the disadvantages:
- the company will need to employ managers to administer the system and mechanics to service the vehicles (although from a union point of view, any increase in employment is a good thing);
- some cars may be roughly used if the drivers will not have them for their private use as well (this is more likely to happen if there are a lot of users);
- on some days, either by chance or because of the organisational needs of the firm, there will be too many or too few cars in the pool.

On the other hand, there are several advantages to both the employer and the employees if:
- the employee has not got his/her own car;
- the employee *has* got a car, but it has broken down, it has been in an accident or is too old or unsuitable for the job;
- there are dirty jobs to be done (e.g. driving across fields, very long-distance jobs) and the employee does not fancy using his/her own car.

There are certainly very many people who do their jobs as efficiently and effectively as they do only because they have a car – or the use of one. If you think that the employer *should* provide cars, and you do not want to be party to an elitist system that survives solely because of the tax situation (which could easily change in the near future), you might:

■ opt for a pooled car system.

A system that does *not* depend on any short-term tax advantages or on any form of tax evasion is:

■ driving your *own* car.

Perhaps you might think that a pooled car system could *complement* members using their own cars (some members may not *want* to own a car). If the employer insists on some employees being able to drive, you can suggest that:

■ they can drive their own cars;

and, if they don't own one, that:

■ the company lends them the money to buy one.

Methods of payment for driving your own car are dealt with in 'Using your own transport' (pages 222–35).

20.

Relocation

Introduction

'Relocation' means going to work in another part of the country *while continuing to be employed by the same company*, and because the boss orders you – or requests you – to go there. This chapter deals with the financial assistance that the employer gives you when you are 'relocated'.

The reasons for moving house and qualifying for 'relocation' expenses might be promotion or what is sometimes called 'reorganisation' (particularly common in the public sector, e.g. the NHS, local government and the Civil Service) – in these circumstances, eligibility is often confined to certain *groups* of employee (e.g. sales personnel) or to broader bands of the workforce (e.g. the white-collar staff). Another important reason for relocation is the wholesale transfer of a department (or firm) to another town; in this case, *potentially all* employees will qualify. A relocation scheme is likely to take into account mortgages in addition to other outgoings (e.g. removal expenses) incurred because of the relocations. This chapter also briefly looks at arrangements made by some companies to give financial assistance to new starters who have to move house.

Fares and other expenses incurred *at work* (i.e. not because of moving house) are dealt with in the chapters on travel (pages 222–60) and in 'Subsistence' (pages 182–95).

The availability of housing finance for relocation, long almost an exclusive perquisite of the finance sector, began to grow in the early 1970s mainly because of the rapidly increasing need of employers to attract *and keep* staff. In 1976, the Alfred Marks Bureau, in its *Survey of Fringe Benefits for Office Staff*, estimated that approximately a quarter of all employers in London and the South-East gave assistance with house purchase and almost half of the employers in the same area helped out with removal expenses. This, though, was a bad year according to the British Institute of Management, who discovered that there was *less* housing finance in 1976 because the overall shortage of money made managements generally unwilling to make cash available to their employees. During the late 1970s, many managements found that they had to change course quite sharply over assistance with house purchase:

■ the GLC, for instance, were confident enough in 1974 to shelve proposals to improve the existing scheme and said they would 'reactivate the matter *if recruitment again became difficult*'. [Emphasis added] In the summer of 1980 they were anxious to update their scheme as 'instances have occurred where our present inability to offer any assistance with the high costs associated with moving home (other than that of a removal van) has been a disincentive to prospective recruits.'

This feeling is widespread: a survey carried out in 1980 by the recruitment consultants MSL discovered that engineers were more likely to back out of a job at the last minute than any other type of worker – often because of relocation problems. The survey also found that engineers' expectations of pay rises on moving to a new job rose from 18 per cent to 25 per cent if it meant moving home. MSL concluded that **the failure of so many employers to provide relocation expenses caused many of their best prospective employees to go elsewhere**. Those firms that do have relocation schemes certainly find that the takeup can be quite considerable; the figures on page 263, quoted in *Industrial Relations Review and Report No 224*, give a good indication of this.

Employers find that there are considerable advantages in relocating: an IDS survey on relocation speculated on certain favourable aspects: 'Improved staff morale appears to be a hidden benefit of relocation reflected in lower turnover and absenteeism, greater efficiency and improved work quality.' Against that, however, there are undoubted social drawbacks:

■ it can be very difficult to make new friends (particularly, perhaps, for *other* members of the family) if only because the firm's invasion may easily have sent local prices rocketing;

■ your spouse's job may be very difficult to replace;

■ the children's education may be badly disrupted.

Social and psychological problems apart, employers have also had difficulty in persuading a lot of trade unionists to accept relocation packages on financial grounds:

	Take up of relocation expenses
Abbey Life	500 over 4 years
BP Oil	400 over 5 years
Berlei (UK)	3 in the last year
British Sugar Corporation	50 in the last year
Carreras Rothmans	52 in the last year
Chelsea Building Society	3 every year
Croda International	30 every year
Dowty Group	60 in the last year
Hambro Life	250 over 5 years
Johnson Matthey Chemicals	12 every year
Norwich Union Insurance	1,000 over 5 years
London Brick Co	30 over 5 years
Johnson Nephew	2–3 every year
J Sainsbury	92 in the last year
Smedley HP	12 over 5 years
Sun Life Assurance	50–60 every year
Henry Sykes	24 over 5 years
United Glass	80–100 every year

■ Workers who already have a *building society* mortgage may not want a *company* mortgage scheme. A 'High Street' scheme *may* be easy to transfer, but problems can arise if the move is to a high-cost area.

■ Members who do not have a building society scheme (perhaps the younger ones) will probably welcome the idea of relocation expenses because of:

> – the inconvenience (or impossibility) of negotiating a mortgage with a building society and
>
> –the probability of having to pay high interest rates.

However, they often have second thoughts when it is brought to their attention that:

> – if/when they leave the firm, they will be saddled with a mortgage they may not want (alternatively, they may just have to stay in the job until the mortgage is paid off).

The Conservative Government elected in 1979 soon produced the slogan 'If you want a job – move!' Trade unionists are more likely to call for the reintroduction and increase of regional development grants to encourage firms to go to *where workers are*. The Manpower Services Commission (MSC) is in no doubt that relocation expenses are essential if many jobs are to be filled: a 1979 survey of the MSC's Employment Service Division managers discovered that two-fifths of them considered that 'inconvenient location' was a fundamental reason for certain vacancies being hard to fill, and the *Department of Employment Gazette* reported in 1979 that 'Districts in areas of high housing cost (such as the South East and North East Scotland) called for *greater assistance with housing*'. [Emphasis added] In 1980, the CBI reached *the same conclusion* in its discussion document *Jobs: Facing the future*. An important source of assistance is the local council covering the area that the firm is relocating to; an interesting and imaginative example of this is the Housing for Industry scheme set up by the Greater London Council. The State, too, gives two kinds of financial assistance to people looking for work:

■ these are the *Employment Transfer Scheme*, which gives financial aid to unemployed and potentially redundant workers who are prepared to move house to a new area because there is a job there; and the *Job Search Scheme*, which gives lodging allowances to help people who are looking for jobs in a new area.

Regrettably, public expenditure cuts mean that these two schemes are unlikely to survive for long.

Lastly, there is an interesting scheme that has been set up by the European Coal and Steel Community using money put up by the European Social Fund: this is to help coal and steel workers who wish to move to new jobs in new areas by giving them loans. So far, two employers have made use of this scheme (which, in this country, links up with the Halifax Building Society): in coalmining, the trade union concerned (the National Union of Mineworkers (NUM)) introduces customers to the Halifax, and in steel it is the British Steel Corporation (BSC) which makes the introductions.

Relocation schemes run *exclusively* by the employer are usually divided into two parts, and companies will sometimes have different names for them. The two parts are:

● housing finance (or housing purchase or company mortgage) and

● removal expenses (or other expenses).

We will now look at one of the more detailed schemes (in the National Health Service) covering employees who move house because of promotion, and then compare other company schemes with it. This first section will finish with a brief discussion of bridging loans and settling-in allowances. After that we will deal with the relocation of a whole company or of an entire department. Lastly, there will be a short section on housing arrangements for new starters.

Promotion

The NHS scheme

If you get promoted in the NHS, you can apply for financial assistance in buying a house. The General Whitley Council Handbook says that the move must be for one of the following reasons:

■ promotion or transfer at management request within the same authority; or

■ promotion or voluntary transfer to a different authority as long as the new job has a higher salary maximum and is above certain specified grades, and as long as the move is 'in the interest of the service'.

The condition that the new post must be above certain grades means, in effect, that all ancillary workers are excluded and only high-ranking medical and administrative staff are eligible; applicants must also have:

■ two years' superannuable service at the time of applying.

The option to take advantage of the scheme is subject to two further restrictions:

■ application for assistance must be made within a year of the promotional transfer taking place;

■ the applicant must provide evidence that s/he has made 'all reasonable attempts to obtain a maximum mortgage' – and that means seeking a mortgage in more than one organisation, including the local housing authority. Some of the relocation expenses, as we shall see, are concerned with the employee's spouse and children, but the agreement is expressly extended to:

■ 'officers with family responsibilities equivalent to those of a married officer'.

The loan does *not* consist of the price of the new house, but the difference between the purchase price and the maximum mortgage advance together with whatever the employee can get hold of from personal sources (including the net proceeds from the sale of any previous property). This 'difference' is also subject to a maximum:

■ if the move is *into* the London Weighting area:
£1,250 or six months' gross salary + £500 (whichever is the greater) – maximum: £4,000;
all other moves:
£750 or six months' gross salary (whichever is the greater) – maximum: £3,500.

If the purchase does not go through for any reason beyond the officer's control, the expenses may be reimbursed 'at the employing authority's discretion'. At all events, the money must be repaid within 10 years, and the period of repayment must not go beyond the officer's minimum age of entitlement to pension.

There is also a series of expenses associated with house hunting, the mechanics of buying and selling property, the actual move and costs that are incurred after the move. These expenses include:

■ *Bridging loans:* 'Interest charges (net after income tax relief) on a bridging loan or proportion of a bridging loan not exceeding the estimated selling price of the old accommodation may be reimbursed in full for up to three months.' The period may be extended if it is proving exceptionally difficult to sell the old accommodation.

■ *Legal and other expenses to do with selling the old house:* solicitor's fees (including legal expenses incurred on the redemption of a mortgage) and house agent's or auctioneer's fees. Where a house agent, solicitor or auctioneer is not used, an officer can claim for reasonable expenses (advertising costs, telephone calls, postage etc) up to a maximum of £125.

■ *Preliminary visit to fix up accommodation:* five days' paid leave and four nights' subsistence allowance (two-thirds of the officer's rate for spouse and children over 12; half of the officer's rate for children aged 12 and under); public transport mileage allowance payable even if you go by car.

■ *Journey from the old home to the new home:* this includes subsistence allowance, if necessary, and covers all dependents *including* those who are under *21* and earning their own living but who are moving house because of the officer's transfer; the travel costs are also provided for 'one servant or nurse'.

■ *Furniture removal:* a minimum of three tenders should be obtained from local removal firms, and the NHS will probably pay the lowest. The expenses exclude relaying carpets and the removal of special items 'e.g. a concert piano . . . livestock'.

■ *Storage:* this includes transport to and from the depot, and cleaning and repacking if storage lasts longer than 18 months. The storage costs may not be totally reimbursed if the new accommodation is *temporary and unfurnished.*

■ *Legal and other expenses to do with buying the new house:* 'The expenses may include solicitor's fees, stamp duty, and registration fees and incidental legal expenses, expenses in connection with mortgage or loan including guarantee and survey fees (but excluding interest), the cost of a private survey, electrical wiring test and drains test.'

■ *Renting, not buying, new accommodation:* the rented accommodation may be furnished or unfurnished, but as long as it is not lodgings the NHS will pay up to £40 for the tenancy agreement, the house agent's fee and the drains test.

■ *Return visit to superintend removal:* paid leave with the usual travelling expenses and subsistence allowances.

■ *Refund of unused season ticket:* if it is not possible to get a refund on an unexpired season ticket, the NHS will make an allowance based on 'the remainder of the quarter current at the time of transfer'.

■ *Arrangements for children's education:* day-school fees for the remainder of the term are reimbursable, as are fees paid in lieu of notice. A child can also be left at the school for one year as a boarder (up to 50 per cent of costs paid to the officer) if s/he is studying for a public examination or is undergoing special education which cannot be provided in the new area.

■ *Moved to the new job but still house hunting:* officers are entitled to normal night subsistence allowances for up to two years, providing that the authority is satisfied that s/he is 'making every effort to find suitable family accommodation', and may also go back home at weekends. If, on the other hand, the officer cannot find any suitable accommodation, s/he can commute from home for up to two years and claim the *extra* travel costs.

■ *Accommodation expenses in two homes:* if, after buying the new home, you still 'unavoidably incur regular expenses' on the *old* home (e.g. rates, ground rent), there is a formula for ensuring that there is no financial loss.

■ *Miscellaneous expenses grant:* this is to cover 'additional expenses after taking up [the] new appointment'; the grant ranges from £215 to £910 a year for junior officers eligible and from £255 to £1,070 a year for senior officers, and varies according to whether there are children.

■ *Retention of rooms allowance:* the NHS will reimburse payment of a retainer fee for an officer who temporarily leaves his/her lodgings in the new area.

Other schemes

Companies in a wide range of industries have formal schemes for relocation expenses:

■ these include Courage, Croda International, Dowty Group, Shell and Henry Sykes.

But schemes are not necessarily open to all employees; most firms discriminate on grounds of seniority:

■ Commercial Union exclude non-clerical staff, training grades and those employees who are not yet on the company's established career structure;

■ the Automobile Association take only staff who are at or above Grade 4 (e.g. personnel assistant, officer supervisor, senior buyer).

Occasionally a firm will stipulate several conditions:

■ the Midland Bank say that married workers must be 23 or more with three years' employment and be at least clerical Grade III or typist Grade IV, while single staff must be 26 with three years' employment and be at least clerical Grade IV or typist Grade V.

Regular expenditure in the new location can be difficult to predict, particularly as different towns have different ways of quoting rent and rates. If it is a question of *buying* accommodation, working out whether the loan is adequate is often more straightforward:

■ The Automobile Association calculates the maximum in the same way as the NHS (see pages 265–66): the difference between what *you* can raise and the purchase price – the loan is interest free.

■ Pilkington Bros lend the difference between the selling price and the purchase price to *existing* householders, and are quoted in *IDS Study 176* as offering a complex scheme to relocated staff who are *first-time buyers*: they qualify for a special loan of 15 per cent of the purchase price (maximum: £2,000) to be repaid over 20 years – or before retirement, if that happens first. The interest is 1 per cent calculated on the amount of money outstanding at the beginning of each 12-month period. Staff who are relocated to within 20 miles of Charing Cross in London are entitled to an interest-free loan of one-third of the price of the new accommodation (maximum: one and a third times annual basic salary).

■ Molins Ltd will lend up to 10 per cent of the purchase price on relocation and charge interest at 1 per cent above Minimum Lending Rate; the money has to be paid back within 10 years.

A special feature of most relocation schemes is what is usually called a 'disturbance allowance' (this is normally held to mean a sum of money to cover such items of expenditure as new fixtures and fittings, the cost of reconnecting gas, electricity, telephone etc). One of the most common ways of fixing this sum of money is to relate it to *new earnings* (i.e. the earnings of the job you have relocated to); here is a list of companies adopting this method (quoted mostly from *Industrial Relations Review and Report No 224*), showing the amount of new earnings that the disturbance allowance consists of:

■ 10 per cent: Allied Breweries, British Aluminium, CPC (UK), Croda International, Dema Glass, Dowty Group, Hambro Life Assurance Co, Smedley HP, United Glass;

■ 1 month: Abbey Life, Alladin Industries, Thomas Cook;

■ 12½ per cent: British Sugar Corporation, Shell;

■ 1½ months: Berlei (UK).

Here are some more examples of other elements of relocation schemes:

■ *legal costs:* Brown & Root pay up to 2½ months' gross earnings;

■ *advertising costs:* General Accident give 0.5 per cent of the selling price, up to a maximum of £150;

■ *house hunting:* the BBC, Croda International, Dema Glass and Johnson Matthey will pay for three visits; Smedley HP will pay for four visits;

■ *surveys:* Abbey Life, the BBC, Smedley HP and Thorn Electrical pay for one survey; Alladin Industries, Thomas Cook and Courtaulds will pay for a second survey if necessary;

■ *removal expenses:* these are paid in full by Abbey Life, Alladin Industries, Brown & Root and Thomas Cook;

■ *storage:* money spent on putting furniture into storage is reimbursed by Alladin Industries, Allied Breweries, Chelsea Building Society, Thomas Cook and Dowty Group (this is particularly important nowadays when conveyancing can take anything up to six months);

■ *mileage allowance:* Gillette Industries pay a special mileage allowance (see page 228) for the first six months of relocation.

While the finance sector invariably provides the money itself for its employees' relocation, other organisations (particularly in the private sector) fix up loans with financial institutions:

■ the Automobile Association have come to an agreement with Woolwich Equitable;

■ Ford have an agreement with Abbey National.

Bridging loans

A bridging loan is the money you may need to borrow if there is a gap of a few weeks, or even months, between paying the mortgage on your original home and taking over responsibility for the next mortgage. This practice is fairly common among those firms that have relocation schemes: according to the British Institute of Management, 76 per cent of firms interviewed granted bridging loans (*Transferring Employees, Policy & Practice in the UK*, BIM 1979). Some firms pay the bridging loan in full and ask for it to be repaid within 3–12 months; for example:

■ Allied Breweries, British Sugar Corporation, CPC (UK), Dowty Group, Gratton Warehouses, Smedley HP;
some firms pay the interest only:

■ BBC, BP Oil, Courtaulds, National Freight Corporation, Henry Sykes.
Details of other bridging loan schemes include:

■ Pilkington Bros pay the interest for two months;

■ Hambro give their own bridging loans, but at current building society rates.

Settling-in allowances

This type of allowance is intended to cover those expenses that have not yet been taken care of – in the NHS scheme, it is called the 'miscellaneous expenses grant' and was to cover general 'additional expenses' (see pages 267–68):

■ in local government, the comparable allowance of £3,000 (maximum) has to pay for such items as unexpired season tickets as well;

■ the British Aluminium Co pays 10 per cent of new earnings for settling in.

One of the many problems facing workers who have been ordered or requested to move house because of the job is having to forego certain advantages enjoyed previously – for example, social facilities or subsidised meals:

■ on moving staff out of London to a location where the London allowance is not payable, Barclays Bank operate a 'rundown' of the allowance: two-thirds in the first year of relocation, one-third in the second year.

Company reorganisation

The 1970s saw a rapidly increasing number of company relocations: they were mainly away from London and in the direction of new industrial estates, 'new towns' or other areas where the Government dangled tax benefits, and development areas where there were Government grants available.

This has often meant that the entire workforce is offered continuity of employment, with the employer giving various degrees of assistance with accommodation and bearing the full cost of the removal. Where firms have had existing relocation schemes, it has been a relatively simple matter to adapt to the wholesale relocation of the workforce; other firms have had to develop schemes from scratch. This is how three companies have dealt with particular problems that have arisen:

■ when IBM moved from London to the South Coast in 1976, they guaranteed the price of property already owned by employees, thereby ensuring that nobody lost when selling;

■ a feature of the package at Abbey Life, which also moved from London to the South Coast in 1976, was the payment of half the interest on mortgages;

■ when Kraft Foods relocated in 1975 from Liverpool to a much more expensive locality (Cheltenham), they paid a special lump sum allowance of £300 to compensate for the higher cost of housing.

When housing belonging to the Greater London Council was transferred from the GLC to most of the London boroughs and certain other councils in the South-East in 1979–80, over 5,000 GLC employees were affected. As is usual in much of the public sector, this reorganisation was a 'statutory transfer' – which means that the conditions of the transfer were governed by statute law: under Section 6(2) of the Greater London Council Housing (Staff

Transfer and Protection) Order 1979, any affected GLC worker could appeal if s/he considered that s/he 'will sustain or has sustained hardship in consequence of [the] transfer'.

The London Housing Staff Commission produced a 'list of suggested circumstances which may need to be taken into account in reaching a decision on these grounds'. The following is a *selection* of these 'circumstances':

moving home: domestic circumstances, e.g. ill-health of appellant, common-law spouse, children;

inconvenience of journey from present home;

interference with employment of spouse or common-law spouse;

change of occupation necessary for older children who are still living at home:

travelling: comparative length and travelling time of the new journey and former journey;

special family responsibility, e.g. attending aged parents;

time spent on home study;

responsibility for invalids or aged persons: availability of other persons able to relieve the officer (a) on payment, (b) without payment;

disturbance of children's education if home is moved: particulars of children and examinations for which they are preparing;

educational facilities in area of the authority to which the officer is to be transferred;

officers in poor health or disabled: comparative length and travelling time of former journey and new journey;

facilities for wheelchairs and invalid cars in former and new posts;

difficulty in moving from a specially adapted home;

availability of other persons to look after officer;

disturbance of arrangements for further education: is the school, college etc at present attended reasonably available from the new place of employment?

if not, are reasonably similar alternative facilities available?

amount of leave available in former post;

distance and time taken to travel to study from former post and from new post.

The existence of statute law gave some added protection to the workers concerned in this housing transfer – it is an advantage that no workers in the *private* sector have ever benefited from. However, housing workers transferred from the GLC frequently had to have recourse to the appeals machinery in order to attain anything like real protection of their existing conditions.

Finally, a note should be made about workers who, as a result of reorganisation, are *not* forced to move house but who suffer financially because of the new travel arrangements:

■ Local government and the Water Service undertake to reimburse *for four years* the difference between the old and the new fare/mileage allowances.

■ The National Coal Board pays a disturbance allowance to workers who have agreed to transfer to a new workplace; previously the allowance was only payable to miners *who had had to move house*. The allowance consists of an initial payment of £600 (employees with 10 years' service or more), £500 (five to ten years), £400 (two to five years) or £200 (less than two years) – followed by three more payments each of £200; the initial payment is made on transfer, and the next three payments are made after six months, a year and two years.

New starters

Special relocation schemes for new starters have been introduced by a large number of firms in order to encourage prospective new employees to move from one area to another: the BIM estimate that approximately 82 per cent of firms do this (*Transferring Employees, Policy & Practice in the UK*, British Institute of Management 1979). It is quite common, though, for the scheme to be less generous for new starters than for established employees:

■ examples of this sort of arrangement are to be found at Courage, Croda International, Dowty Group and Henry Sykes. But this is not always the case;

■ Smith Kline & French offer a scheme which is almost identical to the one for existing employees;

■ Gratton Warehouses include new starters in their scheme if the move involves them moving more than 25 miles.

Other firms have arrangements which are specially tailored to the needs of employees who, in many cases, have just moved into the area; one scheme lays particular emphasis on the need for the new starter to make up his/her mind up before taking on big financial responsibilities:

■ at Cadbury Schweppes, the first 13 weeks are spent in what is called a 'training' period, and during this time the new employee can decide whether to move house.

Other benefits for new starters include:

■ Kraft Foods give no assistance in house buying, but do give a disturbance allowance of 10 per cent of new earnings;

■ Abbott Laboratories pay travelling expenses to graduates in their first month;

■ Allied Breweries pay 50 per cent of legal fees and 50 per cent of estate agent's fees on the sale of the old house;

■ Molins pay four months' interest on a bridging loan and give a house purchase loan of 10 per cent of the buying price at 1 per cent above the Minimum Lending Rate; the money has to be repaid within five years.

Preparing for negotiations

Employment legislation

There is no law that obliges or recommends your employer to give you any financial assistance on relocation. However, the Sex Discrimination Act 1875 and the Race Relations Act 1976 (see page 13) outlaw any sex or racial discrimination with regard to access to, or benefits of, a relocation scheme.

Income tax

Your income tax liability on a loan to buy private accommodation on relocation is usually exactly the same as if you were buying properly through a building society.

Removal and other expenses – as illustrated in this chapter – are tax-free under Extra-Statutory Concession A6(a), as long as the company pays for the expenses when you either first join the firm or transfer to another job in the same firm; the expenses must be properly administered and 'reasonable'. The Inland Revenue also allow a tax-free lump sum payment to cover miscellaneous expenses caused by the move; the actual sum concerned depends on the number and age of people in the family, but the maximum is currently £950. In certain cases, expenses of the type dealt with in this chapter need to be negotiated with the Inland Revenue *first*, before they are incurred.

Sitting down with management

There is only one reason for an employer acceding to a request for a relocation scheme, and that is:

■ recruitment and retention of staff.

Quite simply, if there is no scheme or if it is not good enough, it will be difficult or impossible to take on – and keep – good staff. In order to know whether you can put this sort of pressure on the management, you will need to be well informed about the company's staffing policies.

As for new starters, whether there is a shortage or a glut of workers at a certain grade, you can remind your employer that:

■ it is much easier to attract new recruits if they do not have the added responsibility – and expense – of moving house.

You could also suggest to management that:

■ company loyalty might be engendered from the very beginning by giving financial assistance.

With regard to people already working for the company, you could point out that:

■ existing employees will quite likely leave if any transfers are cumbersome *and expensive*;

■ if a rival employer can offer a better relocation scheme, that can swing the balance between staying and moving to another firm.

When the whole company (or department) is being relocated, you are in a very much stronger position. It is likely that you have been left out of the discussions leading up to the decision to move, but:

■ the management is now in great need of 'cooperation' from the workforce.

If the company wants a large proportion of the workforce to move with it, then quite simply it must pay for this – or else:

■ the inevitable short-term operational difficulties caused by the move will be exacerbated and any financial advantage in moving will be lost.

If you can spend a few days in the area to which you are being relocated, so much the better:

■ *you* have time on your side (it's the employer who needs the quick decision) – and if the members are not satisfied with the deal, they are less likely to cope with the new working conditions (they may even decide at the last moment not to go).

The three most important elements of a scheme are:
- a high sum of money to be borrowed;
- a generous repayment period;
- a concessionary interest rate.

Because of rising prices and movements of the Minimum Lending Rate, there will be frequently a need to adjust the scheme; for this reason it will be necessary to monitor the scheme, keeping an eye particularly on any areas where living costs are unusually high.

21.
Private health insurance

Introduction

Medical insurance schemes agreed between employers and private health insurance firms undermine the National Health Service; they are strongly opposed by the TUC – even though a few unions have succumbed to their attractions. These schemes are examined in this book so that trade unionists can see why the TUC – and many other organisations – object to them so strongly.

This chapter deals with private health insurance schemes organised by the employer, and partly or wholly paid for by him. Scheme members are entitled to have medical treatment in private wings of hospitals, and the bill – or part of it – is paid by the insurance company. This is not the same as free medical checkups or the availability on site of a doctor or nurse; nor is it the same as *insured sick-pay schemes* (see 'Sick leave' (pages 61–64)).

Of all 'fringe benefits', the employer's provision of private health insurance has been one of those to come into favour most dramatically in the last few years: for managers alone, the provision rose (according to Inbucon/AIC, the management salary research unit) from 14.5 per cent in 1969 to 38.8 per cent in 1977 – a rise of over $2\frac{1}{2}$ times in only eight years – and this included a *drop* in 1975–76, according to the British Institute of Management, due probably to a sudden increase in charges. There are now about a dozen companies in the field of private health insurance, the best known of which are BUPA (the British United Provident Association) with over 70 per cent and PPP (Private Patients Plan) with about 24 per cent; between them, the dozen or so firms reckon to have over 3 million members.

Part of the motivation behind supplying health insurance schemes is recruitment and retention of staff –

■ as BUPA says in a publicity booklet to employers, 'Apart

from being one way to encourage employees to stay with the company, private medical treatment protection helps attract high-calibre staff.'

Part of the attractiveness during the 1970s was that:

■ it was a way round the various pay policies of that time,

but much of the appeal today is:

■ a very much shorter queue for certain operations – particularly for such conditions as a slipped disc, piles and gallstones;

■ (maybe) the opportunity to choose the time for the operation to take place.

Other advantages quoted include:

■ greater comfort and privacy;

■ more flexible visiting hours;

■ accessibility via a private telephone.

The mechanics of a private health insurance scheme involves the company taking out a 'group scheme' to cover all or some employees. Members will thereafter be able to have certain costs paid – e.g. fees for nurses and specialists (surgeons, anaesthetists, physiotherapists etc) and accommodation charges; these costs are paid either in total ('full refund') or subject to maximum limits. The company may pay the entire premium for an employee (e.g. a manager) or offer a discount (e.g. to employees below a certain level), and there may be an option to include one's spouse and other members of the family: similarly, this may be free or offered at a discount. Unless the employer decides to undertake the administration of the scheme, there is little more for him to do – the insurance company will generally run that side of things. It seems that there is always the right to *opt out* of a private health insurance scheme.

Any growth in private health insurance encourages doctors and specialists to go precisely to those places where there are people who can *buy* good health care; it also causes much-needed money to be diverted from the National Health Service – after all, it is the NHS which carries out all medical training and funds virtually all research. As the Socialist Medical Association has said: 'Can you justify paying for health treatment which enables you to "jump the queue" and means someone else in greater need waits still longer?'

The private health insurance companies also make much of their disinterest in financial gain: they say, for instance, that 'Private patients still contribute millions of pounds annually to the financially stretched National Health Service.' As 'Fightback' (a campaign against public expenditure cuts and for a free NHS) has stated: 'The fees from private patients only *partly* cover the running costs of these pay beds. They contribute *nothing* to the capital costs in the hospital.' [Emphasis in original] Most of these insurance firms are non-profit-making bodies – they are registered under the Companies Act as 'pecuniary loss insurance companies' – but BUPA and PPP support charitable trusts (the Nuffield Nursing Homes Trust and the Eynsham Trust respectively) to fund and build private hospitals and to renovate old ones: these hospitals, together with laboratory services, can and do make money.

Private medical care is not without its own complications, one of them being the availability of beds:

■ the insurance companies have had difficulty in providing enough beds and facilities for their rapidly increasing membership. Other problems are of a financial or strictly medical nature, and directly affect members:

■ when there is an upper money limit (for example, BUPA have limits on some of the accommodation charges *and* a maximum of £250 for the surgeon's fee for a major operation), scheme members can unsuspectingly be running up bills which they *themselves* will have to pay;

■ there can also be a 'cash flow' problem if there is a gap between your paying the bill and the insurance company reimbursing you – the PPP scheme at Hoechst (UK) reads:

'– PPP will send you the money claimed normally within 2 weeks;

– Operations and hospital residence can be very expensive and although PPP settle promptly, it may be difficult for you to clear your account without inconvenience . . .

– You pay the bills direct to the hospital, nursing home or specialist, as required.'

There are also a large number of things you *cannot* claim for:

■ private medical insurance firms are not too keen on old people: sometimes there is an upper age limit, and even if there isn't, the presence of a large number of older people in the scheme can put the premium up quite considerably (particularly when the insurers ask for medical histories); the treatment of *geriatric illness* is explicitly excluded from some schemes.

Esoteric needs such as cosmetic surgery and visits to health farms are never covered, it seems; but there are much more everyday matters which are often *excluded* as well, for example:

■ 'sight testing, routine medical examinations, treatment by osteopaths and chiropractors, normal dental treatment' (the PPP scheme at Hoechst (UK);

■ 'maternity, except in abnormal cases; expenses incurred for treatment of war- or self-inflicted injuries or disabilities . . . hearing aids or surgical appliances' (a scheme run by Western Provident Association at GKN).

Ill-health that is going to take a long time to cure is also going to be excluded in many schemes, for example:

■ treatment of long-term mental illness, and long-term radiation treatment or kidney dialysis – what one firm in the field has described as 'long-term chronic conditions which show no hope of improvement'.

An executive-oriented study of private health insurance concedes that '[in] cases of chronic or urgent medical need, the NHS usually comes up trumps' (*Business Matters*, February 1980); and even more impressive is the admission of BUPA's Medical Adviser:

'The question is whether the [private] premises, staff and backup equipment is comparable in quality to that in the NHS hospitals – and it rarely is. Very few private homes have resident staff and you can't expect a private hospital, however good, to have all the backup equipment of a 500-bed NHS hospital.'

Access to private health insurance schemes varies enormously from one employer to another:

■ occasionally, all employees have equal rights (e.g. Marks & Spencer and Black & Decker);

■ it is more normal for senior staff to have their subscriptions paid for them by management and other staff to be eligible for the group discount (e.g. the Automobile Association, the Thomas Cook Group and Gillette Industries);

■ sometimes, it is simply open only to supervisory grades and above (e.g. the finance sector).

Sometimes members' families can be covered by the company scheme:

■ usually scheme members *themselves* have to pay for the rest of their families to be included (e.g. Smith Kline & French).

This practice is not universal, however:

■ Abbott Laboratories give free cover to wives of senior staff;

■ the families of directors at Cole of Bilston is paid for by the firm.

The direct cost of membership depends on age – and sometimes on medical history as well: annual subscriptions at PPP range from £77 to £235 employee only) or from £155 to £470 (employee and spouse). Discounts are sometimes available. Companies are traditionally secretive about the amounts of money spent on health insurance, although there are occasional exceptions:

▪ Abbott Laboratories say that the average annual cost for a member of their junior staff and his/her spouse is about £100. Despite the great cost, firms will apparently go to considerable lengths to preserve certain employees' access to private health schemes; a number of examples of this came to the surface during the 1979–80 public expenditure cuts:

▪ Hampshire County Council hoped to 'save' about £6m in 1980–81 through the reduction and/or abolition of school meals, but membership of BUPA at a group discount would continue for senior staff;

▪ Kent County Council put its school meal charges up in September 1980, thereby 'saving' £3.7m, but the premium for top officers' membership of their private health insurance scheme (totalling £4,700 a year) is exempt from the cuts.

▪ Berkshire has put up a large number of its charges, particularly for the physically and mentally handicapped, but BUPA membership remains available to staff.

It is certainly most unusual for manual workers to be included in a scheme, but there are signs that it is on the increase – particularly where there is little or no trade union organisation. Ironically, the best known case of manual workers being granted admission was with the controversial connivance of the union concerned: the agreement which came into force on 1 January 1980 between the Electrical Contractors' Association and EETPU members in the electricity contracting industry. A distinctive feature of the deal is the right to voluntary health screening; EETPU members do not have to pay for it, but have to take unpaid leave in order to have the tests carried out.

Preparing for negotiations

Employment legislation

There is no law in this country dealing with the provision by the employer of a private health insurance scheme; however, any discrimination on the part of the employer on the grounds of sex or race is illegal under the Sex Discrimination Act 1975 and the Race Relations Act 1976 respectively (see page 13).

Income tax

Under Section 68 of the Finance Act 1976, *all* scheme members must pay tax on the amount of money that the *employer* pays into the scheme on the employee's behalf. This applies also to any premiums paid in respect of other members of the family, and employees are equally liable *whether or not they are higher-paid* (see pages 9–10). There is no tax liability on any *benefits* received (e.g. hospital treatment) as a consequence of membership of the scheme.

Employers can claim full corporation tax relief on the subscriptions they pay to the insurance firms.

Sitting down with management

It is impossible to justify a trade unionist negotiating a private medical insurance scheme. In the words of the TUC General Council Report 1979,

'The principle of health care of the highest quality free at the point of use [is] a fundamental tenet of the NHS, and [has] been endorsed by the Royal Commission on the National Health Service as the best way to ensure equity of care to all sick people whatever their financial circumstances.'

The Royal Commission, in fact, supported the socialist principle that the National Health Service should be freely available throughout the land without any impediment on the grounds of age, sex, class, race or religion; it was also the Commission's view that it should be funded entirely out of taxation.

First, though, trade unions must put their own house in order and, for instance:

▪ cease giving financial support to a private hospital (Manor House Hospital in North London);

▪ put a stop to queue jumping for operations (as indulged in by some NHS employees).

They also need to turn away from deals that assist the private sector to flourish: 'unions who accept deals with private medicine are acting as insurance touts and undermining the basic principles of free and equal access' (*Whitleyism and Health – The NHS and its Industrial Relations*, Daniel Vulliamy and Roger Moore, WEA 1979).

A better health service will not be achieved by aiding the private sector to grow. Without private medicine, the Government – of *any* political persuasion – would not be able to avoid shortening the NHS queues.

Glossary

AA: Automobile Association

absence-related: an absence-related benefit is one that is reduced according to the amount of time you have been off work

ACTSS: Association of Clerical, Technical and Supervisory Staffs, part of the Transport and General Workers' Union – a TUC-affiliated trade union

ADHAC: Agricultural Dwelling House Advisory Committee.

APEX: Association of Professional, Executive, Clerical and Computer Staff – a TUC-affiliated trade union

APT&C: Administrative, Professional, Technical and Clerical Services – the white-collar grades in local government

associated employer: two employers are associated if one *controls* the other or if *both* are controlled by a *third* company; for example, *all* the firms owned by a holding company such as Massey-Ferguson (Holdings) or the Ford Motor Company are 'associated employers'; similarly all city, county and district councils are 'associated employers', as are all Area Health Authorities.

ASTMS: Association of Scientific, Technical and Managerial Staffs – a TUC-affiliated trade union

basic pay: earnings *excluding* bonus, allowance for shift, overtime etc, commission; sometimes just referred to as 'basic'.

BIM: British Institute of Management

BMA: British Medical Association

Board of Inland Revenue: see 'Inland Revenue'

BSC: British Steel Corporation

CBI: Confederation of British Industry

Centerprise: a community centre and bookshop in Hackney (London)

CIU: Clubs and Institutes' Union – the body responsible for administering most working men's clubs in Britain

Clegg Commission: the real name of the Clegg Commission was 'The Standing Commission on Pay Comparability'; it was set up in March 1979 to examine the terms and conditions of employment of various groups of workers (including nurses and midwives) and to report on the possibility of establishing acceptable bases of comparison with terms and conditions of employment in other comparable jobs; the Commission was chaired by Professor H A Clegg. It was disbanded by the 1979 Tory Government in 1980.

collective bargaining: negotiations between trade union(s) and the employer related to, or connected with, the terms and conditions of employment listed in Section 29 of the Trade Union and Labour Relations Act 1974; they include wages, holidays, sick pay, discipline, dismissal, membership of trade unions, facilities for shop stewards and negotiating procedures.

company: see page 13.

continuous employment: working, or contracting to work, for a specified number of hours each week, with no gaps in the period covered by the contract – i.e. holidays and sick leave are usually *not* gaps, but if you resign (even if only for a few weeks) it *will* be counted as a gap unless your contract says anything to the contrary.

CPAG: Child Poverty Action Group

CPSA: Civil and Public Servants' Association – a TUC-affiliated trade union.

crêche: a nursery for young children

CSEU: Confederation of Shipbuilding and Engineering Unions

CUPE: Canadian Union of Public Employees

decile: 1/10th of a sample; the survey on page 224 shows that the *bottom* 1/10th of companies surveyed give an average of 10p a mile as a flat-rate payment and the *top* 1/10th give an average of 15p a mile.

defendant: a person who is accused in court of breaking certain laws (e.g. for causing personal injury) or who is sued (e.g. for debt).

DES: Department of Education and Science

DHSS: Department of Health and Social Security

DoI: Department of Industry

EEC: European Economic Community (also known as the Common Market)

EEF: Engineering Employers' Federation

EOC: Equal Opportunities Commission

ERS: earnings-related supplement

ESSP: Employers' Statutory Sick Pay – a term sometimes used for the scheme outlined in the Tory Government's Green Paper for new sick-pay arrangements (see pages 57–61)

ETUC: European Trade Union Conference

ex gratia: 'ex gratia payments' are payments from your employer that you do not have a right to under the terms of your contract – they are totally at management's discretion.

finance sector: banking and insurance

firm: see page 13

full-timer: a full-timer in the *legal* sense is a worker who works 16 or more hours a week *or* between 8 and 16 hours a week with five years' continuous service. This should not be confused with local and national agreements which may stipulate *any* number of hours below which you count as a part-timer for *locally agreed* benefits: a part-timer in these circumstances may be anybody who works less than 40 hours a week, or anybody who works less than 30 or 25 – or any number agreed between your union and the employer.

GCE: General Certificate of Education

GLC: Greater London Council

GMWU: General and Municipal Workers' Union – a TUC-affiliated trade union

GP: General Practitioner – sometimes called the 'family doctor'

Grievance Procedure: a procedure agreed between the trade union(s) and the employer which attempts to solve the 'grievances' (i.e. complaints or disagreements) of workers – the procedure usually consists of at least three stages starting with the union member approaching his/her immediate supervisor/manager, followed by the member seeing the immediate supervisor/manager accompanied by the shop steward, and ending up with the matter being negotiated by the union's full-time organiser and top management.

gross earnings: wages/salary *before* deductions for income tax and National Insurance

Hay/MSL: a firm of management consultants specialising in terms and conditions of employment

higher-paid employees: see pages 9–10

HMSO: Her Majesty's Stationery Office – the Government's publishing house

HNC: Higher National Certificate
HND: Higher National Diploma
hourly-paid: see page 12

IAM: Institute of Administrative Management
IBA: Independent Broadcasting Authority
IDS: Incomes Data Services
ILEA: Inner London Education Authority
independent recognised trade union: an independent trade union is one that has received a certificate of independence from the Certification Officer (Section 8 of the Employment Protection Act 1975); an organisation has to *apply* for the certificate of independence and the Certification Officer can turn it down, for example, on the grounds that it is under the *control* of the employer or suffers from some *interference* from the employer. A *recognised* trade union is one that has a 'recognition agreement' with the employer – this means that the union is recognised for negotiating all (occasionally just some) conditions of employment; the agreement is usually signed by representatives of the union and management.
in kind: a 'benefit in kind' is one with no money *directly* involved (e.g. free meals, time off work, company car).
Inland Revenue: the Government department that tax inspectors work for
in lieu: instead – 'payment in lieu' is payment instead of having a day off, for example; 'time off in lieu' means time off at another time to make up for missing a public holiday.
in loco parentis: somebody who stands 'in loco parentis' to you is a person who is *not* one of your parents (or step- or fosterparents) but who is doing the *job* of being a parent to you.
IPC: International Publishing Corporation
IPM: Institute of Personnel Management
IRRR: *Industrial Relations Review and Report*
ITB: Industry Training Board

JC: Joint Council – see 'NJIC'
JIB: Joint Industrial Board – see 'NJIC'
JIC: Joint Industrial Council – see 'NJIC'
JP: Justice of the Peace – a magistrate

litigation: taking legal proceedings against somebody – for example, against a car dealer who you think has sold you a car that doesn't work properly

local agreement: either (i) an agreement made at a single-site company or (ii) an agreement at one site of a larger company or public sector undertaking to *improve* on the company-wide agreement or the national agreement; see 'national agreement'.

LRD: Labour Research Department, an independent body that publishes a large number of books and pamphlets of interest to all trade unionists, and which will give advice and assistance to subscribers

LV: Luncheon Voucher

management: see pages 12–13
manual workers: see page 12
means-tested: a Social Security benefit is means-tested when the DHSS can disqualify you from receiving *some or all* of it because of the amount of money you earn or receive from other sources.

median: in a survey, the point at which exactly half of the samples are *above* and exactly half are *below*; the survey on page 225 shows that exactly half the payments for 1,501–1,750cc cars were *above* 13p a mile and exactly half were *below* 13p a mile. The 'median' is *not* the same as the 'average': the average would be calculated by adding all the allowances in the survey together and dividing the total by the number of companies.

monthly-paid: see page 12
MP: Member of Parliament
MSC: Manpower Services Commission

NALGO: National and Local Government Officers' Association – a TUC-affiliated trade union
NATFHE: National Association of Teachers in Further and Higher Education – a TUC-affiliated trade union
national agreement: an agreement covering a company that is spread across the country, or covering a public-sector undertaking (e.g. local government, gas, electricity, health etc); see 'local agreement'.
NCB: National Coal Board
net earnings: wages/salary *after* deductions for income tax and National Insurance
NHS: National Health Service
NI: National Insurance
NJC: National Joint Council – see 'NJIC'

NJIC: National Joint Industrial Council – the name given to national negotiating bodies for certain industries; other national negotiating bodies have other names such as JC, JIB, JIC and NJC.
NNEB: National Nursery Examination Board
NUJ: National Union of Journalists – a TUC-affiliated trade union
NUM: National Union of Mineworkers – a TUC-affiliated trade union
NUPE: National Union of Public Employees – a TUC-affiliated trade union
NUS: National Union of Seamen – a TUC-affiliated trade union
NUS: National Union of Students
NUT: National Union of Teachers – a TUC-affiliated trade union
NUTGW: National Union of Tailors and Garment Workers – a TUC-affiliated trade union.

offset: 'sick-pay rates are offset against National Insurance payments' means *either* the normal sick pay in the company agreement *minus* State sickness benefits, *or* the normal sick pay in the company agreement with an *obligation* for you to hand over to the employer the National Insurance payments you receive from the State.
ONC: Ordinary National Certificate
OPC: Opinion Research Centre
OU: Open University

p.a.: per annum – see 'per annum'
per annum: a year or every year: '£100 per annum' means '£100 a year'.
PAYE: Pay As You Earn – the normal income tax system for employees.
payroll costs: the costs to the employer of wages/salaries paid to employees; some employers keep certain non-wage benefits (such as holiday pay and sick pay) *out of* payroll costs so as to make the cost of non-wage benefits look larger.
perks: the short form of 'perquisites' – page 2
perquisites: see page 2
petitioner: a person who sues in court (e.g. for divorce).
PHI: Permanent Health Insurance
plaintiff: a person who accuses in certain types of court case (e.g. in tenant-versus-landlord cases).
private sector: private-sector companies are owned and run by individuals – or groups of individuals – independent of the State.

pro rata: in a workplace where full-time workers do 40 hours a week and part-timers do 30 hours a week (i.e. three-quarters of what the full-timers do), if the part-timers get three-quarters of holiday pay they are being paid pro rata.

public sector: public sector: public-sector concerns are owned and run by the State at national or local level: public-sector organisations at *national* level include Government departments like the DHSS, the NHS and the Department of Employment, and trading companies like the National Coal Board, the British Gas Corporation, British Steel and British Airways; the public sector at *local* level includes all work carried out by local councils (e.g. education, housing, roads etc).

qualification period: the period of time you need to have been employed in order to be eligible for a benefit (sometimes called 'qualifying period')

quartile: a quarter of a sample; the survey on page 224 shows that the *bottom* quarter of companies surveyed give an average of 10p a mile as a flat-rate payment and the *top* quarter give an average of 13p a mile.

RAC: Royal Automobile Club

recognised union: see 'independent recognised trade union'

remuneration: see pages 3–4

respondent: a defendant in certain types of lawsuit (e.g. divorce).

retail: the 'retail trade' consists of shops and department stores that sell goods to the public; the 'retail price' is the price charged to the public in shops; see 'wholesale'.

retention: 'retention of staff' is keeping workers for a reasonable period of time after they are first employed.

RPI: Retail Price Index, the Government's calculation of the cost of living based on the prices of certain goods and services.

service: a word that a lot of employers (and the law) use to mean 'employment' (e.g. 'service qualification period' and 'service-related'); it implies a submissive attitude which must be unacceptable to most trade unionists. The word is used in this book solely because it is the word frequently used in contracts.

service industry: an industry which *provides services* rather than manufactures goods; examples are catering, education, public utilities (gas, electricity, water), street cleaning etc.

service qualification period: the minimum period of employment needed to qualify for a benefit; see 'service'.

service-related: a service-related benefit is one that is linked to the number of months or years you have been employed by the company – e.g. the longer you have been employed, the more holidays (or sick pay) you will get; see 'service'.

shop steward: the person elected by the trade union members in a workplace or department to represent them before management on matters concerning their terms and conditions of employment; see 'Grievance Procedure'.

staff: see page 12

staff shop: a shop on company premises selling goods such as groceries *and/or* goods produced by the company itself

status quo: a status quo agreement between the trade union(s) and the employer states that, in the event of a disagreement, *neither* side will take further action (e.g. industrial action or disciplinary action) until the matter has been negotiated further.

statutory: according to statute law; for example, a 'statutory minimum' is the legal minimum according to an Act of Parliament; a 'statutory duty on the employer' is a legal obligation on the employer; 'statutory bodies' include industrial tribunals, water authorities and boards of school governors.

subpoena: a summons to appear as a witness in court; if you don't go, you may be fined or even imprisoned.

superannuation: pension – this word is used mainly in the public sector.

tax avoidance: see page 9

tax evasion: see page 9

tenure: 'tenure of accommodation' is the period of time you can have the accommodation; tenure can last for months, or years or for an indefinite period.

total remuneration: see pages 3–4

TUC: Trades Union Congress

USDAW: Union of Shop, Distributive and Allied Workers – a TUC-affiliated trade union

VAT: Value Added Tax, a Government tax added to the price of certain goods and services

Wages Councils: see pages 13–14
weekly-paid: see page 12
white-collar workers: see page 12
Whitley Council: the national negotiating machinery for the National Health Service
wholesale: the 'wholesale price' is the price at which manufacturers sell goods to shops; see 'retail'.

Index